The International Responsibility of NATO and Its Personnel during Military Operations

Legal Aspects of International Organizations

Edited by

Niels Blokker

VOLUME 58

The titles published in this series are listed at *brill.com/laio*

The International Responsibility of NATO and Its Personnel during Military Operations

By

David Nauta

BRILL
NIJHOFF

LEIDEN | BOSTON

The views and opinions expressed in this book are those of the author and do not necessarily reflect the official policy or position of the North Atlantic Treaty Organization.

Library of Congress Cataloging-in-Publication Data

Names: Nauta, David, 1976-
Title: The international responsibility of NATO and its personnel during military operations / by David Nauta.
Description: Leiden ; Boston : Brill Nijhoff, 2018. | Series: Legal aspects of international organizations ; volume 58 | Based on author's thesis (doctoral - Radboud Universiteit Nijmegen, 2016). | Includes bibliographical references and index.
Identifiers: LCCN 2017041307 (print) | LCCN 2017041650 (ebook) | ISBN 9789004354647 (e-book) | ISBN 9789004354616 (hardback : alk. paper)
Subjects: LCSH: North Atlantic Treaty Organization. | Tort liability of international agencies. | Peacekeeping forces. | War damage compensation--Law and legislation.
Classification: LCC KZ5930 (ebook) | LCC KZ5930 .N385 2018 (print) | DDC 341.6/3--dc23
LC record available at https://lccn.loc.gov/2017041307

Typeface for the Latin, Greek, and Cyrillic scripts: "Brill". See and download: brill.com/brill-typeface.

ISSN 0924-4883
ISBN 978-90-04-35461-6 (hardback)
ISBN 978-90-04-35464-7 (e-book)

This book is printed on acid-free paper and produced in a sustainable manner.

Contents

List of Figures

List of Abbreviations

ACHR	American Convention on Human Rights
ACIL	Amsterdam Centre for International Law
ACO	Allied Command Operations
ACT	Allied Command Transformation
AD	Allied Doctrine
AI	Amnesty International
AIHRC	Afghanistan Independent Human Rights Commission
AIRCOM	Air Command
AJP	Allied Joint Publication
AMIS	African Union Mission in Sudan
AMISOM	African Union Mission in Somalia
ANP	Afghan National Police
AP	Allied Publication
API	Additional Protocol I
ARIO	Draft Articles on the Responsibility of International Organizations
ASR	Articles on State Responsibility
AU	African Union
AWACS	Airborne Warning and Control System
BCCLA	British Columbia Civil Liberties Association
BDA	Battle Damage Assessment
CAOC	Combined Air Operations Centre
CFI	Coalition Forces Iraq
CIS	Commonwealth of Independent States
CN	Counter Narcotics
COMISAF	Commander International Security Assistance Force
COMKFOR	Commander Kosovo Force
CONOPS	Concept of Operations
CPA	Coalition Provisional Authority
CRC	Crowd and Riot Control
CSCE	Commission on Security and Cooperation in Europe
DC	Defence Committee
DDCPO	Disciplinary Directive Civilian Personnel Office (UN)
DFAIT	Department of Foreign Affairs, Trade and Development (CAN)
DIIS	Danish Institute for International Studies
DPA	Department of Political Affairs
DPC	Defence Policy Committee (NATO)
DPKO	Department of Peacekeeping Operations (UN)

EAPC	Euro-Atlantic Partnership Council
EC	European Council
ECCC	Extraordinary Chambers in the Courts of Cambodia
ECHR	European Convention on Human Rights
ECJ	European Court of Justice
ECMM	European Community Monitor Mission
ECOSOC	Economic and Social Council
EJIL	European Journal of International Law
ESDP	European Security and Defense Policy
EU	European Union
EUNAVFOR	European Union Naval Forces
EUPM	European Union Police Mission
EUPOL	European Union Police Mission
GPS	Global Positioning System
HQ	Headquarters
HRC	Human Rights Council
IACHR	Inter-American Court of Human Rights
ICC	International Criminal Court
ICCPR	International Covenant on Civil and Political Rights
ICJ	International Court of justice
ICMPD	International Centre for Migration Policy Development
ICRC	International Crescent and Red Cross
ICTR	International Criminal Tribunal for Rwanda
ICTY	International Criminal Tribunal for the former Yugoslavia
ID	Identification
IFOR	Implementation Force
IHL	International Humanitarian Law
IHRL	International Human Rights Law
ILA	International Law Association
ILC	International Law Commission
IMP	International Military Police
IMS	International Military Staff
IPAP	Individual Partnership Action Plans
ISAF	International Security Assistance Force
JCE	Joint Criminal Enterprise
JFCB	Joint Force Command Brunssum
JFCBS	Joint Force Command Brunssum
JFCNP	Joint Force Command Naples
JTAC	Joint Tactical Air Controller
JTWG	Joint Targeting Working Group

KFOR	Kosovo Force
LANDCOM	Land Command
MARCOM	Maritime Command
MC	Military Committee
MNB	Multi-national Brigade
MONUC	Mission de l'Organisation des Nations Unies en République Démocratique du Congo
MOU	Memorandum of Understanding
MP	Military Police
MTA	Military Technical Agreement
NAC	North Atlantic Council
NACC	North Atlantic Cooperation Council
NAEW	NATO Airborne Early Warning
NATO	North Atlantic Treaty Organization
NCPR	NATO Civilian Personnel Regulations
NCS	NATO Command Structure
NDS	National Directorate of Security
NNCN	Non NATO Contributing Nation
NPG	Nuclear Planning Group
NSPA	NATO Support Agency
NTM	NATO Training Mission
OEF	Operation Enduring Freedom
OHCHR	Office of the High Commissioner on Human Rights
ONUC	Opération des Nations Unies au Congo
OPCOM	Operational Command
OPCON	Operational Control
OPLAN	Operation Plan
OSCE	Organization for Security and Co-operation in Europe
PCIJ	Permant Court of International Justice
POHRF	Post-Operations Humanitarian Relief Fund
PRT	Provincial Reconstruction Team
RC	Regional Command
REV	Revision
ROE	Rules of Engagement
SACEUR	Supreme Allied Commander Europe
SACLANT	Supreme Allied Commander Atlantic
SACT	Supreme Allied Commander Transformation
SC	Supreme Command
SCR	Senior Civilian Representative
SFOR	Stablisation Force

SHAPE	Supreme Headquarters Allied Powers Europe
SOFA	Status of Forces Agreement
SOMA	Status of Mission Agreement
SOF	Special Operations Forces
SRSG	Special Representative to the Secretary General
STANAG	Standardization Agreement
TCN	Troop Contributing Nation
TEU	Treaty on European Union
TF	Task Force
TFU	Task Force Uruzgan
TPIU	Trafficking and Prostitution Investigation Unit
UDHR	Universal Declaration on Human Rights
UN	United Nations
UNAMA	United Nations Assistance Mission in Afghanistan
UNCC	United Nations Compensation Commission
UNDP	United Nations Development Programme
UNDPKO	United Nations Department of Peacekeeping Operations
UNFICYP	United Nations Forces in Cyprus
UNHRC	United Nations Human Rights Council
UNIFEM	United Nations Women's Fund
UNISOM	United Nations in Somalia
UNMIK	United Nations in Kosovo
UNODC	United Nations Office on Drugs and Crime
UNOHCHR	United Nations Office of the High Commissioner of Human Rights
UNOSOM	United Nations Operations in Somalia
UNPROFOR	United Nations Protection Force
UNSC	United Nations Security Council
UNSCR	United Nations Security Council resolution
WEU	Western European Union
WHO	World Health Organization

Table of Cases

I Permanent Court of Justice

- *Lotus*, PCIJ, Series A, no. 10, 1927

II International Court of Justice

- *Corfu Channel (United Kingdom of Great Britain and Northern Ireland v Albania)*, Judgment, 25 March 1948
- *Reparation for injuries suffered in the service of the United Nations*, Advisory Opinion, 11 April 1949
- *Advisory opinion on the interpretation of the agreement of 25 March 1951 between the WHO and Egypt*, Advisory opinion, 20 December 1980
- *Applicability of Article VI, Section 22, of the Convention on the Privileges and Immunities of the United Nations (Mazilu Case)*, Advisory Opinion, 15 December 1989
- *Certain Phosphate Lands in Nauru (Nauru v Australia)*, Judgment, 26 June 1992
- *East Timor (Portugal v Australia)*, Judgment, ICJ Reports 1995, 30 June 1995
- *Legality of the Threat or Use of Nuclear Weapons*, Advisory Opinion, 8 July 1996
- *Case Concerning the Arrest Warrant of 11 April 2000*, Democratic Republic of the Congo v. Belgium, Judgment, 14 February 2002
- *Legal Consequences of the Construction of a Wall in the Occupied Palestinian Territory*, Advisory Opinion, 9 July 2004
- *Cases concerning the Legality of Use of Force* (The title refers to several cases before the ICJ, initiated by Serbia and Montenegro / Yugoslavia against ten NATO member States on 29 April 1999 regarding the bombing of Yugoslav territory as part of the NATO operation "Allied Force"), 15 December 2004
- *Democratic Republic of the Congo v. Uganda, Case Concerning Armed Activities on the Territories of the Congo*, Judgment, 19 December 2005.
- *Case Concerning the Application of the Convention on the Prevention and Punishment of the Crime of Genocide*, Judgment, 26 February 2007
- *Belgium v. Senegal, Questions relating to the obligation to prosecute or extradite*, Judgment, 20 July 2012

III European Court of Human Rights

- *Soering v. United Kingdom*, Application no. 14038/88, 7 July 1989
- ECtHR, *Stocke v. Germany*, Application no. 28/1989/188/248, 12 October 1989
- *Drozd and Janousek v. France and Spain*, Application no. 12747/87, 26 June 1992
- *Loizidou v. Turkey*, Application no. 40/1993/435/514, 18 December 1996
- *Bankovic, Stojadinovic, Stoimenovski, Joksimovic and Sukovic v. Belgium, The Czech Republic, Denmark, France, Germany, Greece, Hungary, Iceland, Italy, Luxembourg, The Netherlands, Norway, Poland, Portugal, Spain, Turkey and The United Kingdom,* Decision of the Grand Chamber to the admissibility of Application no. 52207/99, ECHR 2001-XII, 12 December 2001
- *Cyprus v. Turkey*, Application no. 25781/94, 10 May 2001
- *Ilascu et al. v. Moldova and Russia*, Application no. 48787/88, 8 July 2004
- *Öcalan v. Turkey*, Application no. 46221/99, 12 May 2005
- Court of First Instance, *Kadi v Council of the European Union and Commission of the European Communities*, Judgment, Case T-315/01, 21 September 2005
- *A. Behrami and B. Behrami against France*, Application no. 71412/01 and *R. Saramati against France, Germany and Norway*, Application no. 78166/01 by, Grand Chamber Decision as to the admissibility of the application, 2 May 2007
- *Behrami v. France*, Application no. 71412/01 and *Saramati v. France, Germany and Norway* (Application no. 78166/01), Admissibility Decision of 31 May 2007
- ECJ (Grand Chamber), *Kadi v Council of the European Union and Commission of the European Communities*, Judgment, action for annulment, appeal, Case C-402/05 P, [2008] ECR I-6351, [2009] AC 1225, 3 September 2008
- European Court of Human Rights, M.S.S. v Belgium and Greece, Application no. 30696/09, Judgment of 21 January 2011
- *Al-Skeini and others v. the United Kingdom,* Judgment, 55721/07, 7 July 2011
- European Court of Human Rights, Al-Jedda v. The United Kingdom, application no. 27021/08, Decision of 7 July 2011
- ECJ (Grand Chamber), *European Commission et al v. Yassin Abdullah Kadi,* Appeal, Joined Cases 584/10, C-593/10, C-595/10, 18 July 2013

IV Inter-American Human Rights Court

- *La Tablada* case, IACHR Report No. 55/97, Case No. 11.137, Argentina, OEA/Ser/L/V/II.97, Doc. 38, 30 October 1997

V International Criminal Tribunal for the Former Yugoslavia

- *Prosecutor v. Dusko Tadić*, Appeals Chamber, IT-94-1-AR72, 2 October 1995
- *Prosecutor v. Dusko Tadic*, Appeals Chamber, IT-94-1-A, 15 July 1999
- *"Čelebići camp" case*, Appeals Chamber, IT-96-21-A, 20 February 2001
- *Prosecutor v. Blagoje Simić, Milan Simić, Miroslav Tadić, Stevan Todrović and Simo Zarić,* Decision on Motion for Judicial Assistance to be Provided by SFOR and Others, Trial Chamber 1, IT-95-9-PT, 18 October 2000
- International Criminal Tribunal for the Former Yugoslavia, Prosecutor v. Blăskić, IT-95-14-A, Judgment of 29 July 2004
- *Prosecutor v. Milutinović et al.*, Case no. IT-05-87-PT, Decision on the Second Application of Dragoljub Ojdanić for Binding Orders Pursuant to Rule 54bis, 17 November 2005
- *Ramush Haradinaj et al.,* Trial Chamber I, IT-04-84-T 3 April 2008
- *Prosecutor v. Boškoski and Tarulovski,* IT-04-82-T, 10 July 2008
- *Prosecutor v Popović et al,* IT-05-88, Judgment of 30 January 2015

VI International Criminal Tribunal of Rwanda

- *Prosecutor v. Kambanda*, Trial Chamber, ICTR 97-23-S, 4 September 1998

VII Extraordinary Chamber in the Courts of Cambodia

- *Decision on the Appeals Against the Co-Investigative Judges Order on Joint Criminal Enterprise* (*JCE*), Case File No: (002/19-09-2007-ECCC-OCIJ), Pre-Trial Chamber, 20 May 2010

VIII Domestic Courts

- *PDS parliamentary group v. Federal Government,* German Federal Constitutional Court, 19 June 2001
- *R (Al Jeddah) v. Secretary of State for Defence,* EWHC 1809, UK Administrative Court, (2005)
- *R (Al Jeddah) v. Secretary of State for Defence*, UK Court of Appeal, EWCA Civ 327 (2007)
- Tribunal of First Instance of Brussels, *El Hamidi & Chlih v. NATO*, R.G. no. 11/9647/A, 21 October 2012

- High Court of England and Wales, *Serdar Mohammed v. Ministry of Defence*, 2014, EWHC 1369, OB
- *Amnesty International et al v. Attorney General of Canada et al*, Federal Court of Canada, T-324-07, 25 January 2008
- *Dredge and Dock* [1985] 1 SCR 662, Canadian Supreme Court, 23 May 1985
- Hoge Raad der Nederlanden, *Short v. Kingdom of The Netherlands*, ECLI:NL:HR1990:AD7494, 30 March 1990
- *Nuhanovic v. De Staat der Nederlanden*, Gerechtshof Den Haag, 200.020.174/01, 5 July 2011
- *Staat der Nederlanden v. Erik O.*, District Court Arnhem, ECLI:RBARN:2004: AR4029, 05/097011-03, 18 October 2004.

CHAPTER 1

Introduction

Few might have envisaged the scope and nature of transformation that the North Atlantic Treaty Organization (NATO) went through since the adoption of the Washington Treaty on the 4th of April 1949. The Alliance was initially created to collectively defend the fundamental values and principles of the Transatlantic member States, embellished in Article 5 of the Washington Treaty, which constitutes the cornerstone of the Alliance:

> [I]f [...] an armed attack occurs, each of them, in exercise of the right of individual or collective self-defence recognised by Article 51 of the Charter of the United Nations, will assist the Party or Parties so attacked by taking forthwith, individually and in concert with the other Parties, such action as it deems necessary, including the use of armed force, to restore and maintain the security of the North Atlantic area.[1]

In the first four decades since its inception, NATO prepared to counter an armed attack from the Soviet Union, but – fortunately – was never required to actually come into action. Ironically, NATO embarked on a large number of military operations that were outside of the original extent of the Treaty. In order to *"safeguard the freedom, common heritage and civilisation of their peoples, founded on the principles of democracy, individual liberty and the rule of law",*[2] the Alliance launched humanitarian assistance missions,[3] anti-piracy operations,[4] peace enforcement operations[5] and military training missions.[6]

1 Article 5, *North Atlantic Treaty 1949*, 34 UNTS 243, 24 August 1949.

2 Preamble, *North Atlantic Treaty 1949*, 34 UNTS 243, 24 August 1949.

3 For example, NATO Relief mission to Pakistan, 11 October 2005–1 February 2006. For a complete list of NATO-led operations, see Appendix A "NATO-led Military Operations" to this book.

4 Operations Allied Provider (24 October–13 December 2008), Allied Protector (24 March–29 June 2009) and Ocean Shield (17 August 2009 – present).

5 Operations Deadeye (30–31 August 1995), Deliberate Force (5–14 September 1995), Joint Endeavour (IFOR, 20 December 1995–20 December 1996), Joint Guard / Joint Forge (SFOR, 20 December 1996–2 December 2004), Allied Force (24 March–20 June 1999), Allied Harbour (26 April–30 August 1999), Joint Guardian (KFOR, 12 June 1999 – present), International Security Assistance Force (ISAF, 11 August 2003 – present).

6 NATO Training Mission – Iraq (NTM-I, 7 August 2004 – present), Operation Resolute Support (June 2014 – present).

 | DOI 10.1163/9789004354647_002

These so-called 'out-of-area, non-article 5' operations are a far cry from the static collective self-defence mission for which the Alliance was originally created in 1949.

With the increased involvement of NATO in operations around the world, the question of responsibility of the Alliance for breaches of international law became more impelling. In fact, the responsibility of international organizations in general started to attract the attention of the public more and more.[7] There are two reasons that explain this recently growing interest, the first being that international organizations are a fairly new phenomenon in international law.[8] Another reason is that international organizations were initially seen only as capable to do "good".[9] It may not have been anticipated that international organizations could also commit wrongful acts.

That perception changed in the last two decades. The idea that international organizations should be held responsible for wrongful acts gained traction in the wake of the failure of the UN to act in places where atrocities, like genocide in Rwanda and Srebrenica, have taken place. Klabbers notes that holding international organizations responsible under international law is not straightforward; *"With NATO dropping bombs over Belgrade in the late 1990s, should one blame NATO? Should one blame its most influential member State for quite possibly pushing the action through? Should one blame all member States? Or only those who actively participated?"*[10] Academic research emerged on the

7 Klabbers, J. (2009), *An introduction to international institutional law.* United Kingdom: Cambridge University Press, pp. 271–273. Klabbers illustrates the relatively new phenomenon of responsibility of international organisations by taking the collapse of the International Tin Council in the mid-1980s as an example. Since then the study on the responsibility of international organisations gained significant attention.

8 The International Telecommunications Union (ITU) is seen as the oldest intergovernmental organisation, established in 1865. In respect of State responsibility, the responsibility of international organisations is a much younger concept and its rules and definitions are less established through practice and jurisprudence. Hartwig, M. (2013), *International organizations or institutions, responsibility and liability.* Available at: http://opil.ouplaw.com/view/10.1093/law:epil/9780199231690/law-9780199231690-e509?rskey=26uGlh&result=6&prd=EPIL (Accessed: 12 May 2016).

9 According to the representative of the Netherlands to the UN General Assembly, it was *"unrealistic to assume that international organizations were by definition 'good doers'. They were capable of internationally wrongful acts. A system and a set of rules on responsibility needed to be established even without extensive practice."* UN General Assembly, press release, *Treaties comprise bulk of international law, so States need guidelines,* GA/L/3354, 30 October 2008.

10 Klabbers, J. (2009), *An introduction to international institutional law.* United Kingdom: Cambridge University Press, p. 274.

responsibility of international organizations, particularly relating to their activities during military operations.[11] International and domestic jurisprudence as well as State practice developed rapidly. NATO became the subject, or at least was the context, in cases before the International Court of Justice (ICJ) and the European Court of Human Rights.[12]

International organizations came under scrutiny of the public for their role regarding criminal conduct of their personnel as well. In 2000, allegations arose of personnel of the United Nations Mission in Kosovo (UNMiK) and of Kosovo Force (KFOR) having committed acts of human trafficking and forced prostitution in Kosovo. The allegations caused certain human rights organizations to call for a re-examination of the reason why, for instance, UN personnel should be accorded immunity that prevented criminal prosecution.[13]

---

11 Schmalenbach, K. (2004) *Die Haftung Internationaler Organisationen: Im Rahmen Von Militaereinsaetzen und Territorialverwaltungen*. Germany: Peter Lang Gmbh, Internationaler Verlag Der Wissenschaften, Zwanenburg, M.C. (2005) *Accountability of peace support operations*, Netherlands: Martinus Nijhoff Publishers, Naert, F. (2010) *International law aspects of the EU's security and Defence policy, with a particular focus on the law of armed conflict and human rights*. Belgium: Intersentia Publishers, International Law Commission (ILC), *Articles on the Responsibility of International Organizations*, 2011.

12 Before the International Court of Justice (ICJ), several respondent States argued that the use of force during the NATO air campaign in 1999 over Kosovo should be attributed to NATO rather than the individual member States, International Court of Justice, *Legality of Use of Force* (Serbia and Montenegro v. Belgium, Canada, France, Germany, Italy, Netherlands, Portugal, Spain, United Kingdom and Yugoslavia v. United States of America), (1999), ICJ Reports 1999, 916. The title refers to several cases before the ICJ, initiated by Serbia and Montenegro / Yugoslavia against ten NATO member States on 29 April 1999 regarding the bombing of Yugoslav territory as part of the NATO operation "Allied Force", *International Court of Justice, Legality of Use of Force (Serbia and Montenegro v. Portugal), Preliminary objections of the Portuguese Republic, 5 July 2000*, Chapter II, para. 40. In *Behrami*, the European Court of Human Rights examined which entity – the UN, NATO or Troop Contributing Nations – should be held responsible for the death and injury of two children caused in 2000 by unexploded ordnance dropped during NATO operation "Allied Force", European Court of Human Rights, *A. Behrami against France*, application no. 71412/01 and *R. Saramati against France, Germany and Norway*, application no. 78166/01, Decision of 2 May 2007.

13 United Nations Mission in Kosovo (UNMiK) Regulation 2000/47, 18 August 2000, "*UNMiK, its property, funds and assets shall be immune from any legal process. 3.2 The Special Representative of the Secretary General, the Principal Deputy, and the four Deputy Special Representatives of the Secretary General, the Police Commissioner, and other high-ranking officials as may be decided from time to time by the Special Representative of the Secretary General, shall be immune from local jurisdiction in respect of any civil or criminal act performed or committed by them in the territory of Kosovo. 3.3 UNMIK personnel, including*

Questions were raised regarding the measures the UN should have taken to prevent this kind of conduct.[14] NATO was similarly criticised for their inaction against KFOR personnel allegedly involved in the same sort of conduct. Both organizations since then have issued policy on combating human trafficking and forced prostitution,[15] but the incidents led to much more academic research on the responsibility of the international organizations in relation to criminal conduct of its personnel and their perceived inability to counter misconduct of their personnel.[16]

The transformation of the Alliance, the substantial increase in out-of-area operations and the emerging interest in the responsibility of international organizations were the main drivers to dedicate a study on NATO's responsibility during military operations.

1.1 The Concept of International Responsibility

International responsibility may be one of the most vast and complex topics of international law.[17] It forms part of an area of international public law, which consists of rules governing the relationship between international subjects of law, i.e. States and international organizations with international legal personality.

International responsibility arises when there is a breach of an international obligation by a State or international organization. The consequences of responsibility may include the obligation to make reparations of damage or injury. The conditions by which international responsibility arises are described

---

locally recruited personnel, shall be immune from legal process in respect of words spoken and all acts performed by them in their official capacity. 3.4 UNMIK personnel shall be immune from any form of arrest or detention. If erroneously detained, they shall be immediately turned over to UNMIK authorities [...]" (emphases added).

14 Amnesty International (2004) *'So does it mean that we have the rights?' Protecting the human rights of women and girls trafficked for forced prostitution in Kosovo*. Available at: http://reliefweb.int/report/serbia/so-does-it-mean-we-have-rights-protecting.

15 NATO, *NATO Policy on combating human trafficking in human beings*, and appendices, 29 June 2004. United Nations Department of Peacekeeping Operations (UN DPKO) *Human trafficking and United Nations peacekeeping*, March 2004.

16 UN, General Assembly, *Comprehensive review of the whole question of peacekeeping in all their aspects*, A/59/710, 24 March 2005.

17 United Nations, International Law Commission, Reports of the Special Rapporteur on State Responsibility, A/CN.4/96, 8th session of the ILC, 1956, p. 175.

in the International Law Commission's (ILC) Articles on State Responsibility[18] and the Articles on the Responsibility of International Organizations.[19]

These articles describe the conditions under which responsibility arises, but do not outline the content of international obligations. This is done for obvious reasons, as the obligations to which each State or international organization may be bound, will vary. This research will examine in Chapter 6 the international obligations binding upon NATO.

International responsibility arises when there is a wrongful act, which is attributable to a State or international organization. Attribution is the link between the organization and individuals through whom the organization acts in the physical world. The ILC's Articles deal with the rules of attribution in detail. This book will focus on how these rules are applied to NATO, with specific attention to the fact that the Alliance relies mainly on military personnel that is placed at its disposal by States.

International responsibility also encompasses mechanisms to invoke responsibility for wrongful acts. Chapter 2 of the ILC's Articles on the Responsibility of States and Chapter 2 of the ILC Articles on Responsibility of International Organizations both deal with the reparation for injury caused by a wrongful act of a subject of international law which include actions such as restitution, compensation and satisfaction. The ILC noted that invocation of such rules is open to States or international organizations. The victim-State can demand reparation from the State or organization that has caused the damage. Notwithstanding this possibility, claims are not frequently made against inernational organizations. The main reason for this – but certainly not the only – is that international organizations often lack legal standing before international tribunals or courts.

International organizations, such as NATO, may cause injury or damage caused to individuals. The ILC's Articles do not mention the possibility of individuals to demand reparation from a State or organization, but States and organizations may take certain measures on behalf of the injured individual. In such cases a right of diplomatic protection may arise. Diplomatic protection consists of the resort to diplomatic action (or other means of peaceful settlement) by a State or organization adopting in its own right the cause of its national in respect of an injury to that national arising from an internationally

18 ILC, Report by Mr. R. Ago, Chairman of the Sub-Committee on State Responsibility, A/CN.4/152, 1963.

19 ILC, Articles on the Responsibility of International Organizations, A/66/10, 2011.

wrongful act.[20] Rights to diplomatic protection may be created in domestic law, opening the possibility for individuals to forward their claims directly against the international organization before domestic courts, after they have exhausted remedies made available within the organization. For example, individuals have recourse against the European Community before the European Court of Justice. Within NATO, however, no such direct recourse for individuals exists.

1.2 Research Objective and Research Questions

1.2.1 *Research Objective*

The book focuses particularly on one specific international organization: the North Atlantic Treaty Organization. It does not cover the responsibility of other international organizations, such as the United Nations and European Union. These organizations may participate with NATO in military operations or may launch operations that are very similar to those of NATO. This research may contribute to existing efforts on the responsibility of the EU and the UN, but the conclusions drawn and observations made in this book are first and foremost only relevant to NATO, given its specific characteristics, such as its institutional framework and decision-making procedures.

A second limitation imposed on the scope of the book is the confinement of responsibility during NATO operations. This book will not examine the responsibility of NATO during peacetime garrison activities. Rather, it will focus on the responsibility during operations. The term 'operations' will include all types of NATO operations (peace support operations,[21] post-conflict stabilisation operations and humanitarian operations). A characteristic of NATO operations is the involvement of the use of (military) force. Therefore, the book will examine in particular the international norms governing the justifications to use force (*jus ad bellum*) and the rules governing the conduct of warfare (*jus in bello*). The sources of these obligations are found in international customary law and conventional law, such as the UN Charter, UN Security Council

20 Article 1(1), Report of the International Law Commission on the Work of its Fifty-Fourth Session, 2002, A/57/10, at 169. The UN and academic writers recognized the possibility that diplomatic protection is also possible against international organizations, *Brief for the United Nations as Amicus Curiae, United Nations Juridical Yearbook 1980,* at 2227, Ritter, J.P., *La Protection Diplomatique à l'Egard d'une Organisation Internationale,* 8 Annuaire Français de Droit International 427 (1962).

21 Peace Support Operations include conflict prevention, peace enforcement, peacekeeping, peace-making, peace building and humanitarian relief operations (Chapter 2, NATO Allied Joint Publication 3.4.1. Peace Support Operations, July 2001).

resolutions, international humanitarian law and international human rights law. The book will not examine other international obligations that may arise for NATO, such as the obligation to request diplomatic clearance for overflight of State aircraft under the Chicago Convention[22] or other international obligations not directly pertaining to the use of military force.

Perhaps needless to say, military operations inevitably have a negative impact on the civilian population. Chapter 2 of this book illustrates the social magnitude of responsibility of NATO for violations of international law. The lack of a clear position – by NATO, its member States as well as in academic literature – as to whether NATO is an international organization with international legal personality and – as such – can be held responsible for violations of international law during its operations, is detrimental to ensuring respect for international humanitarian law and international human rights law and undermines efforts to prevent and repress violations of international law. It is the intention of this research to examine whether NATO is responsible for breaches of international law during its operations, and to determine whether NATO should adopt a more proactive role in taking up that responsibility. In the current situation where there is no unambiguous position as to whether the Alliance can be responsible for breaches of international law, NATO consequently barely takes action to prevent, investigate or repress violations of international law committed or about to be committed during its military operations. It leaves this responsibility almost entirely to the individual troop contributing nations, resulting in a very fragmented approach to address breaches of international law. For instance, there is no single approach in NATO operations regarding the treatment and transfer of detainees, nor is there an overarching policy relating to the investigation and repression of misconduct of personnel. These issues are entirely left to the member States, which does not support an efficient and effective implementation to guarantee the respect of international law during NATO operations.

Beyond the social relevance of examining the responsibility of NATO during operations, the book aims at contributing to the scientific development of responsibility of international organizations in international law. Other international organizations, for instance the European Union (EU), the United Nations (UN) and African Union (AU), are equally involved in military operations. There is increasing academic research relating to their responsibility under international law. Although NATO is not identical to other international organizations, some of the conclusions made in this book may equally be valid to other international organizations. Another aspect that this book examines,

22 *Convention on Civil Aviation*, 1944, 15 UNTS 295, 4 April 1947.

is the position of States vis-à-vis NATO, which may contribute to the general academic understanding of responsibility of international organizations for violations of international law. States may act as members of the international organization, while at the same time the international organization can be an independent legal entity separate from the member States. The position of States in relation to the international organization of which they are members, is not always clear. This book aims to contribute to the general academic efforts of the responsibility of international organizations.

Since NATO operations are carried out by individuals, i.e. its personnel, it seems appropriate to define what is meant with 'NATO personnel'. In the most basic form, NATO personnel consist of personnel in the employment of the Alliance. Their salaries are paid by the Alliance and the employment is regulated by a contract between the organization and the employee. Currently (as of 2017), there are over 6.000 international civil servants working for NATO.

The largest part of the NATO work-force consists, however, of military personnel. NATO does not have military forces of its own, but depends on contributions of States. Military personnel may be seconded to NATO headquarters in Europe and the United States. Additionally, for the execution of its operations, it relies on military forces made available by Troop Contributing Nations, i.e. States that place their military forces under the command of NATO for a specific operation. Since military personnel remain in the service of their respective States, a prominent question is to determine to which entity their conduct should be attributed. This issue has been a central question before various international and domestic courts,[23] most recently before the Supreme Court of The Netherlands which decided that the conduct of Dutch military personnel attached to the United Nations Protection Force in Srebrenica is attributable to both the United Nations as well as The Netherlands' government.[24]

This study will, in addition, examine NATO's responsibility for violations of the rules of international humanitarian and human rights involving international criminal responsibility. It is important to note here that the study will not examine individual criminal responsibility nor criminal responsibility under national law. Instead it will focus on the responsibilities and obligations that NATO has in respect of criminal acts committed by its personnel.

---

23 ECtHR, Grand Chamber, Decision, *Admissibility of Application no. 71412/01 by A. Behrami and B Behrami against France and Application no. 78166/01 by R. Saramati against France, Germany and Norway*, 2 May 2007. European Court of Human Rights, *Al-Jedda v. The United Kingdom*, application no. 27021/08, Decision of 7 July 2011.

24 Hoge Raad der Nederlanden, *H. Nuhanović v. the Netherlands*, ECLI:NL:HR:2013:BZ9225, 6 September 2013.

There are two reasons for including this topic, which relates partially to international criminal law, in a study that covers the responsibility of NATO under international public law.

The first reason is that international crimes constitute the most severe form of wrongful conduct that could possibly take place during NATO operations. International crimes constitute gross or serious violations of international human rights law and international humanitarian law. The Statute of the International Criminal Court includes four such core crimes: the crime of genocide, war crimes, crimes against humanity and the crime against of aggression.[25]

The second reason is found in the development of rules establishing a positive obligation to prevent and suppress international crimes.[26] This obligation may be to prevent, criminalise, criminally investigate, prosecute and punish perpetrators of human rights violations, whether these have been committed by public officials or private individuals.[27] As a result, criminal offences perpetrated by public officials or private individuals can lead to the responsibility of States and international organizations under international law.[28]

While it is perhaps interesting to analyse the available remedies for damages resulting from wrongful conduct by international organizations,[29] this book will not examine the mechanisms that exist to invoke the responsibility of NATO. Legal literature doctrinally separates procedural and material aspects of responsibility. A study on the conditions under which responsibility for NATO arises does not necessarily require a study on the potential remedies available to invoke that responsibility. Moreover, the inclusion of available procedural mechanisms to invoke the responsibility of NATO would demand an additional

---

25 E.g. Article 6, article 8, article 7, article 8 *bis* 202 *Rome Statute of the International Criminal Court*, 2002, 2187 UNTS 90, 1 July 2002.

26 The UN has promulgated a set of principles for the protection and promotion of human rights through action to combat impunity, ECOSOC report E/CN.4/2005/102/Add.1. The principles refer to serious crimes under international law and include grave breaches of the Geneva Conventions of 1949 and other violations of international humanitarian law that are crimes under international law such as genocide, crimes against humanity and other violations of internationally protected human rights that are crimes under international law.

27 E.g. Article 2(3) of the *International Covenant on Civil and Political Rights*, 1966, 999 UNTS 171, 23 March 1976, or the *Optional Protocols to the Convention on the Rights of the Child on the Involvement of Children in Armed Conflict*, 2002, 1577 UNTS 3, 12 February 2002.

28 Responsibility in this case will arise from a violation of a primary rule.

29 Zegveld, L. (2003) *'Remedies for victims of violations of international humanitarian law'*, International Review of the Red Cross, 85(851) Optional Protocols to the Convention on the Rights of the Child on the Involvement of Children in Armed Conflict.

and separate volume to this book. Such research would be well served in a separate study specifically dedicated to that aspect.

1.2.2 *Research Questions*

The central question of this research is: what is the scope and the extent of NATO's responsibility for violations of the rules of public international law and international criminal law during military operations? This central question can be broken down into four sub-questions.

The first sub-question is whether NATO is a subject of international law to which a wrongful act can be attributed. Is the Alliance an association of States or an international organization, existing as a subject of international law and separate from its member States? Without international legal personality, only the member States – and not NATO – could be held legally responsible. The criteria to establish the existence of international legal personality are formulated by the ICJ in the *Reparations* case[30] and further developed in academic research.[31] These criteria will be used to determine NATO's status under international law.

The second sub-question is: Which international obligations exist for NATO under international law, in particular during its military operations? A breach of an international obligation relating to military operations may result in a wrongful act of the Alliance. NATO's military operations typically take place in situations of crisis or of armed conflict and consist of military personnel, authorised to use force. Given these characteristics, the norms of international humanitarian law and international human rights law are particularly relevant. Other international obligations may exist, such as obligations under the UN Charter and UN Security Council resolutions, providing in many cases the authorization for NATO operations.

The third sub-question is: When and under which conditions can wrongful conduct of NATO personnel committed during military operations be attributed to NATO? As stated above, NATO personnel consists of military and civilian personnel, either in the employment of NATO or placed at the disposal of the Alliance. Under certain conditions their conduct can be attributed either to NATO, to other international organizations – such as the UN – or to States. It

30 International Court of Justice, *Reparations for Injuries suffered in the Service of the United Nations*, (1949), ICJ Reports 1949, 174.

31 Crawford, J. (2012) *Brownlie's principles of public international law*. 8th edn. Oxford: Oxford University Press, USA, Klabbers, J. (2009) *An introduction to international institutional law*. United Kingdom: Cambridge University Press, Shaw, M.N. (2014) *International law*. United Kingdom: Cambridge University Press.

is also conceivable that the conduct can be attributed to multiple entities. Recent developments in academic research[32] and jurisprudence[33] have resulted in a set of generally accepted criteria by which conduct is assessed to be attributable and to which entity.

The fourth sub-question regards the possible responsibility under international public law of NATO in case of international crimes committed by its personnel deployed in military operations. NATO may be responsible for an international crime under international law only if it has violated an obligation to take measures to prevent, investigate or punish the perpetrator.

1.3 Methodology and Materials

Article 38 of the Statute of the International Criminal of Justice (ICJ) lists the sources of international law. These sources have also been used to analyse and determine the scope and content of the responsibility of NATO during its operations.[34] There are four sources enumerated: (1) international conventions, (2) international custom, (3) general principles of law recognised by civilised nations and, as a subsidiary source, (4) judicial decisions and the teachings of the most highly qualified publicists of the various nations. In addition, the

32 International Law Commission (ILC), *Draft Articles on the Responsibility of International Organizations*, Sixty-third session, A/CN.4/634, 2011. Nollkaemper, A. and Nedeski, N. (2012) *'Responsibility of international organizations "in connection with acts of states"'*: 'SSRN', Amsterdam Centre for International Law, 31 May 2012.

33 ECtHR, Grand Chamber, Decision *Admissibility of Application no. 71412/01 by A. Behrami and B Behrami against France and Application no. 78166/01 by R. Saramati against France, Germany and Norway*, 2 May 2007. European Court of Human Rights, *Al-Jedda v. The United Kingdom*, application no. 27021/08, Decision of 7 July 2011. International Court of Justice, *Legality of Use of Force* (Serbia and Montenegro v. Belgium, Canada, France, Germany, Italy, Netherlands, Portugal, Spain, United Kingdom and Yugoslavia v. United States of America), (1999), ICJ Reports 1999, 916.

34 Article 38, *Statute of the International Court of Justice*, 1945, 33 UNTS 993, 26 June 1945, *"(1) The Court, whose function is to decide in accordance with international law such disputes as are submitted to it, shall apply: a. international conventions, whether general or particular, establishing rules expressly recognized by the contesting states; b. international custom, as evidence of a general practice accepted as law; c, the general principles of law recognized by civilized nations; d. subject to the provisions of article 59, judicial decisions and the teachings of the most qualified publicists of the various nations, as subsidiary means for the determination of rules of law."*

Vienna Convention on the Law of Treaties has been used to interpret these primary sources.[35]

International responsibility of international organizations is a topic that is not yet fully developed in international law, despite the adoption of the Draft Articles on Responsibility of International Organizations by the ILC in 2011. To date, there is only little State practice and there are only few clearly developed principles of law in that field. Despite these limitations, the Articles are the only document which can serve in the analysis of international responsibility of NATO.

The subsidiary sources, i.e. academic research and judicial decisions of the international courts and tribunals, have been used more extensively to arrive at the conclusions made in this research.

As for the reliance on academic sources, this study uses the ILC's "Draft Articles on the Responsibility of International Organizations" extensively.[36] There are several reasons for this choice. First, the ILC is an institute established by the UN General Assembly in 1946. It is mandated – among other tasks – to promote the codification of international law. As such, the ILC has a special status among others, as the international community directly tasks the ILC to codify and develop international law directly. Secondly, particularly in the area of responsibility of international organizations – where practice of States and international organizations is little available – it is important to receive agreement, or at least acquiescence, from these actors that the rules represent a degree of *opinio iuris*. The ILC inquired States and international organizations and requested them to submit their comments and observations on the Articles. This interaction adds extra value to the work of the ILC and may to some extent compensate for the lack of State practice. Moreover, the Articles have been used as a reference by judicial institutions, such as the European Court of Human Rights,[37] the International Court of Justice[38] and domestic courts,[39] in their judgments. While there are other sources relating to the international

35 Section 3, *Interpretation of Treaties, Vienna Convention on the Law of Treaties*, 1980, 1155 UNTS 331, 27 January 1980.

36 ILC, *Draft Articles on the Responsibility of International Organizations*. UN General Assembly (GA) Resolution A/RES/66/100, 27 February 2012.

37 ECtHR, Grand Chamber, Decision, *Admissibility of Application no. 71412/01 by A. Behrami and B Behrami against France and Application no. 78166/01 by R. Saramati against France, Germany and Norway*, 2 May 2007.

38 International Court of Justice, *Case Concerning the Application of the Convention on the Prevention and Punishment of the Crime of Genocide*, (2007), ICJ Reports 2007, 43.

39 UK Court of Appeal, *R (Al Jeddah) v. Secretary of State for Defence*, EWCA Civ 327 (2007), 12 December 2007.

responsibility of international organizations, such as the works of the International Law Association,[40] the work of the ILC can be seen as most authoritative in this respect. The ILA's work is primarily academic in nature and does not serve governments in the same respect as the ILC does.

The ILC adopted the Articles on the Responsibility of International Organizations during its 63rd session in August 2011 and recommended to the UN General Assembly to elaborate of a convention on the basis of these Articles.[41] The General Assembly adopted without vote Resolution 66/100 in which it takes note of the Articles and considered the recommendation of the ILC. The General Assembly did not decide on the form that might be given to the Articles.[42] Therefore, the Articles do not have the status of an internationally legally binding document for States and international organizations. It seems that it depends on the international legal community, including scholars, judicial institutions and state practice, whether the Articles will be considered and treated as an authoritative source.

Other sources, not covered by Article 38 of the ICJ Statute, include decisions of international organizations, in particular of the UN Security Council and NATO's North Atlantic Council. The study also relies on NATO policy, doctrine and operating procedures. Most of the key materials, such as the Strategic Concepts, have been declassified and are publicly available. Other material may be classified, however its content is publicly available as it may have been disclosed in judicial proceedings,[43] parliamentary inquiries[44] or investigations that have been made public.[45] While the author also had other material

---

40 International Law Association, *Study Group on the Responsibility of International Organizations,* Sofia Conference 2012.

41 ILC, *Report of the International Law Commission on the work of its sixty-third session,* 26 April–3 June and 4 July–12 August 2011, General Assembly, Sixty-Sixth Session, Supplement no. 10, A/66/10/Add.1.

42 UN General Assembly, *Resolution adopted by the General Assembly on 9 December 2011,* A/RES/66/100, 27 February 2012.

43 E.g. the ISAF detention procedures are classified, but publicly made available to a large extent in the case of the Canadian Federal Court of Appeal, Amnesty International Canada and British Columbia Civil Liberties Association and Chief of the Defence Staff for the Canadian Forces, Minister of National Defence and Attorney General of Canada, A-149-08, 10 December 2008.

44 E.g. Parliamentary reports describe operations in fairly detailed manner, referring to classified material in some instances. See, Tweede Kamer der Staten-Generaal, *Bestrijding internationaal terrorisme,* vergaderjaar 2007–2008, 27925, nr. 272 on the ISAF operation in Chora, Afghanistan.

45 For example, ISAF targeting directives are classified but publicly available when the newspaper Spiegel obtained the reports on the investigation on an allegedly indiscriminate

available in his positions as a legal adviser to the Netherlands Ministry of Defence and to NATO, the study has relied primarily on publicly available documents to allow academic review to take place. The preparation of the book has taken place through collection and critical analysis of documents, legal texts, jurisprudence, academic publications and other information.

1.4 Object of Study

This study examines the responsibility of NATO for wrongful conduct of its personnel during NATO operations and the responsibility for international crimes committed by its personnel within the context of these operations. Since this study is limited to responsibility during "NATO operations", it is appropriate to define here in more detail, which operations qualify as such and which do not.

NATO uses the term "NATO operations" to encompass any operation that is conducted under the command and control of NATO.[46] Operations that fall outside of this definition are those operations under the command and control of a State,[47] a coalition of States[48] or other international organizations.[49]

A broad range of activities fall under the definition of NATO operations.[50] They include collective defence operations, peace support operations, security sector reform, interim-governance, disaster relief operations[51] and even surveillance activities during certain popular events such as the Olympics and Football championships.[52]

---

airstrike in Kunduz, Afghanistan, Spiegel Online, *New allegations against German officer who ordered Kunduz air strike,* 21 September 2009.

46 http://www.nato.int/cps/en/natolive/official_texts_75565.htm, accessed 15 July 2014.

47 E.g. Operation Enduring Freedom, an operation conducted in *inter alia* Afghanistan, since 7 October 2001 against terrorism, under command and control of the United States of America.

48 E.g. Multinational Force Iraq, an operation conducted in Iraq, from 14 May 2004 to 31 December 2009, to implement UN Security Council resolution 1546(2004), under the command and control of the United States of America, United Kingdom, Australia and Poland.

49 E.g. Operation Atalanta, an operation conducted in the Horn of Africa, since 8 December 2008, to combat piracy, under the command and control of the EU.

50 NATO Allied Joint Publication 3(A) *Allied Joint Operations,* 2 July 2007.

51 Such operations include the humanitarian relief operations in Pakistan in response to the flooding in 2010, and in the US in response to the disaster caused by hurricane Katrina in 2005.

52 NATO air surveillance was requested for the 2004 Summer Olympics in Greece, 2004 European Football Championship in Portugal, 2006 World Cup Football Championship in Germany, 2012 Euro Football Championship and other important meetings and events.

Arguably, responsibility may arise equally during all of these activities and even during peacetime garrison activities.[53] However, there are three reasons why the study covers only NATO military operations. The first reason is that NATO is uniquely equipped to command large-scale, high-intensity military operations. These operations will justifiably have a prominent place in research on the responsibility of NATO. Secondly, the book focuses on the responsibility under public international law, which is defined as the law between states and / or international organizations, especially within the context of the law of war, peace and security, and the protection of territories.[54] Therefore, the book particularly focuses on the responsibility of NATO during operations within the context of the maintenance of international peace and security or during collective self-defence operations. Finally, a considerable source of relevant international obligations for NATO during military operations is found in international humanitarian law, international human rights law and *jus ad bello*, which includes the UN Charter and UN Security Council resolutions. For these three reasons, the book will primarily focus on NATO-operations in which the use of military force plays a central role.[55] Broadly speaking, there are three types of operations that fall in this category. These are (1) collective defence operations,[56] (2) peace enforcement operations[57] and (3) peace operations.[58] A short description of these operations is appropriate here.

---

53 The term "peacetime garrison activities" refers to the activities undertaken by NATO during peacetime. They include activities relating to the sustainment of the headquarters.

54 Vinopal, K. (2013) *'Researching Public International Law'*, American Society of International Law, Electronic Research Guide.

55 Operations such as Peace building (NATO Allied Joint Publication 3.4.1, *Peace Support Operations*, Section VI), Humanitarian relief – (NATO Allied Joint Publication 3.4.1, *Peace Support Operations*, Section VII) and and Non-combatant Evacuation Operations (NATO Allied Joint Publication 3.4.2, *Non-combatant Evacuation Operations*, 2014) are not included, as these operations, in principle, do not involve the use of military force.

56 AJP 3.4, *Allied Joint Operations.*

57 AJP 3.4.1, *Peace Support Operations*, Section IV.

58 The latter category is not a NATO defined category, but encompasses peacekeeping (AJP 3.4.1, *Peace Support Operations*, Section IV), peacemaking (AJP 3.4.1, *Peace Support Operations*, Section V) and conflict prevention (AJP 3.4.1, *Peace Support Operations*, Section III). The terminology by NATO reflects the terminology used by the UN Department of Peacekeeping Operations, *UN Peacekeeping Operations, Principles and Guidelines*, 18 January 2008. All three have as a characteristic that the force operates upon the consent of the host State and additionally is subject to the principles of impartiality and restricted to the use of force in self-defence, T.D. Gill, The UN Collective Security System, in Gill, T.D. and Fleck, D. (eds.) (2010) *The handbook of the international law of military operations*, United Kingdom: Oxford University Press.

Collective defence operations are operations based on Article 5 of the Washington Treaty, which refers to the right of collective self-defence against an armed attack on one or more of its member States as recognised by Article 51 of the UN Charter.[59] Member States agreed that they would assist each other by taking actions as they deem necessary, including the use of armed force, to restore and maintain the security of the North Atlantic area. Article 5 leaves it up to the member States to choose which actions to take in this respect. They may choose to limit their action to, for example, political or economic support. Article 5 neither obliges the member States to achieve consensus within the North Atlantic Council (NAC) to approve an operation in the case of an armed attack. The provision merely affirms that an armed attack on one of the member States is considered an armed attack on each of them and that each of them may render assistance either individually or collectively. Two collective self-defence operations (Operation Eagle Eye and Operation Active Endeavour) have been conducted under NATO command and control, both in response to the attacks on the US by a terrorist organization "Al Qaida" on 11 September 2001.[60]

Peace enforcement and peace operations do not find their basis explicitly in the Washington Treaty. Instead, on the basis of a decision taken during the NATO Summit in Washington D.C. in 1999, the member States included conflict

---

59 Article 5, *North Atlantic Treaty* 1949, 34 UNTS 243, 24 August 1949, *"The Parties agree that an armed attack against one or more of them in Europe or North America shall be considered an armed attack against them all and consequently they agree that, if such an armed attack occurs, each of them, in exercise of individual or collective self-defence recognised by Article 51 of the UN Charter of the United Nations, will assist the Party or Parties so attacked by taking forthwith, individually or in concert with the other Parties, such action as it deems necessary, including the use of armed force, to restore and maintain the security of the North Atlantic area. Any such attack and all measures taken as a result thereof shall immediately be reported to the Security Council. Such measures shall be terminated when the Security Council has taken the measures necessary to restore and maintain international peace and security."*

Article 51, *Charter of the United Nations*, 1945, 1 UNTS XVI, 24 October 1945, *"Nothing in the present Charter shall impair the inherent right of individual or collective self-defence if an armed attack occurs against a Member of the United Nations, until the Security Council has taken measures necessary to maintain international peace and security. Measures taken by the Members in the exercise of this right of self-defence shall be immediately reported to the Security Council and shall not in any way affect the authority and responsibility of the Security Council under the present Charter to take at any time such action as it deems necessary in order to maintain or restore international peace and security."*

60 Operation Active Endeavour and Eagle Assist, see for an overview of all NATO operations the appendix to this book.

prevention and crisis management missions as part of NATO's fundamental security tasks.[61] The purpose of a peace enforcement operation is to maintain or restore international peace and security through the employment of a necessary degree of force.[62] Peace enforcement operations are undertaken on the basis of Chapter 7 of the UN Charter. If the UN Security Council determines that there is a threat to or breach of the international peace and security,[63] it may decide to take measures – including the use of armed force – to restore or maintain international peace and security.[64] The UN Security Council can choose to authorise member States or international organizations, such as NATO, to undertake a peace enforcement action.

Peace operations do not find their basis in the UN Charter, but have become an established and generally accepted instrument in the maintenance of peace.[65] Lacking a formal basis, these operations require the consent of the host State in order to deploy and operate on that State's territory.[66] The principles of peace operations are, next to the necessity of consent of the host nation, is that the operation is impartial towards the parties of the conflict and that the use of force is in principle restricted to that of self-defence.[67]

Accordingly, this study will deal with the responsibility of NATO during NATO operations, which are defined here as those operations conducted under the command and control of the Alliance and limited to collective defense operations, peace enforcement- and peace operations.

---

61 Strategic Concept 1999, 24 April 1999, paras. 10, 31–32.

62 Gill, T.D. and Fleck, D. (eds.) (2010) *The handbook of the international law of military operations, United Kingdom*: Oxford University Press, p. 82.

63 Article 39, Charter of the United Nations, 1945, 1 UNTS XVI, 24 October 1945, *"The Security Council shall determine the existence of any threat to the peace, breach of the peace, or act of aggression and shall take recommendations, or decide what measures shall be taken in accordance with Article 41 and 42, to maintain or restore international peace and security."*

64 Article 42, Charter of the United Nations, 1945, 1 UNTS XVI, 24 October 1945, *"Should the Security Council consider that measures provided for in Article 41 would be inadequate or have proven to be inadequate, it may take such action by air, sea, or land forces as may be necessary to maintain or restore international peace and security. Such action may include demonstrations, blockade, and other operations by air, sea, or land forces of Members of the United Nations."*

65 Gill, T.D. and Fleck, D. (eds.) (2010) *The handbook of the international law of military operations, United Kingdom*: Oxford University Press, p. 138.

66 Gill, T.D. and Fleck, D. (eds.) (2010) *The handbook of the international law of military operations, United Kingdom*: Oxford University Press, p. 136.

67 UN Department of Peacekeeping Operations, *UN Peacekeeping Operations, Principles and Guidelines*, 18 January 2008, p. 31.

1.5 Outline of the Study

The study starts with setting out three cases, providing practical examples of events that have occurred during NATO operations. The events relate to alleged violations of international law and show the reaction of States, NATO and other entities to those allegations. The purpose of the cases is threefold. First, they are intended to show the relevance of the topic of the book. The cases illustrate that responsibility of NATO is not a purely hypothetical issue, but is also practically relevant. Secondly, by providing examples of responsibility of NATO, the cases will make all that is discussed more concrete. Lastly, the cases will be used throughout the book to exemplify conclusions, analyses or positions. For these reasons, the three cases are presented at the beginning of this dissertation. In the concluding chapter of this study, a brief assessment of the cases is provided that apply the conclusions and recommendations made in this book to the cases.

Research on NATO itself logically starts with an overview of the organization and the way it has come into being. Therefore, Chapter 3 provides an overview of key historical events that have shaped the Alliance. It outlines the transformation of NATO as an alliance of member States to collectively defend themselves against a perceived threat emanating from the Soviet Union to an international organization capable to respond to various security threats, even beyond the borders of the territory of the member States. The chapter serves to provide a general understanding of the principles and objectives of NATO, but even more to provide the historical background to the analysis and conclusions made in subsequent chapters. For instance, the conclusion made in Chapter 5 that NATO is an international organization with international legal personality separate from its member States, may not be fully appreciated from reading NATO's founding documents. Neither would the analysis of the current institutional framework in Chapter 4 be fully appreciated, if no historical context had been provided. This context is an essential part for the analysis throughout the book and is – for this reason – given in Chapter 3.

Chapter 4 discusses the current institutional framework of NATO. This includes a study on the various organs of the Alliance and their authority in the planning and execution of NATO operations, but also the relationship of NATO with other international entities, such as States and international organizations. Moreover, a brief overview is given on the various categories of personnel employed by or attached to NATO. The conclusions and findings made in Chapters 3 and 4 are relevant to the rest of the research. For instance, the finding that the organization has grown into an independent actor distinct from its member States is relevant to Chapter 5 to determine whether NATO has international legal personality. The institutional framework discussed in Chapter 4 will be used in Chapter 7 to determine, for example, whether NATO has effective control over agents and organs placed at its disposal.

Chapter 5 deals with the international legal personality of the Alliance. Legal personality is relevant as only organizations that possess legal personality can be held responsible for violations of international legal norms.[68] Without international legal personality, conduct cannot be attributed to NATO and the organization cannot bear responsibility under international public law. In order to determine NATO's status under international law, recourse is made to the conditions set by the ICJ in its Advisory Opinion on the *Reparation for injuries suffered in the Service of the United Nations.*[69] Having examined the historic developments that the Alliance has gone through and the current institutional framework in Chapter 4, conclusions may be drawn whether NATO enjoys such status under international law.

Chapters 6 and 7 examine the responsibility of NATO for wrongful conduct under international public law. Chapter 6 identifies the international obligations binding upon the Alliance as far as they are relevant to its operations. It will discuss in particular obligations as they apply during military operations. Chapter 7 deals with the attribution of conduct of agents and organs to the Alliance. Again, the previous analysis on the Alliance's institutional framework discussed in Chapter 4 is used to determine for which conduct NATO can be held responsible.

The final chapter, Chapter 8, gives the conclusions and recommendations drawn from the previous chapters as well as an analysis of the three cases provided in the beginning of the book. It is also intended to provide practical recommendations to some of the challenges on the issue of responsibility that NATO might face during NATO-led operations.

68 Zwanenburg, M.C. (2005) *Accountability of peace support operations*, Netherlands: Martinus Nijhoff Publishers, p. 35.

69 International Court of Justice, *Reparations for Injuries suffered in the Service of the United Nations*, (1949), ICJ Reports 1949, 174.

CHAPTER 2

Three Illustrative Cases – Facts and Questions

2.1 Introduction

This chapter describes three situations taken from NATO operations in Kosovo and Afghanistan. The cases are introduced at the beginning of the book, because their intent is to illustrate the relevance of the research into the responsibility of NATO and to provide practical examples of that responsibility, which are then used throughout the rest of the book. Moreover, the practical examples make all that is discussed throughout the book more concrete.

While other cases were also available and could have been relevant, the selection of the three cases has been made based upon three criteria. First, for obvious reasons, the cases must relate to a NATO operation as this research deals with the responsibility of NATO during its operations. More specifically, the three cases relate to those NATO operations in which the international norms governing the justification to use force and the conduct of warfare are applicable. As mentioned in the previous chapter, NATO operations typically take place in situations of crisis or of armed conflict and in which personnel is authorised to use force. Given these characteristics IHL and IHRL are of particular relevance.

Second, each case covers several topics that will be examined throughout the book. The "Kunduz" incident (Afghanistan), covers the aspect of binding obligations[1] to NATO as well as attribution of conduct to either NATO or the member State. The case is also relevant to the role of NATO towards criminal conduct of its personnel.[2] The case relating to the transfer of detainees in Afghanistan deals primarily with the issue of attribution of conduct to several Troop Contributing Nations and NATO as well as a breach of an international obligation under the Convention against Torture and Other Cruel, Inhuman

1 In particular, articles 52 and 57 *Protocol Additional to the Geneva Conventions of 12 August 1949, and relating to the Protection of Victims of International Armed Conflicts*, 1977, 1125 UNTS 3, 8 June 1977.

2 The alleged indiscriminate attack on the fuel truck in Kunduz may be considered a crime under national host nation law (Afghanistan) and under German law, as well as an international crime under article 8 of the *Rome Statute of the International Criminal Court*, 2002, 2187 UNTS 90, 1 July 2002.

 | DOI 10.1163/9789004354647_003

or Degrading Treatment or Punishment.[3] The case on human trafficking that allegedly has occurred in Kosovo by KFOR members is relevant, primarily, to the question on the role that NATO plays regarding criminal conduct of its personnel as well to the issue of attribution to either the contingents involved or to the Alliance.

The third criteria for the selection of the cases is that the incidents have led to inquiries, e.g. by non-governmental organizations, judicial institutions, national parliaments, or international organizations, such as the UN Human Rights Council. This gives insight in how responsibility of NATO is viewed by others.

The cases are presented in a structure consisting of three parts. The first part explains the legal basis of the mission, the command structure and the status of mission personnel. The second part deals with the factual background of the incident that has occurred during the mission and which is relevant to this research. Finally, the third part describes the reaction by NATO and Troop Contributing Nation or third parties to these incidents.

2.2 Case 1: Human Trafficking and Forced Prostitution in Kosovo

2.2.1 *Background, Legal Framework of the Operation and Command Relationships*

Following the NATO air-campaign "Operation Allied Force" in Kosovo in 1999,[4] representatives of the European Union and the Russian Federation presented a peace plan to the United Nations, which resulted in the conclusion of a Military Technical Agreement (MTA) between the Federal Republic of Yugoslavia and NATO establishing the cessation of NATO air strikes upon the condition that Yugoslav forces would withdraw from the territory of Kosovo.[5]

The MTA anticipated that the United Nations Security Council would authorise an international security presence to be deployed in order to establish and maintain a secure environment in Kosovo.[6] Pending this authorization, the

3 *Convention against Torture and Other Cruel, Inhuman or Degrading Treatment or Punishment*, 1984, 1465 UNTS 85, 26 June 1987.

4 Operation Allied Force, 24 March–20 June 1999.

5 Military Technical Agreement between the International Security Force ("KFOR") and the Governments of the Federal Republic of Yugoslavia and the Republic of Serbia, 9 June 1999.

6 Article I, para 2, Military Technical Agreement between the International Security Force ("KFOR") and the Governments of the Federal Republic of Yugoslavia and the Republic of Serbia, 9 June 1999.

agreement stipulated that the Federal Republic of Yugoslavia and the Republic of Serbia *"understand and agree that the international security force ("KFOR") will deploy [...] and operate without hindrance within Kosovo and otherwise carry out its mission"*.[7]

Neither the MTA or the peace plan were intended to legitimise an international security presence in Kosovo, but rather to serve as a guarantee to the United Nations Security Council that the Federal Yugoslav Republic would agree to the deployment of such a presence.

By its resolution 1244(1999) of 10 June 1999 the UN Security Council authorised the creation of an international civil presence and an international security presence in Kosovo. The international civil presence was to be established by the *"Secretary General, with the assistance of relevant international organisations"*[8] and would have the task to provide for an interim administration for Kosovo. On 12 June 1999, the UN Secretary General presented a concept for the organization of the civil presence, which became known as the United Nations Interim Administration Mission in Kosovo (UNMiK)[9] led by the UN Special Representative of the Secretary General for Kosovo (SRSG). The concept outlined four pillars of activity,[10] individually led by the United Nations High Commissioner for Refugees (humanitarian assistance, Pillar I), the United Nations (civil administration, Pillar II), the Organization for Security and Co-operation in Europe (institution-building, Pillar III) and the European Union (reconstruction, Pillar IV).[11]

In contrast to the international civil presence, not the UN Secretary General but the *"member States and relevant international organisations"* would establish the international security presence.[12] The tasks of this presence included "*[d]eterring renewed hostilities,[...] [d]emilitarizing [...] armed Kosovo Albanian groups, [...] [e]nsuring public safety, [...] [s]upervising demining, [...] [s]upporting, [...] and coordinating [...] with [...] the international civil presence,*

---

7 Article I, para 2, Military Technical Agreement between the International Security Force ("KFOR") and the Governments of the Federal Republic of Yugoslavia and the Republic of Serbia, 9 June 1999.

8 United Nations Security Council resolution 1244(1999), 10 June 1999, para 10.

9 United Nations Security Council, Report of the Secretary General pursuant to paragraph 10 of the Security Council resolution 1244(1999), S/1999/672, 12 June 1999.

10 Article I, para 3, Military Technical Agreement between the International Security Force ("KFOR") and the Governments of the Federal Republic of Yugoslavia and the Republic of Serbia, 9 June 1999.

11 United Nations Security Council, Report of the Secretary General on the United Nations Interim Administration Mission in Kosovo, S/1999/779, 12 July 1999, para 43.

12 United Nations Security Council resolution 1244(1999), 10 June 1999, para. 7.

[c]onducting border monitoring duties [and] [e]nsuring the protection and freedom of movement of itself, the international civil presence, and other international organizations;"[13] These tasks reflect the tasks set out in the MTA and, as was envisaged in the peace plan, NATO would have a substantial participation in the international security presence.[14]

The international security presence and the international civil presence were placed under two separate commands, with a task to coordinate and support each other.[15] UNMiK is placed within the command chain of the UN and subordinate to the UN Special Representative of the UN Secretary General,[16] while NATO would have the responsibility over KFOR. This separation in command is emphasised by the UN Secretary General in its first report to the UN Security Council where it remarked KFOR as an "outside agency", with whom close coordination is required.[17]

KFOR is headed by the Commander KFOR, who sits within the NATO command structure. Political oversight of the operation is given by the NAC, while the NATO Supreme Allied Commander Europe (SACEUR) gives strategic military direction and guidance. Operational command and control is delegated to the Commander Joint Force Command Brunssum (at the time Commander in Chief South, NATO's Commander in Chief over the Southern region).

KFOR, at the time, was divided into four regionally based contingents, called Multinational Brigades (MNBs), each led by a "lead nation".[18] The composition of the nations leading the MNBs varied over time. In 2008, Finland led MNB Centre, France led MNB North, MNB South was led by Austria, MNB West was led by Italy and the USA led MNB East. Although the brigades were responsible for their area, they all fall under *the "unified command and control"* of the Commander of KFOR (COMKFOR).[19]

The mandate and tasks of KFOR were given in the UNSCR 1244(1999), which were transposed in NATO's operational plan 10413 (Operation Joint Guardian). The tasks encompassed the deterrence of renewed hostilities and

13 United Nations Security Council resolution 1244(1999), 10 June 1999, para. 9.

14 Annex, para 4, Letter dated 7 June 1999 from the Permanent Representative of Germany to the United Nations addressed to the President of the Security Council, S/1999/649, 7 June 1999.

15 United Nations Security Council resolution 1244(1999), 10 June 1999, paras. 6, 9(f) and 20.

16 United Nations Security Council resolution 1244(1999), 10 June 1999, para. 6.

17 Report of the Secretary General on the United Nations Interim Administration in Kosovo, S/1999/779, 12 July 1999, para. 47.

18 The US, UK, France, Germany and Italy would each lead a Multinational Brigade.

19 United Nations Security Council resolution 1244(1999), 10 June 1999, annex 2, paras. 4 and 76.

the establishment of a safe and secure environment in Kosovo, but also the marking and clearing of minefields and obstacles, and liaison with the UN and the Organization for Security and Co-operation in Europe (OSCE).[20] KFOR's operational plan envisaged four phases, starting with a preparatory phase, followed by the deployment of the force. The third phase consists of monitoring the withdrawal of the Yugoslav forces, ensuring a safe and secure environment, supervising the demining efforts until the international civil presence takes over this task and supporting and coordinating with the work of the international civil presence. The end-state of the KFOR operation is reached when these tasks of KFOR are either completed or handed over.[21]

2.2.2 *Status of Forces*

To regulate the status of UN personnel on mission, the UN ordinarily concludes a Status of Mission Agreement (SOMA) with the host nation,[22] which would refer to the Convention on Privileges and Immunities of the United Nations and accords immunity to UN personnel on mission from the host State jurisdiction for words spoken and acts performed by them in their official capacity. The Convention authorises the Secretary General to waive immunity for UN personnel on mission if the course of justice would be obstructed. For UNMiK, the procedure has been slightly different, but with a similar result. As the legislative functions of the host State in Kosovo were taken over by UNMiK,[23] the UN did not pursue a bi-lateral SOMA, rather it issued UNMiK Regulation 2000/47 referring to the UN Convention on Privileges and Immunities and accorded functional immunity to UNMiK personnel.[24]

The status of KFOR personnel is different from UNMiK personnel. Although initially an agreement (Status of Forces Agreeent, SOFA) with the host nation was envisaged in Article 3 of annex B of the MTA, this was never concluded. Instead, UNMiK and KFOR came to a joint declaration that *"KFOR personnel*

20 Operational Plan 10413, Operation Joint Guardian, pp. 4–5, [non-classified version], 12 February 1999.

21 KFOR is currently (beginning of 2017) still in Kosovo, which has been given a different set of tasks, including the standing down of the Kosovo Protection Corps and the creation of the Kosovo Security Force, www.aco.nato.int/kfor.

22 Status of Forces Agreement (SOFA) and Status of Mission Agreement (SOMA) is seemingly used inter-changeably. The UN uses the term SOMA for Chapter VI UN Charter operations commanded by the UN (JAG's Legal Center & School, U.S. Army, *Operational Law Handbook,* 2011, p. 62).

23 UNMiK Regulation No. 1999/1, 25 July 1999.

24 UNMiK Regulation No. 2000/47, UNMiK/REG/2000/47, 18 August 2000, on the status, privileges and immunities of KFOR and UNMiK and their personnel in Kosovo, Section 3.3.

shall be subject to the exclusive jurisdiction of their respective sending States. They shall be immune from local criminal, civil and administrative jurisdiction and from any form of arrest or detention other than by person acting on behalf of their sending States".[25] The joint declaration was readily agreed upon, since UNMiK was the sole entity possessing legislative powers in Kosovo to grant such immunity to KFOR. Subsequently, UNMiK issued Regulation 2000/49[26] providing KFOR immunity from the host nation and exclusive jurisdiction to the sending States.[27]

2.2.3 *Background of the Incident*

KFOR entered Kosovo on 12 June 1999 and deployed around fifty thousand troops from thirty-six NATO and non-NATO nations.[28] Given the fact that in 1999 Kosovo counted around two million inhabitants, the international security presence is in comparison very large; accounting for 2,5% of the local population. The amount of international personnel involved indicates the magnitude of the abovementioned tasks given to NATO to maintain and preserve security in Kosovo.

The large presence of relatively well-paid personnel from KFOR and various other international (non-governmental) organizations gave a significant impetus to the local economy.[29] At the same time, the international presence also drew the attention from individuals engaged in criminal activities such as prostitution and human trafficking. Several studies on Kosovo link the presence of personnel from international organizations such as NATO and the UN to an increase in human trafficking and forced prostitution.[30] A number of non-governmental organizations reported that Kosovo became a major destination

---

25 UNMiK/KFOR Joint Declaration, CJ(00)0320, 17 August 2000, reprinted in Fleck, D. (ed.) (2001) *The handbook of the law of visiting forces*, United Kingdom: Oxford University Press, p. 596.

26 UNMiK Regulation No. 2000/47, UNMiK/REG/2000/47, 18 August 2000, on the status, privileges and immunities of KFOR and UNMiK and their personnel in Kosovo, Section 2.

27 UNMiK Regulation No. 2000/47, UNMiK/REG/2000/47, 18 August 2000, on the status, privileges and immunities of KFOR and UNMiK and their personnel in Kosovo, Section 2.4(a).

28 KFOR is deployed under NATO's operation "Joint Guardian".

29 The number of international personnel amounted to 2.5% of the total population of Kosovo, H.M. Smith, C.A. Smith, *"Human trafficking; the unintended effects of United Nations intervention"*, International Political Science Review, Issue 34(2), March 2013, p. 14.

30 Amnesty International (2004) *'So does it mean that we have the rights?' Protecting the human rights of women and girls trafficked for forced prostitution in Kosovo.* Available at: http://reliefweb.int/report/serbia/so-does-it-mean-we-have-rights-protecting, Human Rights Watch, *"World Report 2003: events of 2002"*, 2003.

for women trafficked into prostitution.[31] Within six months of KFOR's arrival, at least four brothels opened within the vicinity of military bases and locations of the international organizations.[32] Eighteen premises were identified where clients included military and international civilian personnel. Since then, prostitution increased with unprecedented expectation; by January 2001, seventy-five premises were identified. Three years later this number climbed to two hundred. Prior to the deployment of the international presences these numbers were significantly lower.[33]

The problem of human trafficking and forced prostitution reached such a severity that UNMiK created a special police unit, called the "UNMiK Police Trafficking and Prostitution Investigation Unit (TPIU)" in November 2000. TPIU's aims were to *"[gather] evidence to assist in the prosecution of those believed to be responsible for trafficking"*.[34] TPIU acted expeditiously; issuing fifty-one indictments for persons involved in human trafficking of which fifteen were convicted. The numbers rose to ninety-two indictments the following year with twenty-seven convictions. The indictments and convictions were not directed at NATO personnel, but to other persons outside the NATO mission. In 2003, sixty persons were indicted for these criminal acts of which sixteen were convicted.[35]

Human trafficking is a crime and a grave violation of an international human right. The Protocol to Prevent, Suppress and Punish Trafficking in Persons to the United Nations Convention against Transnational Organized Crime obliges member States to prevent, suppress and punish human trafficking.[36]

---

31 Amnesty International (2004) *'So does it mean that we have the rights?' Protecting the human rights of women and girls trafficked for forced prostitution in Kosovo*. Available at: http://reliefweb.int/report/serbia/so-does-it-mean-we-have-rights-protecting and UNIFEM, *"No safe place: an assessment on violence against women in Kosovo"*, 2000.

32 UNIFEM, *"No safe place: an assessment on violence against women in Kosovo"*, 2000, p. 93.

33 UNIFEM, *"No safe place: an assessment on violence against women in Kosovo"*, 2000, p. 94, *"Prostitution took place in Kosovo before the advent of the international agencies but appears to be fairly limited [...] In four years investigating prostitution before 1998, my evidence is for 75–85 women in Kosovo [...] Professor, Pristina."*

34 Amnesty International (2004) 'So does it mean that we have the rights?' Protecting the human rights of women and girls trafficked for forced prostitution in Kosovo. Available at: http://reliefweb.int/report/serbia/so-does-it-mean-we-have-rights-protecting, p. 8.

35 TPIU reports 2001, 2002 and 2003, available on the UNMiK website.

36 The United Nations Convention against Transnational Organized Crime, entered into force on 29 September 2003 is supplemented by the Protocol to Prevent, Suppress and Punish Trafficking in Persons, Especially Women and Children and the Protocol against the Smuggling of Migrants by Land, Sea and Air. Article 5 of the Convention obliges States to establish as criminal offences the participation in an organised criminal group.

The Statute of the International Criminal Court classifies forced prostitution as a crime against humanity,[37] as well as a war crime.[38] Human trafficking is also a violation of international humanitarian law.[39]

The United Nations received criticism that – in relation to trafficking and the linked issue of sexual exploitation and abuse of trafficked women and women forced into prostitution – peacekeepers were rather part of the problem than of the solution.[40] While exact figures on the involvement of UN personnel are not available, Amnesty International and other NGOs have reported that UNMiK personnel – including UNMiK police – were involved in human trafficking and forced prostitution or were frequenting brothels suspected of being involved in human trafficking and forced prostitution.[41] The OSCE reported that in 1999, 80% of the clients in brothels were international personnel. This number diminished in subsequent years to 30% in 2003,[42] but the brothels remained heavily dependent on their international clientele, as they comprised 80% of the revenues.[43] The UN SRSG took measures to halt the involvement of UN personnel in prostitution by issuing a code of conduct[44]

Article 5 of the Protocol to Prevent, Suppress and Punish Trafficking in Persons particularly obliges States parties to enact legislation to criminalise the act of human trafficking. The Convention and Protocols did not enter into force at the time of misconduct of KFOR. Therefore, there was no international obligation of the member States, or NATO, to prevent, suppress and punish human trafficking at that time.

37 Article 7(1)(g), *Rome Statute of the International Criminal Court*, 1998, 2187 UNTS 38544, 1 July 2002.

38 Article 8(2)(vii), *Rome Statute of the International Criminal Court*, 1998, 2187 UNTS 38544, 1 July 2002.

39 Articles 49 and 146, *Geneva Convention Relative to the Protection of Civilian Persons in Time of War* (Geneva Convention IV), 1949, 75 UNTS 287, 12 August 1949.

40 Department of Peacekeeping Operations, *"Human Trafficking and United Nations Peacekeeping"*, DPKO Policy Paper, March 2004.

41 Amnesty International (2004) 'So does it mean that we have the rights?' Protecting the human rights of women and girls trafficked for forced prostitution in Kosovo. Available at: http://reliefweb.int/report/serbia/so-does-it-mean-we-have-rights-protecting.

42 Unicef (2002) *Trafficking in human beings in south eastern Europe 2002*, available at: http://www.iom.md/materials/1_traff_human_beings_se.pdf (Accessed: 14 May 2016), p. 96; Organization for security and Co-operation in Europe mission in Kosovo department of human rights (2001) *Kosovo: Review of the Criminal Justice System*, p. 51.

43 Amnesty International (2004) 'So does it mean that we have the rights?' Protecting the human rights of women and girls trafficked for forced prostitution in Kosovo. Available at: http://reliefweb.int/report/serbia/so-does-it-mean-we-have-rights-protecting.

44 Issued on 24 January 2001.

together with a monthly updated "off-limits" list of premises that UNMiK staff is forbidden to access.

The problems did not pertain exclusively to the United Nations; the outcomes of TPIU investigations revealed that KFOR military personnel were frequenting the brothels as well.[45] According to TPIU, KFOR was – moreover – involved in the human trafficking process.[46]

2.2.4 *Reaction by NATO, TCNs and / or Others*

As early as 2001, the OSCE recommended UNMiK and KFOR to adopt a stronger response to the involvement of their personnel in trafficking activities.[47] Internal disciplinary measures were, according to the OSCE, insufficient to address the problem adequately. UNMiK adopted a "code of conduct" which set as a consequence for UN personnel's involvement in human trafficking a waiver of immunity, followed by disciplinary measures or criminal proceedings. A specific order prohibiting military personnel from committing acts of sexual exploitation – in similar fashion as the UN SRSG did by declaring a Code of Conduct – was never issued by COMKFOR.[48] COMKFOR issued a general order not to leave the military base except for official duty, which left ample room to circumvent the International Military Police that had to implement the order.[49]

In an interview with Amnesty International, one NATO official admitted that the issue of soldiers frequenting prostitutes was *"hard to end"* and stated that disciplinary action was a matter for the respective national authorities.[50] COMKFOR directed commanders of TCNs *"to publish national policies that*

45 Unicef (2002) *Trafficking in human beings in south eastern Europe 2002*, available at: http://www.iom.md/materials/1_traff_human_beings_se.pdf (Accessed: 14 May 2016), p. 96, *"According to the police, the majority of the customers are local men, although members of the international community constitute a sizeable 40 per cent of clientele, mostly KFOR soldiers".*

46 Amnesty International, *"'So does it mean we have rights?', Protecting the human rights of women and girls trafficked for forced prostitution in Kosovo"*, 5 May 2004, p. 66.

47 Organization for security and Co-operation in Europe mission in Kosovo department of human rights (2001) *Kosovo: Review of the Criminal Justice System.*

48 UN Code of Conduct for UNMiK staff, 24 January 2001, which was based on a previously issued UNMiK Regulation 2001/4, *On the prohibition of Trafficking Persons in Kosovo,* 12 January 2001.

49 The International Military Police (IMP) is a collaboration between of military police units of various TCNs. By combining MP units in the IMP a more efficient use of MP units is achieved.

50 Amnesty International (2004) *'So does it mean that we have the rights?' Protecting the human rights of women and girls trafficked for forced prostitution in Kosovo.* Available at: http://reliefweb.int/report/serbia/so-does-it-mean-we-have-rights-protecting, p. 53.

regulate against the use of prostitutes for sexual services and to ensure that such regulations are enforceable through national disciplinary sanctions",[51] but did not refer to the possibility that violating the anti-trafficking regulation could lead to criminal proceedings.

COMKFOR relied mainly on national commanders to issue policies to ensure that KFOR personnel would not be involved in human trafficking and forced prostitution. If national commanders would deem it necessary, they would take disciplinary action, or waive immunity for KFOR personnel followed by repatriation and criminal prosecution before national courts.[52] This raises the question which role NATO has in the prevention and repression of misconduct committed by military personnel placed at its disposal. Does NATO have an international obligation to prevent crimes from happening and to punish the perpetrators during NATO operations and does the Alliance have any measures at its disposal to effectively prevent and repress misconduct committed by its personnel? The prevention and repression of crimes is an oblgation found in various international human rights treaties and is discussed further in Chapter 6.

While there have been indictments against persons involved in human trafficking and forced prostitution, the majority of these persons concerned were nationals of Kosovo. However, already in 2000, reports emerged that peacekeeping personnel were also involved in the trafficking of women and girls.[53] The UN Secretary General noted that often *"contributing States fail to prosecute their nationals accused of wrongdoing while on services for the* [UN]*"*[54] The report noted the inaction of sending States to exercise jurisdiction over, in particular, their military forces. More recently, the UN General Assembly urged States to exercise jurisdiction over crimes of a serious nature, committed by their nations while serving as UN officials or experts on mission.[55] Of note is

---

51 Amnesty International (2004) *'So does it mean that we have the rights?' Protecting the human rights of women and girls trafficked for forced prostitution in Kosovo.* Available at: http://reliefweb.int/report/serbia/so-does-it-mean-we-have-rights-protecting, p. 54.

52 The Times, *Colonel caught in brothel*, 6 July 2000; AFP, *Royal Marines sent home from Kosovo after strip-club booze up*, 11 January 2001; Associated Press, *10 French NATO peacekeepers caught at off-limits bar*, 6 December 2002.

53 UN Secretary General, *Women, Peace and Security, Study submitted by the Secretary General pursuant to Security Council resolution 1325 (2000)*, 2002, para. 268. The report refers to the report of the UN Commission on Human Rights, *Report of the Special Rapporteur on violence against women, its causes and consequences*, E/CN.4/2001/73, 23 January 2001.

54 UN Secretary General, *Women, Peace and Security, Study submitted by the Secretary General pursuant to Security Council resolution 1325 (2000)*, 2002, paras. 267–272.

55 UN General Assembly Resolutions A/RES/62/63 and A/RES/63/119, para. 3.

that neither the UN Secretary General nor the commanders of national elements have ever issued a waiver of immunity. At the same time, neither are there records of indictments issued against KFOR personnel. According to some sources, at least in one instance, the US has investigated the involvement of its troops in this criminal behaviour but has found no substantial evidence of such.[56] Investigations by other TCNs are not known of.

2.3 Case 2: Detention Operations in ISAF

2.3.1 *Background, Legal Framework of the Operation and Command Relationships*

Following the terrorist attacks on 11 September 2001 on American territory by members of the Al Qaida, the United States initiated *Operation Enduring Freedom-Afghanistan* (OEF-A) to conduct together with its allies a counter-terrorism operation in Afghanistan. OEF-A started 7 October 2001 and by 13 November 2001, Coalition Forces and the Afghan Northern Alliance removed the Taliban regime from its power in the capital Kabul. In December 2001, Afghan representatives participated in the so-called "UN Talks on Afghanistan" to formulate arrangements intended as first steps towards the establishment of a new Afghan government. An interim government would be established on 22 December 2001 with a mandate of six months. Within this period a *Loya Jirga* would convene to allow for a smooth and orderly transfer of power to a legitimate transitional government.[57] The arrangements were laid down in the *"Agreement on provisional arrangements in Afghanistan pending the re-establishment of permanent government institutions"*, also referred to as the Bonn Agreement.[58] The United Nations Security Council later endorsed the Bonn Agreement in Security Council resolution 1383(2001).[59]

56 In 2003, the US Department of Defense Inspector investigated human trafficking in Bosnia Herzegovina and concluded that there was "negligible evidence that US Armed Forces in the Balkans patronized prostitutes or engaged in other activities on a wide-spread basis that supported human trafficking", Assessment of the US Department of Defense efforts to combat trafficking in persons, http://www.hrw.org/reports/2002/bosnia/ig.pdf (accessed 14 October 2012).

57 A *Loya Jirga* is a meeting by representatives of the Afghan population, usually for prepared for major events such as electing a president.

58 Agreement on Provisional Arrangements in Afghanistan pending the Re-establishment of Permanent Government Institutions, 5 December 2001.

59 United Nations Security Council resolution 1383(2001), 6 December 2001.

The participants recognised that *"the responsibility for providing security and law and order throughout the country resides with the Afghans themselves."*[60] Considering that some time may be required for the new Afghan security and armed forces to be fully constituted and functioning, they requested the UN Security Council to mandate an international force to assist in the maintenance of security in Kabul and its surrounding areas.

On 20 December 2001, the UN Security Council determined that the situation in Afghanistan continued to pose a threat to the international peace and security and issued resolution 1386(2001). The resolution established the International Security Assistance Force (ISAF) with a mandate to take all necessary measures to *"assist the Afghan Interim Authority in the maintenance of security in Kabul and its surrounding areas"*[61] and invited member States to contribute forces to ISAF and to take leadership of the mission.

In January 2002, the Interim Administration of Afghanistan and the Commander of ISAF concluded a Military Technical Agreement (MTA), setting out the terms of deployment of ISAF.[62] ISAF would primarily be responsible for maintaining security in Afghanistan. On 16 April 2003 NATO took lead over the operation, which was previously led on a six-month rotational basis by an individual 'lead nation'. SACEUR promulgated Operational Plan 10302[63] and appointed Allied Joint Force Command[64] Brunssum as the operational commander.

On 13 October 2003, the Afghan government welcomed NATO's assumption of strategic command, control and coordination of ISAF and the prospect of an expansion of NATO's ISAF mission.[65] Several days later, the UN Security Council authorised the expanded mission through adoption of resolution 1510(2003).[66] The resolution reiterates the call to ISAF to work closely with the UN Special Representative in Afghanistan and requires ISAF to report to the Security Council on the implementation of the mandate.

NATO deployed in August 2003, and on its peak in 2013, commanded over 100.000 ISAF troops.

---

60 Agreement on Provisional Arrangements in Afghanistan pending the Re-establishment of Permanent Government Institutions, 5 December 2001, annex I, para 3.

61 UNSCR 1386(2001) 20 December 2001, para 1.

62 Military Technical Agreement between the International Security Assistance Force (ISAF) and the Interim Administration of Afghanistan ('Interim Administration'), 4 January 2002.

63 OPLAN 10302, 18 December 2003.

64 In 2003, Allied Joint Force Command Brunssum was called "Regional Command North".

65 Letter dated 10 October 2003 from the Minister for Foreign Affairs of Afghanistan addressed to the Secretary General, S/2003/986, 13 October 2003.

66 United Nations Security Council resolution 1510(2003), 13 October 2003.

2.3.2 *Status of Forces*

Annex A to the MTA regulates the status of ISAF's presence in Afghanistan. The agreement accords immunity from personal arrest as necessary for the independent exercise of their functions during the period of their mission. Paragraph 3 of Annex A to the MTA mentions that *"ISAF and supporting personnel fall under the exclusive jurisdiction of their respective national elements in respect of any criminal or disciplinary offences committed within the territory of Afghanistan".*[67] The provision of exclusive jurisdiction by the sending State over their personnel is commonly found in SOFAs and often a prerequisite for States to send their personnel on deployment.[68]

Furthermore, the MTA stipulates that *"ISAF and its personnel will not be held liable for any damages to civilian or government property caused by any activity in pursuit of the ISAF mission."*[69] Although the MTA does not mention it explicitly, NATO interprets this clause as such that this provision also applies to injury or death of persons in Afghanistan caused by ISAF.

In an exchange of letters in 2004 between the NATO Secretary General and the Afghan Minister of Foreign Affairs the provisions of the already existing MTA and its Annex A regarding the status of ISAF are *mutatis mutandis* applicable to NATO, NATO forces and NATO personnel. The immunities and privileges accorded in the MTA were even extended to NATO contractors.[70] A contractor is limited to those – other than locally – contracted by NATO, NATO member States and non-NATO member States participating in the ISAF.

2.3.3 *Background of the Incident*

SACEUR's Operational Plan 10302 includes the Rules of Engagement (ROE) for ISAF, which are approved by the North Atlantic Council (NAC). The ROE allow ISAF to detain persons who pose a threat to the mission or where detention is necessary for the purposes of execution of the mission. The NAC directed in the ROE that detained persons would subsequently either be released or

67 Military Technical Agreement between the International Security Assistance Force (ISAF) and the Interim Administration of Afghanistan ('Interim Administration'), 4 January 2002, Annex I, Section 1, para 3.

68 Mason, C.R. (2012) *CRS report for congress, status of forces agreement (SOFA): What is it, and how has it been utilized?* Available at: https://www.fas.org/sgp/crs/natsec/RL34531.pdf (Accessed: 14 May 2016).

69 Military Technical Agreement between the International Security Assistance Force (ISAF) and the Interim Administration of Afghanistan ('Interim Administration'), 4 January 2002, Annex I, Section 3, para 10.

70 Exchange of Letters between the Secretary General of NATO and the Afghan Minister of Foreign Affairs, dated 5 September 2004 and 22 November 2004.

transferred as soon as possible to Afghan authorities. The aim is to detain such persons for no longer than 96 hours, unless logistical conditions dictate otherwise.[71] The Council likely wished to avoid the need of instituting a costly ISAF-led prison facility. Moreover, there was little political appetite to have a detention facility under the command of NATO after the incident at Abu Ghraib in Iraq, where prisoners were tortured by US forces and caused significant political embarrassment.

Between 2002 and 2005, ISAF operated in Kabul and its surroundings. Due to the limited area of operations, ISAF initially did not detain many individuals. Only after the expansion throughout the country in 2005, detention operations became more frequent and COMISAF saw the need to issue detailed procedures setting out standards and conditions of treatment of detainees during their – relatively short – period of detention. The procedures also provided guidance on the transfer of detainees to Afghan authorities or their release.[72]

When ISAF became more and more involved in detention operations, differences in political views of the various NATO member States on the detention policy became more apparent. It became clear that even without the burden of having to deal with long-term detention of individuals, NATO and its member States could not avoid challenges associated with detention. In particular, the hand-over procedures to Afghan authorities became a complicated issue.

In fact, some TCNs refused to hand over detainees to Afghan authorities, in direct contradiction to the direction of the NAC. Two factors seemed to preclude them to transfer detainees to Afghan authorities. The first factor related to the circumstance that the Government of Afghanistan did not have effective measures in place to guarantee that transferred detainees would be treated humanely in Afghan-run detention facilities. UN Secretary General and several human rights organizations reported on frequent abuse of detainees and instances of torture, especially within facilities led by the Afghan National Directorate of Security.[73] In its report of June 2004 until May 2005, the Afghan

71 Deeks, A. (2008) *Detention in Afghanistan: The need for an integrated plan*, available at: http://csis.org/files/media/csis/pubs/080213_deeks_afghanistan.pdf (Accessed: 12 May 2016).

72 ISAF Standard Operating Procedure 362, *Detention of non-ISAF personnel*, dated 31 August 2006, revised on 24 July 2007.

73 Amnesty International (2007) *Afghanistan, Detainees transferred to torture: ISAF complicity*, available at https://www.amnesty.org/en/documents/asa11/011/2007/en/ (Accessed: 16 May 2016). Report of the United Nations Secretary General, *"The situation in Afghanistan and its implications for international peace and security. Emergency international assistance for peace, normalcy and reconstruction of war-stricken Afghanistan"*, A/60/712 – S/2006/145, 7 March 2006 para. 29, *"Complaints of serious human rights violations*

Independent Human Rights Commission (AIHRC) identified 439 cases of torture.[74] By 2006, torture of detained or imprisoned persons was still frequent, although the number declined.[75] The UN Secretary General reported these concerns again in 2006.[76]

According to certain authors, the transfer of detainees from one State to another, when there is a risk of torture in the latter, would be a violation of international humanitarian law, refugee law, extradition treaties and international human rights law.[77]

Another reason for TCNs not complying with the ISAF's limitation on the detention period and handover to Afghan authorities was the existence of the death penalty in Afghanistan for certain criminal acts. States party to the conventions that abolish the death penalty – such as Protocol 6 and 13 to the European Convention for the Protection of Human Rights and Fundamental Freedoms concerning the abolition of the death penalty – can not transfer detainees to another State when the detainee risks to be exposed to the death penalty.[78] The ICCPR prohibits the transfer of detainees to a State where they

---

committed by representatives of national security institutions, including arbitrary arrest, illegal detention and torture are numerous." Economic and Social Council, Commission on Human Rights, *Report of the independent expert on the situation of human rights in Afghanistan,* 11 March 2005, para. 46. United Nations Human Rights Council, *Report of the High Commissioner for Human Rights on the situation of human rights in Afghanistan and on the achievements of technical assistance in the field of human rights,* A/HRC/4/98, 5 March 2007, para 66.

74 AIHRC, Annual Report, 2004–2005, p. 43.

75 AIHRC, Annual Report, 2003–2004, p. 53.

76 Report of the United Nations Secretary General, *The situation in Afghanistan and its implications for international peace and security. Emergency international assistance for peace, normalcy and reconstruction of war-stricken Afghanistan,* 7 March 2006, p. 7.

77 Droege, C., *Transfer of detainees: legal framework, non-refoulement and contemporary challenges,* International Review of the Red Cross, Vol 90, no. 871, September 2008, p. 670.

78 Protocols 6 and 13 to the *European Convention for the Protection of Human Rights and Fundamental Freedoms* adopted respectively on 1 November 1998 and 3 May 2002, European Court of Human Rights, *Soering v. The United Kingdom,* Application no. 14038/88, Judgment of 7 July 1989, "[*t*]*he likelihood of the feared exposure of the applicant to the "death row phenomenon" has been shown to be as such as to bring Article 3 into play", para 99.* In the case of Afghanistan, the question rises whether the ECHR has extra-territorial applicability. This is discussed in extent in case: European Court of Human Rights, *Vlastimir and Borka Bankovic and others v. Belgium, the Czech Republic, Denmark, France, Germany, Greece, Hungary, Iceland, Italy, Luxembourg, the Netherlands, Norway, Poland, Portugal, Spain, Turkey and the United Kingdom,* Application no. 52207/99, 12 December 2001.

would face the imposition of the death penalty without fundamental guarantees of a fair trial.[79] A similar provision is found in Article 3 ECHR.

These two factors caused certain nations to issue far-reaching restrictions on detention operations, essentially excluding themselves from those operations. In those cases where there were substantial grounds for believing that the detainee would be in danger of being subjected to torture or ill-treatment if transferred, or running the risk to be charged with the death penalty, some nations refused to transfer detainees within the proscribed 96 hours set forth in the ISAF rules of engagement.[80]

The issue raises several questions regarding the relationship between the member States and NATO, which are examined more elaborately in the following chapters of this book. It shows that TCNs are able to re-assume command over their forces, without terminating their commitment to the NATO mission. This flexibility illustrates the separate status of NATO from the member States, which will be further analysed in Chapter 4 and 5. Another question that arises relates to the attribution of conduct. To whom a potential breach of the obligation not to transfer detainees in case of a likelihood of torture, should be attributed? Is it NATO – for having issued the directive to transfer – or States – that have implemented the directive, or both. This question and the issue of multiple attribution is examined in Chapter 7.

A practice emerged in which individual TCNs entered into bilateral agreements with the Afghan authorities to ensure adherence to human rights standards by the Afghan government after the individual was transferred.[81] This instrument was criticised by NATO commanders as the bilateral agreements created a substantial risk that different, and possibly contradictory, standards and procedures regarding the treatment of detainees would develop. The preferred idea was to conclude a single overarching agreement between ISAF and the Government of Afghanistan. Unfortunately, the NAC could not reach consensus on its content.

---

79 Droege, D., *Transfer of detainees: legal framework, non-refoulement and contemporary challenges,* International Review of the Red Cross, Vol 90, no. 871, September 2008, p. 672.

80 *Convention against Torture and Other Cruel, Inhuman or Degrading Treatment or Punishment,* 1984, 1465 UNTS 85, 26 June 1987, article 3 para 1 state that *"no State shall expel, return or extradite a person to another State where there are substantial grounds for believing that he would be in danger of being subjected to torture".*

81 An example is the Memorandum of Understanding between the Minister of Defence of the Islamic Republic of Afghanistan and the Minister of Defence of the Kingdom of The Netherlands concerning the transfer of persons by The Netherlands military forces in Afghanistan to Afghan authorities, concluded on 21 November 2005 and amended on 13 June 2006.

2.3.4 *Reaction by NATO, TCNs and / or Others*

Human rights organizations criticised the continued transfer of detainees from NATO to Afghanistan. In particular, Amnesty International and the British Columbia Civil Liberties Association (BCCLA) brought a case before the Canadian Federal Court to end Canadian Forces' practice of transferring detainees to Afghan authorities as there were concerns that the prisoners would face the risk of torture and other human rights violations. The civil rights organizations claimed that the transfers were in breach of the Canadian Charter of Rights and Freedoms. BCCLA and Amnesty International did not invoke a breach of Article 3 of the United Nations Convention Against Torture, which obliges parties to the Convention not to return ("refouler") a person to another State where there are substantial grounds for believing that he or she would be in danger of being subjected to torture. While Canada is party to this convention, the extra-territorial applicability of the Convention is disputed, which likely persuaded the applicants to base their claim on the Canadian Charter of Rights and Freedoms. This Charter provides in similar protection of human rights as the ECHR.

The Canadian Court did not decide on the substance of the matter, as it ruled that the Canadian Charter of Rights and Freedoms did not apply to Canadian Forces in Afghanistan due to lack of extra-territorial applicability.[82] Nevertheless, the case is illustrative to the position of TCNs in NATO-led operations.

Canadian forces have been deployed in Afghanistan in support of both OEF-A[83] and ISAF.[84] Canada concluded an agreement with the government of Afghanistan to outline the objectives of the Canadian forces – participating in OEF-A as well as ISAF – in Afghanistan and to regulate the status of their military forces.[85] In this agreement, Canadian forces are, under all circumstances, immune from Afghan law, arrest or detention. Canadian forces may take *"such measures as are considered necessary to ensure the accomplishment of their operational objectives".* The agreement further stipulated that

82 Canadian Federal Court of Appeal, Amnesty International Canada and British Columbia Civil Liberties Association and Chief of the Defence Staff for the Canadian Forces, Minister of National Defence and Attorney General of Canada, A-149-08, 10 December 2008, paras. 24–35.

83 Operation Archer.

84 Operation Athena.

85 Technical arrangements between the government of Canada and the government of the Islamic Republic of Afghanistan, 18 December 2005, *cited in* Federal Court of Canada, Amnesty International *et al* v. Attorney General of Canada *et al,* T-324-07, 12 March 2008, para. 44.

> Canadian personnel may need to use force (including deadly force) to ensure the accomplishment of their operational objectives, the safety of the deployed force, including designated persons, designated property, and designated locations. Such measures could include the use of close air support, firearms or other weapons; the detention of persons; and the seizure of arms and other materiel. Detainees would be afforded the same treatment as Prisoners of War. Detainees would be transferred to Afghan authorities in a manner consistent with international law and subject to negotiated assurances regarding their treatment and transfer.[86]

It is unclear what additional value the arrangements could have, seen in the light of the existing ISAF MTA, but likely the Canadian government preferred to regulate the status with the Afghan government for all Canadian forces, whether they operate within ISAF or OEF, in one single document.

Canada, in addition, has concluded several agreements with the Government of Afghanistan on the treatment of transferred detainees. The first Arrangement of 19 December 2005 established procedures to be followed in the event that a detainee was transferred from the custody of the Canadian Forces to a detention facility operated by Afghan authorities. On 3 May 2007, Canada and Afghanistan concluded a second Arrangement governing the transfer of detainees held by the Canadian Forces, requiring that detainees transferred by the Canadian Forces be held in a limited number of detention facilities, to assist in keeping track of individual detainees, to allow access of the AIHRC, ICRC and Canadian officials to the facilities and to require approval by Canadian officials before any detainee to be transferred on to the custody of a third country. The Agreement provides that allegations of abuse are to be investigated by the Government of Afghanistan.[87]

In 2006, Canadian-led Provincial Reconstruction Teams (PRT) and the Canadian embassy in Afghanistan sent reports to the Canadian Ministry of Defence warning on the maltreatment of detainees in Afghan custody.[88] The Canadian detachment commander (Commander Task Force Afghanistan) issued a national detention policy for Canadian Forces participating in ISAF,

86 Technical arrangement between the government of Canada and the government of the Islamic Republic of Afghanistan, 18 December 2005, para 12.

87 Federal Court of Canada, Amnesty International *et al* v. Attorney General of Canada *et al*, T-324-07, 12 March 2008, para. 66 and 70.

88 Colvin, R., *Supplementary written evidence to the Special Committee on Afghanistan*, 16 December 2009.

which, in general terms, is similar to the ISAF Detention SOP.[89] Canada retains the power to decide not to transfer detainees, and it has done so on various occasions.[90]

Canada informed ISAF that it unilaterally *"had suspended detainee transfers until such time as transfers could be resumed 'in accordance with Canada's international obligations'. The decision to suspend detainee transfers came about as a result of a 'credible allegation of mistreatment' having been received on November 5, 2007 by Canadian personnel monitoring the condition of detainees transferred to Afghan authorities."*[91]

Likely, Canada, when acknowledging its obligations under international law in relation to the transfer of detainees, referred to its obligations under customary IHL and IHRL, as stated in Canada's response in the case Amnesty International *et al* v. Attorney General of Canada cited above.[92]

The suspension was temporary; lasting from 5 November 2007 until 26 February 2008.[93] The Canadian contingent, by holding the detainees for a longer period than 96 hours, contravened ISAF ROE and NATO detention procedures. Notwithstanding its unilateral decision, Canada declared to remain committed to the ISAF policy of transferring detainees to the custody of Afghan authorities and would resume the transfers when they would be in accordance with Canada's international legal obligations.[94] From 26 of February 2008, transfers have resumed as the Canadian Forces had implemented additional measures to reduce the risk to detainees transferred into the custody of Afghan authorities.[95]

---

89 Joint Task Force Afghanistan, Theatre Standing Order 321A, *Detention of Afghan nationals and other persons,* 19 March 2007.

90 Federal Court of Canada, Amnesty International *et al* v. Attorney General of Canada *et al,* T-324-07, 25 January 2008, para. 61.

91 Federal Court of Canada, Amnesty International *et al* v. Attorney General of Canada *et al,* T-324-07, 25 January 2008, paras. 75–76, p. 21.

92 Amnesty International *et al* v. Attorney General of Canada *et al,* Respondents factum re: determination of two questions, pursuant to rule 107 of the Federal Courts Rules, regarding the application of the Canadian Charter of Rights and Freedoms, T-324-07, 18 January 2008, *para.* 84.

93 Federal Court of Canada, Amnesty International *et al* v. Attorney General of Canada *et al,* T-324-07, 25 January 2008, paras. 81–82, p. 21–22.

94 Federal Court of Canada, Amnesty International *et al* v. Attorney General of Canada *et al,* T-324-07, 25 January 2008, para. 80, p. 21.

95 Federal Court of Canada, Amnesty International *et al* v. Attorney General of Canada *et al,* T-324-07, 25 January 2008, para. 83.

The case between BCCLA and the Canadian government resulted in the establishment of a parliamentary investigation, the *"Study of the transfer of Afghan detainees from the Canadian Forces to Afghan authorities"* by the Special Committee on the Canadian Mission in Afghanistan.[96] Canada selected the facilities of the Afghan National Directorate of Security (NDS) *"as the first place in the transfer chain for Afghans detained by Canada."*[97] The choice to use these facilities was done in order to assist in keeping track of the individual detainees.[98] Despite reports on the propensity of NDS to torture detainees, Canadian forces continued to transfer to this agency. According to evidence submitted by – primarily – the Embassy of Canada to the United States of America, the Canadian government has been made aware of the substantial risk of torture that detainees run when being transferred to the NDS. Nevertheless, the reports did not lead to a change in position of the Canadian government. According to a statement of the Canadian Embassy,

> as of May 2007, Canada had transferred to the Afghan authorities six times as many detainees as the British, [...] and 20 times as many detainees as the Dutch [but] did not monitor our own detainees after their transfer. Canada's memorandum of understanding on detainees in 2005 had no provision for Canadian officials to follow up detainees after being handed over.[99]

Furthermore,

> senior officials in DFAIT and the Canadian Forces did not welcome our reports or advices. [...] By April 2007, we were receiving written messages from the senior Canadian government coordinator for Afghanistan to the effect that we should be quiet and do what we were told and there was a

---

96 Canadian House of Commons, Special Committee on the Canadian Mission in Afghanistan, Order of Reference of 17 November 2009, *Study of the transfer of detainees from the Canadian Forces to Afghan Authorities.*

97 Scott, D., *Presentation to the House of Commons Special Committee on the Canadian Mission in Afghanistan,* 10 February 2010, p. 5.

98 Federal Court of Canada, Amnesty International *et al* v. Attorney General of Canada *et al,* T-324-07, 25 January 2008, para. 71.

99 House of Commons, Special Committee on the Canadian Mission in Afghanistan, Order of Reference of 17 November 2009, *Study of the transfer of detainees from the Canadian Forces to Afghan Authorities,* Evidence number 15, 19 November 2009. A new detention policy with a clause to monitor transferred detainees was signed between the Canadian and Afghan government on 3 May 2007.

> phone message from the DFAIT assistant deputy minister suggesting that in future we should not put things on paper but, instead, use the telephone.

The Canadian House of Commons Special Committee on the Canadian Mission in Afghanistan was prorogued from 10 December 2009. It is unclear whether *"the committee charged with investigating* [the] *claims will be resurrected once Parliament reconvenes in March given that the unanimous consent of all parties in House of Commons would be needed to re-establish it."*[100]

NATO decided to suspend the transfer of detainees to certain Afghan detention facilities on 6 September 2011[101] on the basis of observations contained in a report of UNAMA.[102] The findings of UNAMA were that in some of the detention facilities, detainees were tortured. NATO conducted its own inspection at six facilities and begun remediation training in one facility.[103] After the inspections and remedial action, the transfers resumed. Two years later, UNAMA re-evaluated the detention facilities and concluded that torture was still taking place in some of the detention centres. NATO again suspended the transfer of detainees.[104] The actions taken by NATO in 2011 and 2013 show that the Alliance was in a position to effectively address the concerns of TCNs in ISAF regarding the treatment of detainees in Afghanistan.

2.4 Case 3: Kunduz Incident

2.4.1 *Background, Legal Framework of the Operation and Command Relationships*

As with the case presented in the previous paragraph, this case relates to the ISAF mission as well. For a background and the legal framework of the operation as well as the command relationship, reference is made to paragraphs 2.3.1 and 2.3.2.

100 Canadian Press, *The cheque's in the mail, Ottawa says it will pay Richard Colvin's legal bills,* 28 January 2010.

101 BBC, *NATO halts Afghan prisoner transfer after torture fears,* 6 September 2011, http://www.bbc.com/news/world-south-asia-14809579.

102 UNAMA, UN Office of the High Commissioner for Human Rights, *Treatment of Conflict-Related Detainees in Afghan Custody,* October 2011.

103 Resolute Support, *ISAF outlines proactive detainee safeguards,* 10 October 2011, http://www.rs.nato.int/article/isaf-releases/isaf-outlines-proactive-detainee-safeguards.html.

104 The Guardian, *NATO stops sending prisoners to Afghan jails after reports of torture,* 18 January 2013.

The command structure of the NATO-led ISAF mission, as outlined in the previous paragraph, is as follows. The NAC retains political control over the ISAF mission, while SACEUR has operational command and control. SACEUR has delegated operational control over the mission to Allied Joint Force Command Brunssum, which has deployed a forward command (HQ ISAF) to Afghanistan. During the period in which this case takes place, the Headquarters of ISAF commanded 5 regional commands, Regional Command North, -East, -South, -West and -Capital. Among other tasks, the Regional Commands coordinate civil-military activities conducted by Provincial Reconstruction Teams (PRTS), in their area of responsibility. Regional Command North at that time had 5 PRTS, one of which in Kunduz.

2.4.2 *Background of the Incident*

In the evening of 3 September 2009, Taliban insurgents hijacked two fuel trucks arriving from Tajikistan and destined to an ISAF PRT compound in Kunduz. When one of the trucks got stuck in the soft soil of a riverbed between Ali Abad and Char Dara districts, the hijackers chose to siphon fuel out of the tankers. Civilians from a village nearby the stranded trucks were either forced to assist the hijackers[105] or – according to the Taliban' version of events[106] – allowed them to loot from the fuel tankers.

According to the German media, an ISAF aircraft spotted the trapped fuel tankers and relayed its location through a Special Forces unit in the area to the ISAF PRT Commander.[107] This unit informed the commander that several high ranking Taliban commanders were among the hijackers of the fuel trucks.

Several hours later, the ISAF PRT Commander authorised an air strike on the two fuel tankers – allegedly neglecting the possibility that civilians might be present among the group gathered around the fuel tankers. A US F-15 aircraft conducting the strike proposed to perform a low flying manoeuvre to warn off the civilians, but this was answered in the negative by the PRT's joint tactical air controller. The question from the pilot whether the individuals posed an immediate threat to ISAF was answered in the affirmative.[108] The latter question indicates that the pilot wanted to ascertain that the risk of civilian

105 Cleveland.com, *U.S.-German rift emerges over Afghan deaths in bombing of hijacked fuel tankers*, 6 September 2009.

106 According to the Taliban investigation report; "Fact finding mission of 'The Islamic Emirate of Afghanistan', *Findings of the investigation Commission of the Islamic Emirate of Afghanistan on the gruesome event of Kunduz and Names of Victims*", 9 September 2009.

107 Bild.com, *German KSK Special Forces involved in deadly bombing*, 10 December 2009.

108 Bild.com, footage from the US aircraft involved.

casualties outweighed the military necessity – such as in case of an imminent danger to friendly troops. Subsequently, the strike was carried out.

Although the PRT Commander did not report that there were any civilians among the deaths caused by the air strike,[109] the higher headquarters at ISAF Regional Command North received information that several children arrived at hospitals in Kunduz with shrapnel wounds, likely caused by the air strike earlier that day.[110] The Regional Command on its turn informed the German Ministry of Defence as well as Headquarters ISAF in Kabul that civilians were amongst the casualties.

Attacks that are not directed at a military objective, or attacks which may cause expected incidental loss of civilian life or injury to civilians which would be excessive in relation to the concrete and direct military advantage anticipated, are prohibited.[111] These violations constitute war crimes under the ICC Statute if the attacks was part of State or organizational policy.[112]

The initial reports from the Afghan Governor of the Kunduz province were that 56 armed men were killed and 12 injured. Notwithstanding this statement, the Afghan President declared the same day that it would appoint a fact-finding mission to investigate the details of this event.[113] The conclusions of this investigation were that at least 30 civilians were among the 119 casualties.[114]

2.4.3 *Reaction by NATO, TCNs and /or Others*

Mainly due to Afghanistan's size, mountainous landscape and ISAF's relatively small amount of military forces,[115] most of the operations are executed,

109 Spiegel online, *Oberst Klein wollte "Feinde des Wiederaufbaus treffen",* 12 December 2009.

110 Bild.de, *Hat Minister Jung die Wahrheit verschwiegen?* 25 November 2009.

111 Article 51(4), 51(5)(b) and 57 *Protocol Additional to the Geneva Conventions of 12 August 1949, and relating to the Protection of Victims of International Armed Conflicts*, 1977, 1125 UNTS 3, 8 June 1977.

112 Article 8(1) *"The Court shall have jurisdiction in respect of war crimes in particular when committed as part of a plan or policy or as part of a large-scale commission of such crimes."* Article 8(2)(b)(iv) *Rome Statute of the International Criminal Court*, 1998, 2187 UNTS 38544, 1 July 2002 *"Intentionally launching an attack in the knowledge that such attack will cause incidental loss of life or injury to civilians or damage to civilian objects or widespread, long-term and severe damage to the natural environment which would be clearly excessive in relation to the concrete and direct overall military advantage anticipated."*

113 Islamic Republic of Afghanistan, Office of the President, Press release, *President Karzai ordered investigation into Kunduz incident,* 4 September 2009.

114 Tageschau.de, *30 Zivilisten und 20 Unbewaffnete getötet,* 23 March 2010.

115 KFOR was composed at its height of 50.000 troops (www.nato.int/issues/kfor/evolution.html, accessed 14 March 2010) to cover Kosovo's size of 10.902 km^2, while ISAF is currently

or at least supported, by air strikes. While airstrikes are not particularly more indiscriminate, the President of Afghanistan expressed his concerns over the civilian lives lost during military operation, in particular those due to the numerous ISAF air strikes.[116]

UNAMA's Special Representative expressed similar concerns on the topic of civilian casualties in 2008.[117] UNAMA's Human Rights Unit recorded 2.118 civilian casualties from 1 January 2008 until 31 December 2008, compared to 1.523 recorded in the same period in 2007. Around 39% is attributed to pro-government forces – which include military forces operating under ISAF, Operation Enduring Freedom and the Afghan Nations Security Forces.[118] UNAMA analysed that air strikes account for the largest percentage of civilian deaths.[119] In its 2009 report UNAMA reported 2.412 civilian deaths.[120] The percentage of civilian casualties attributed to pro-government forces has diminished to 25%, but *"air strikes remain a concern; they are responsible for 61% of civilian deaths attributed to pro-Government forces in 2009".*[121]

The UN Human Rights Council voiced the same concerns.[122] In 2007, the Council directed attention to defensive air strikes, which allegedly were particular disproportionate in some cases. The UN High Commissioner for Human

---

composed of 85.795 troops (www.nato.int/isaf/docu/epub/pdf/placemat.pdf, accessed 14 March 2010), twice the size of KFOR but Afghanistan is 60 times larger.

116 BBC News online, *Karzai anger over civilian deaths,* news.bbc.co.uk/2/hi/south_asia/6615781.stm, accessed 14 March 2010, 2 May 2007 and CBS News/60 Minutes, *Karzai: stop the air strikes,* 28 October 2007.

117 Briefing to the UN Security Council by the Special Representative of the Secretary General for Afghanistan: *"First and foremost, every effort must be made to reduce the number of civilian casualties to a minimum. I am in a regular dialogue with COMISAF concerning this and other topics."* 10 July 2008.

118 UNAMA Human Rights Unit, *Afghanistan, Annual report on protection of civilians in armed conflict, 2008,* January 2009.

119 UNAMA, Human Rights Unit, *Afghanistan, Annual Report on Protection of Civilians in Armed Conflict,* 2008, January 2009 *"Air-strikes account for the largest percentage of civilian deaths attributed to pro-governments forces. UNAMA recorded 552 civilian casualties of this nature in 2008. This constitutes 64% of the 828 non-combatant deaths attributed to actions by pro-government forces in 2008 and 26% of those killed overall",* p. 16.

120 UNAMA Human Rights Unit, *Afghanistan, Annual report on protection of civilians in armed conflict, 2009,* p. 1.

121 UNAMA, Human Rights Unit, *Afghanistan, Annual Report on Protection of Civilians in Armed Conflict,* 2008, January 2009, p. 3.

122 United Nations Human Rights Council, *Report of the High Commissioner for Human Rights on the situation of human rights in Afghanistan and on the achievements of technical assistance in the field of human rights,* A/HRC/7/27, 27 February 2008.

Rights concluded that the *"alarming levels"* of civilian casualties caused by ISAF and OEF operations *"breach international law"*.[123] The Special Rapporteur on extrajudicial, summary or arbitrary executions to the Human Rights Council criticised ISAF on its obscure procedures on the vetting of military targets, which prevented him to assess compliance with international law. The Rapporteur noted that

> [t]he international forces have procedures for vetting targets and selecting an appropriate method of attack [but] it is not clear that sufficient caution is shown in practice to ensure that attacks are not indiscriminate and that civilian casualties will not be excessive in relation to the military advantage anticipated.[124]

The UN Secretary General reiterated the concerns voiced by the UN agencies in Afghanistan in its reports to the UN General Assembly. On various occasions, the Secretary General pointed at ISAF and other pro-government forces that they caused a significant percentage of the civilian casualties in the armed conflict.[125] The Secretary General recommended that *"[c]ivilians must be protected, not only from terrorists and insurgency, but also from unintended consequences of pro-Government military operations"*.[126] The Secretary General's Special Representative has also been active in raising this issue and seeking solutions with COMISAF.[127]

Human rights organisations, such as Human Rights Watch, equally reported on the rise in civilian casualties due to military operations conducted by ISAF. Human Rights Watch specifically recommended NATO in 2008 to *"ensure air attacks comply with the legal obligation to take all feasible precautions to minimise*

---

123 Reuters, *"U.N. blames all sides for Afghan civilian deaths"*, 20 November 2007.

124 Report of the Special Rapporteur on extrajudicial, summary or arbitrary executions, addendum, *"Mission to Afghanistan"*, A/HRC/11/2/Add. 4, 6 May 2009, p. 7.

125 Report of the Secretary General, *The situation in Afghanistan and its implications for international peace and security*, para 54, A/62/345 – S/2007/555, 21 September 2007; para 53, A/63/372 – S/2008/617, 23 September 2008; para 66, A/64/751 – S/2009/135, 10 March 2009; para 54, A/64/364 – S/2009/475, 22 September 2009; para 24, A/64/705 – S/2010/127, 10 March 2010.

126 Report of the Secretary General, *The situation in Afghanistan and its implications for international peace and security*, A/63/372 – S/2008/617, para 68, 23 September 2008.

127 Report of the Secretary General, *The situation in Afghanistan and its implications for international peace and security A/63/751 – S/2009/135*, para 88, 10 March 2009.

harm to the civilian populations".[128] The ICRC has expressed similar concerns to COMISAF in confidential correspondence as early as in 2007.[129]

The Afghan government called for a change in the MTA to obtain influence in the planning and execution of ISAF operations, but without result. The proposed amendments would give the Afghan government influence in the conduct of operations, escalation of force procedures and operations that have a serious impact Afghan's personal lives culture, like night raids of civilian houses.[130] NATO remained of the opinion that the MTA did not need to be changed. Instead, COMISAF issued a Tactical Directive, demanding a more cautious approach in the use of force.[131]

In light of this prudent approach in the Tactical Directive, the air strike on 4 September 2009 in the Kunduz province, causing between 30[132] to 74[133] civilian deaths, came as a surprise to the ISAF commander. Early reports indicated that the strike would be in contravention of the latter directive.

COMISAF – in conformity with Standard Operating Procedures[134] – received reports on the strike and since there was a possibility of civilian casualties, convened an Initial Action Team to conduct a review of the incident. The Initial Action Team would verify whether the PRT Commander abided by targeting procedures and more specifically the terms of the Tactical Directive.[135] The investigation did focus on the abidance to international humanitarian law but rather on the more operational aspects, since TCNs retain criminal jurisdiction over their personnel.[136] COMISAF took administrative measures by suspending

128 Human Rights Watch, *"Troops in Contact", airstrikes and civilian deaths in Afghanistan,* September 2008, p. 37.

129 Letter from the head of mission of the ICRC in Afghanistan and COMISAF of 5 September 2007 and response from COMISAF of 20 September 2007.

130 Letter from the Minister of National Defence to the Secretary General of NATO, 30 August 2008.

131 COMISAF Tactical Directive, 6 July 2009, unclassified version.

132 Bild.de, *Amtlich! 30 Zivilisten wurden getötet,* 13 September 2009.

133 UNAMA Human Rights Unit, *Annual report on protection of civilians in armed conflict, 2009,* p. 18, January 2010.

134 Standard Operating Procedure 302, *CJ3 – Operational Reports and Returns,* 29 August 2007 and Standard Operating Procedure 307, *I-IQ ISAF CIVCAS Battle Drill.*

135 NATO Press release of 9 September 2009, PR# 2009–681, NATO Website: http://www.nato.int/isaf/docu/pressreleases/2009/09/pr090908-681.html

136 Annex A (Arrangement regarding the status of the International Security Assistance Force) to the Military Technical Agreement of 4 January 2002, shows that: *"The ISAF [...] personnel [...] will under all circumstances and at all times be subject to the exclusive jurisdiction of their respective national elements in respect of any criminal or disciplinary offences which may be committed by them on the territory of Afghanistan.",* p. A-1.

the German Joint Tactical Air Controller, who directed the US aircraft on the targets, pending the ISAF investigation.[137] The ISAF investigation, brought to a close in October 2009, concluded that there were between 30 to 40 civilians among the casualties. The statement by the Joint Tactical Air Controller to the American aircraft that there was an imminent threat was insufficiently founded. The ISAF investigative team concluded that both the PRT Commander and the Joint Tactical Air Controller operated outside ISAF directives and procedures.[138]

The question arises whether COMISAF was required to take additional measures beyond the investigation of the incident in Kunduz. International human rights law requires commanders to take measures within his or her power to prevent or repress the commission of breaches of international human rights law and to submit the matter to competent authorities for investigation and prosecution.

The German Military Police led a separate criminal investigation against the PRT Commander and the Joint Tactical Air Controller.[139] The German investigators noted that the Commander of the PRT acted mostly on its own behalf, without informing Regional Command North. Furthermore, it remained unclear for the Military Police why "battle damage assessment"[140] was conducted several hours after the attack, which should have been done within two hours. At the time when the battle damage assessment was performed, the bodies were already removed. The German Ministry of Defence requested the Commander of Regional Command North how it was ascertained that no civilians were present at the fuel tankers. The Commander responded that an Afghan informant confirmed that the persons nearby the fuel trucks were all insurgents.[141]

Criminal proceedings against the PRT Commander and the Joint Tactical Air Controller were initiated in Germany in March 2010[142] for launching an attack, which caused excessive loss of civilian lives in relation to the concrete

137 ISAF Memorandum, *Red Baron 20 Suspended from controlling ISAF aircraft*, 4 September 2009,

138 Spiegel online, *Ein deutsches Verbrechen*, 1 February 2010.

139 20. Deutsches Einsatzkontingent ISAF, *"Undersuchungsbericht zum 'Close Air Support KUNDUZ' vom 04.09.2009"*, 9 September 2009.

140 AAP-6, NATO Glossary of Terms and Definitions, 22 March 2010, *"The assessment of effectis resulting from the application of military action, either lethal or non-lethal, against a military objective"*, p. 2-B-2.

141 20. Deutsches Einsatzkontingent ISAF, *"Untersuchungsbericht zum 'Close Air Support KUNDUZ' vom 04.09.2009"*, 9 September 2009.

142 Spiegel online, *"Nichtinternationaler bewaffneter Konflikt"*, 15 March 2010.

military advantage anticipated.[143] The German Federal Prosecutor terminated the investigations for potential war crimes on grounds that there were no indications of violations of either international or domestic criminal law.[144]

In March 2013, several survivors of the air strike initiated civil proceedings against the German government before the regional court in Bonn, Germany. The victims claimed compensation for the death of their family members caused by the airstrike. On 11 December 2013 the court rejected the claims, stating that the Commander PRT acted correctly.[145]

The incident has had serious political consequences in Germany, but not due to the possible illegitimacy of the air strike, rather because of the failure to provide accurate information to the German parliament by the German Ministry of Defence and military leadership. The Minister of Defence as a consequence thereof, resigned.[146] Germany's new Defence Minister announced that a new examination of the air strike would be undertaken.[147] In the report issued on 25 October 2011, it was concluded – again – that there was no breach of national or international law.[148]

Besides investigations conducted by the involved Troop Contributing Nations involved and ISAF, several human rights organisations, as well as the ICRC have issued reports on this incident. Amnesty International based its findings on interviews with relatives of the deceased and survivors of the incident. It also provided a list of names of 83 people killed. No assessment was given on whether the principles of international humanitarian law were violated.[149]

---

143 The relevant article in the German criminal code: "Paragraf 11 des Völkerstrafgesetzbuch" reflects article 51 of *Protocol Additional to the Geneva Conventions of 12 August 1949, and relating to the Protection of Victims of International Armed Conflicts*, 1977, 1125 UNTS 3, 8 June 1977.

144 German prosecution office, Generalbundesanwalt, *Ermittlungsverfahren wegen des Luftangriffs vom 4. September 2009 eingestellt,* August 2010. http://www.generalbundesanwalt.de/de/showpress.php?themenid=12&newsid=360.

145 Landgericht Bonn, Pressemitteilung, 11 December 2013, *Kein Schadenersatz für zivile Opfer des NATO-Luftangriffs in Kundus/Afghanistan*, http://www.lg-bonn.nrw.de/presse/420_Aktuell/index.php, Website of representative of the victims, K. Popal; http://www.kanzlei-popal.de/aktuelles.php.

146 BBC, 26 November 2009, *Germany's top soldier quits of Afghanistan raid;* BBC, 27 November 2009, *German minister Franz Josef Jung resigns over raid.*

147 Deutsche Welle (dw-world.de), *Zu Guttenberg promises new investigation into Kunduz airstrike,* 30 November 2009.

148 Deutscher Bundestag, *Besschlussungsempfehlung und Bericht,* Drucksache 17/7400, 25 October 2011.

149 Amnesty International, *Afghanistan: Background to the Kunduz airstike of 4 September 2009*, 30 October 2009.

The ICRC reported that around 75 civilians were killed in the air strike and – according to the German media – concluded that the attack was not in conformity with standards of international humanitarian law.[150]

UNAMA announced that it would investigate the incident as well,[151] however with the exception of the Annual Report on the Protection of Civilians in Armed Conflict of 2009, the UN made no further reference of any results of the intended investigation on the air strike.[152] The UN Human Rights Council (UN HRC) lamented the lack of transparency by ISAF forces when investigating incidents with a high loss of civilian life and specifically referred to the incident in Kunduz.[153] The Council recommended *"pro-government forces* [to] *pursue and strengthen procedures in place to mitigate the impact of the conflict on the civilian population."*[154]

Each investigation has examined the facts of the Kunduz airstrike from a different perspective. While the German authorities have investigated whether any criminal offences may have occurred, the UN HRC and other NGOs examined more in general breaches of international humanitarian and human rights law. ISAF, on the other hand, investigated whether the TCN has abided by NATO ROE and other policies of the Alliance. Similarly, the outcome of each investigation has had diverging consequences. The ISAF investigation has led to the suspension of the Joint Tactical Air Controller, while the German prosecution did not lead to a further prosecution of German military personnel.

---

150 Stern.de, *Rot-Kreuz-Bericht erhöht Druck auf Guttenberg*, 10 December 2009.

151 UN News Centre, *UN calls for probe after air strike in northern Afghanistan kills dozens*, 4 September 2009.

152 UNAMA Human Rights Unit, *Afghanistan, Annual Report on protection of civilians in armed conflict, 2009*, p, 17 and 18, January 2010.

153 UN Human Rights Council, *Report of the United Nations High Commissioner for Human Rights on the situation of human rights in Afghanistan and on the achievements of technical assistance in the field of human rights*, para 15, 11 January 2010.

154 UN Human Rights Council, *Report of the United Nations High Commissioner for Human Rights on the situation of human rights in Afghanistan and on the achievements of technical assistance in the field of human rights*, para 69, 11 January 2010.

CHAPTER 3

Overview of the Key Moments in the Development of NATO

3.1 Introduction

This chapter provides a historical overview of the most important events that have shaped the Alliance into the organization it is today. The chapter serves to provide a better understanding of NATO's functions, legal framework and objectives. A reading of NATO's constituent document alone would not be sufficient to understand the Alliance' tasks that it currently undertakes and organization that it currently requires. A brief analysis of historical events is therefore required.

More specifically, the chapter examines whether the organization has evolved to such an extent that the Alliance should be regarded as an autonomous actor in its own right and distinct from the policies of its member States. Such an examination is relevant to the question whether NATO has international legal personality,[1] which is pivotal to whether NATO can be held responsible under international public law.

The chapter is divided into two parts separated by a key historical milestone that influenced the course of action for NATO: the end of the Cold War. The first part of this chapter will outline the establishment of the Alliance and its purpose to counter the threat coming from the Soviet Union. During this period, NATO was often described as a static alliance of individual nations that convened to formulate a common military strategy against the Warsaw Pact. With the fall of the Berlin Wall in 1989, this strategy came to an end as well and NATO needed to realign itself in order to stay relevant.

The end of the Cold War introduced a new era for NATO in which it reinvented itself into a flexible organization capable of deploying military forces far from NATO territory. Paragraph 3.3 examines the transformation that the Alliance has gone through and discusses the differences between NATO version

---

1 The question whether NATO has international legal personality will be dealt with Chapter 5 *The International Legal Personality of NATO*.

 | DOI 10.1163/9789004354647_004

"1.0" and "2.0".[2] The final paragraph of this chapter will provide observations and conclusions.

3.2 NATO from 1949 until 1989

One of the motives for the United States of America and Western Europe to create a system of collective defence was the perceived threat coming from the Soviet Union and the ideological aims of the Soviet Communist Party.[3] The Western European nations and the United States sought ways to restrain the expansionist movement by the USSR evidenced by the occupation of the Baltic States during the Second World War and the direct threats against the sovereignty of Norway, Greece, Turkey and other European countries in the period of 1947 to 1949. In particular, the covert backing from the Soviet Union of the coup d'état by the Communist Party of Czechoslovakia in 1948 and the illegal blockade of Berlin in the same year gave significant impetus to the USA and western European countries to develop a common defence system. Although the United Nations' Charter explicitly prohibits the use of force between States, many Western countries felt that eventual appeals for respect of the UN Charter would not guarantee national sovereignty and independence of democratic States when faced with a threat like that of the Soviet Union.

A collective security system was necessary against a two-fold threat: the renewal by Germany of a policy of aggression and the possible invasion of Europe by the Soviet Union. For this purpose, the North Atlantic Treaty Organization was established. NATO, founded by twelve States on the 4th of April 1949,[4] was aimed at safeguarding the freedom of the NATO community[5] by

2 NATO, Speech by NATO Secretary General Anders Fogh Rasmussen at the German Marshall Fund of the United States (GMF), Brussels, *The New Strategic Concept: Active Engagement, Modern Defence,* 8 October 2010, http://www.nato.int/cps/en/natohq/opinions_66727.htm?

3 NATO Handbook, 2006, p. 16. Other motives to create the North Atlantic Treaty Organizations were to forbid the revival of national militarism in Europe through a strong North American presence on the continent, and second to encourage European political integration, www.nato.int/history/nato-history.html.

4 The North Atlantic Treaty entered into force on 24 August 1949, after the deposit of ratifications of all signatory States. The founding Member States were Belgium, Canada, Denmark, France, Iceland, Italy, Luxembourg, The Netherlands, Norway, Portugal, United Kingdom and The United States of America.

5 Preamble to the North Atlantic Treaty 1949, 34 UNTS 243, 24 August 1949.

acting collectively in self-defence against an armed attack against one or more on the territory of a NATO member State.[6]

NATO's *raison d'être* is explained in a mere fourteen articles in the North Atlantic Treaty. The size reflects the practical resolution and the idealism of the founding nations to confront the threat at the time posed by the USSR.[7] The cornerstone of NATO is its collective defence mechanism is contained in Article 5 of the North Atlantic Treaty:

> The Parties agree that an armed attack against one or more of them in Europe or North America shall be considered an armed attack against them all and consequently they agree that, if such an armed attack occurs, each of them, in exercise of the right of individual or collective self-defence recognised by Article 51 of the Charter of the United Nations, will assist the Party or Parties so attacked by taking forthwith, individually and in concert with the other Parties, such action as it deems necessary, including the use of armed force, to restore and maintain the security of the North Atlantic area.
>
> Any such armed attack and all measures taken as a result thereof shall immediately be reported to the Security Council. Such measures shall be terminated when the Security Council has taken the measures necessary to restore and maintain international peace and security.

The Treaty acknowledged that any decision to use force by its member States would be taken in accordance with the provisions of the United Nations Charter. In fact, the Treaty makes reference to the Charter no less than nine times, emphasizing the primary responsibility of the UN for the maintenance of international peace and security.

Once NATO was established, the members set out how the goals of the Alliance would be achieved. The first strategic document issued by the North Atlantic Council in 1949 became known as "*The Strategic Concept for the*

6 Article 5 of the North Atlantic Treaty 1949, 34 UNTS 243, 24 August 1949.

7 The Russian government inveighed against the establishment of NATO and warned the Europeans *"that a North Atlantic Alliance was simply an instrument for furthering the imperialist aims of the Anglo-Saxon Powers."* The founding NATO members replied that the text of the treaty was the *"best answer to Soviet allegations, since it showed beyond a shadow of doubt that the Alliance was not aimed against any nation or group of nations, but only against armed aggression."*, Lord Ismay, *NATO: the first five years 1949–1954*.

Defence of the North Atlantic Area" (DC 6/1).[8] The document had two main topics. First, an emphasis was put on the re-strengthening of European military capacity. Secondly, since the USSR had far outnumbered the Alliance's military power and it would take years before the European allies would match those numbers, plans were drawn up on the use of thermonuclear weapons to compensate for the numerical inferiority.[9] At this time NATO mostly functioned as vehicle of military assistance – in the form of monetary aid – by the US to European allies. The Alliance was more a promise by the US of assurance and assistance to Europe rather than an institutionalised organization.

The first Strategic Concept didn't last long. The North Korean invasion of South Korea in 1950 grew fears that such communist expansion could occur in Europe as well. It was recognised that Western European forces were too loosely organised in the NATO structure. Structural changes were necessary if the European allies were to be able to withstand a Soviet invasion. A process started that resulted in a increase in defence efforts, deployment of US forces in Europe and rearmament of Germany.[10] Institutional changes were made to NATO, including the establishment the Supreme Allied Command Europe (SACEUR) integrating all European military forces under one command. In wartime, SACEUR would assume command over all allied forces in Western Europe. The new structure led to a new Strategic Concept – MC 3/5.[11] Prior to that, there was neither a headquarters structure nor an overall commander that could provide in the vital element of integrated command and control. Even in the new command structure, military forces were commanded by national authorities, but the new structure changed the Alliance from a loosely political alliance into a North Atlantic Treaty Organization with an elaborate political and military structure.[12] The new structure, in which SACEUR has unified command over European military forces, is the start of a development showing the transformation from an Alliance of member States towards a separate entity with international legal personality. As some authors noted: it had put the "O"

8 The Strategic Concept for the Defense of the North Atlantic Area, DC 6, 1 December 1949.

9 Although no reference to the use of atomic bombs can be found in DC 6/1, the phrase "[...] *to carry out strategic bombing promptly by all means possible with all types of weapons, without exception*", includes the potential use of nuclear weapons.

10 Reinalda, B. and Verbeek, B. (eds.) (1998) *Autonomous policy making by international organizations*, New York: Taylor & Francis, p. 124.

11 The Strategic Concept for the Defense of the North Atlantic Treaty Area, MC 3/5, 3 December 1952.

12 Pedlow, G.W. (no date) *NATO Strategy Documents 1949–1969*. Available at: http://www.nato.int/archives/strategy.htm (Accessed: 12 May 2016), p. 1.

in NATO.[13] Early literature is generally pessimistic on the achievements on the institutional change of NATO from 1949 to 1989.[14] However, the establishment of SACEUR spurred the institutionalization of NATO in such a way that it could act on its own initiatives.[15]

To which extent SACEUR has gained separate powers and purposes from the member States is examined in detail in Chapter 4 on the institutional framework of NATO. While SACEUR commanded military forces in Europe, in 1951 two new organs were created: Supreme Allied Commander Atlantic (SACLANT) commanding forces in the United States and Commander in Chief Channel (CINCHAN), commanding forces in the (English) Channel (See figure 1).

The crisis in 1956 between France and the UK on one side, and Egypt on the other, regarding the blockade of the Suez Canal led to a reconsideration of the Strategic Concept. France requested, *"to include sections dealing with the effects upon NATO of Soviet political and economic activities outside the NATO area."*[16] In a political directive of the NAC, two conclusions were drawn: not all cases of aggression by the USSR would necessarily lead to the use of nuclear weapons;[17] conventional forces would deal with incursions, infiltration and hostile acts. Secondly – reflecting on the Suez crisis – NATO's defence planning would need to take into account developments outside its North-Atlantic area. The conclusions were implemented in MC 14/2. While recognizing that NATO military authorities have no responsibilities or authority except with respect to incidents

FIGURE 1 *NATO's command structure 1951–1991.*

13 Reinalda, B. and Verbeek, B. (eds.) (1998) *Autonomous policy making by international organizations*, New York: Taylor & Francis, p. 124.

14 Maier, K.A., Wiggerhaus, N., *Das Nordatlantische Bündnis 1949–1956*, 1993, quoted in Reinalda, B. and Verbeek, B. (eds.) (1998) *Autonomous policy making by international organizations*, New York: Taylor & Francis, p. 127.

15 Reinalda, B. and Verbeek, B. (eds.) (1998) *Autonomous policy making by international organizations*, New York: Taylor & Francis, p. 127.

16 Pedlow, G.W. (no date) *NATO Strategy Documents 1949–1969*. Available at: http://www.nato.int/archives/strategy.htm (Accessed: 12 May 2016), p. XIX.

17 CM(56)138, 13 December 1956.

covered by Article 5 of the Treaty, they would need to take into account the dangers that may arise from crises as the abovementioned.[18]

The final change to the strategic plans of NATO before the end of the Cold War was MC 14/3 of 1968.[19] The advent of Russian long-range bombers and the successful developments in space aviation brought the US' territory into the reach of Russian nuclear weapons. The US subsequently sought to avoid an all-out nuclear weapons exchange and probed the NATO allies in changing the strategic policy of "massive retaliation". The US already implemented certain plans with regard to Berlin to de-escalate situations. The new proposed strategy included more flexibility in the use of nuclear weapons. The French government opposed the proposals of the US, as it went too far from the original idea of massive retaliation. If France had not withdrawn as a member of the NAC, the strategy would likely not have been accepted. The Strategic Concept MC/14/3 of 1968 remained in place until after the fall of the Berlin Wall in 1989 and the disintegration of the Warsaw Pact in 1991. These developments resulted into drastic changes in NATO's strategic thinking. The Strategic Concept of 1991 started to part from the original idea of the founders of NATO, which was oriented against a threat from the Eastern Bloc. It also was the prelude to a change into a more distinct role for NATO than it has been during the Cold War Period. NATO was shifting away from a pact between member States to defend each other in case of an armed attack to a vehicle capable of undertaking much broader functions, powers and decision-making structure.

3.3 NATO in the Period after the Cold War

The fall of the Berlin Wall in 1989 and the gradual dissolution of the Soviet Union from 1990 to 1991 led to the thought that NATO's *raison d'être* would seize to exist. The members nonetheless believed that NATO could continue to be of use in maintaining the security in the North-Atlantic area.

At the London summit in July 1990, a new strategic direction of NATO was discussed.[20] The members summed up a range of changes that could guarantee

---

18 Overall Strategic Concept for the Defense of the North Atlantic Treaty Organization Area, MC 14/2 23 May 1957, para. 22.

19 Overall Strategic Concept for the Defense of the North Atlantic Treaty Organization Area, MC 14/3 16 January 1968.

20 *Declaration on a Transformed North Alliance issued by the Heads of State and Government participating in the meeting of the North Atlantic Council* ("The London Declaration"), 6 July 1990.

NATO's continuity, which led to the promulgation of the New Strategic Concept of 1991.[21] One change – which is of particular importance here – was the shift of focus in possible threats facing the Alliance' security.[22] The Strategic Concept committed itself to a broad approach to stability and security. For the first time it addressed security threats beyond the area as defined by Article 6 of the Washington Treaty. The Strategic Concept of 1991 envisioned contingencies that might occur outside NATO's member States' territory. The Alliance noted that security couldn't be guaranteed if it would not take the global context into account. The *"proliferation of weapons of mass destruction, disruption of the flow of vital resources and actions of terrorism and sabotage"* could all take place well beyond NATO's borders, but with an impact on the security of Alliance.[23] The 1991 Strategic Concept identified security challenges and risks coming from mainly countries in Central and Eastern Europe, due to *"serious economic, social and political difficulties, including ethnic rivalries and territorial disputes".*[24] This served as a basis for peacekeeping and joint crisis management operations.

This change meant that NATO could be involved in tasks not purely related to Article 5 collective self-defence operations. Due to the political sensitivity of the topic at the time, no consensus could be reached to include "non-article 5 crisis response operations" as an explicit new task in the 1991 Strategic Concept.[25] Despite the omitted reference in the 1991 Strategic Concept, certain

---

21 The Alliance's New Strategic Concept agreed by the Heads of State and Government participating in the Meeting of the North Atlantic Council, 7–8 November 1991.

22 Another important change was that NATO would cooperate with the countries of Central and Eastern Europe, through a *Partnership for Peace Program* (PfP), *NATO's Ministerial Communiqué; Partnership with the Countries of Central and Eastern Europe – 6–7 June 1991*.

23 The Alliance's New Strategic Concept agreed by the Heads of State and Government participating in the Meeting of the North Atlantic Council, 7–8 November 1991, para. 12.

24 The Alliance's New Strategic Concept agreed by the Heads of State and Government participating in the Meeting of the North Atlantic Council, 7–8 November 1991, para. 9.

25 At the signing of the Washington Treaty, these contingencies that might occur outside NATO's borders would not lead to any obligation of the NATO member States to assist one another. Articles 5 and 6 state that only in case of an armed attack on the territory of a member State in Europe and North America (and on forces in or over the Mediterranean Sea or the North Atlantic area north of the Tropic of Cancer) would result in an obligation for the other member States to assist in the collective self-defence. Even at the time certain member States had vested interests outside of the territory specified in article 6 – France in Indochina, Britain at Suez and America in Vietnam – these interests were not guaranteed by the provisions of the NATO constituent treaty. With the advent of the 1991 Strategic Concept, the possibility to intervene in situations that pose a threat to the Alliance' security became a possibility. In these – later so-called – non-article 5

Alliance members remained convinced that *"if NATO does not address the primary security challenges facing Europe today, it will become increasingly irrelevant. NATO must go out of area or it will go out of business."*[26]

The shift in focus introduced by the 1991 Strategic Concept is significant to the topic of this book, because it set in motion several changes in the military planning procedures resulting in NATO functioning more independently from its members and, hence, developed towards an international legal subject, as will be examined in Chapter 5 furtheron.

The Strategic Concept required NATO to be prepared to respond to a variety of contingencies. During the Cold War, the Alliance was focussed on one adversary, requiring a single military plan and military forces on stand-by. Military planners working at the member States' Ministries of Defence contributed to and developed a single war plan which was then approved by the NAC and to which member States assigned forces in case the plan would be executed. They also agreed on several alarm plans that spelled out the conditions under which they would transfer their operational command of assigned forces to Allied commanders.[27] These pre-delegation procedures, however, would not meet the requirements of the post-Cold War security environment. The planning of operations, the committal by Member States to contribute their forces to a mission and the transfer of authority over these forces to SACEUR would need to take place on a more *ad hoc* basis and likely more frequent as well. Planning shifted away from national Defence planners to the NATO Command Structure, which was able to produce on an *ad hoc* basis operational plans for a variety of operations. The influence and role that the member States had in the planning of operations and the identification of capabilities and resources was hence significantly reduced and shifted to NATO. These measures effectively resulted in that NATO would acquire a more distinct role from the member States. The changes in operational planning was put to the test almost immediately.

---

operations, the geographical limitations set by article 6 would not apply. The expansion to "out-of-area" operations was politically sensitive. Thies, W.J. (2009) *Why NATO endures*. New York: Cambridge University Press, p. 202.

26 Asmus, R.D., Kugler, R.L. and Larrabee, F.S. (1993) *'Building a New NATO'*, Foreign Affairs, 72(4), p. 28.

27 Chr. Tuschhoff, *The Impact of NATO's Defence Planning and Force Generation on Member States*, in Mayer, S. (ed.) (2014) *NATO's post-cold war politics: The changing provision of security*, United Kingdom: Palgrave Macmillan, Chapter 11.

When, at the beginning of the 1990s, the Socialist Federal Republic of Yugoslavia started to disintegrate and a multi-ethnic conflict emerged, NATO saw itself for the first time operating outside the member States' territory and outside the traditional tasks mentioned in the Washington Treaty. As the events rapidly succeeded each other, NATO was forced to go beyond merely portraying its capabilities. NATO had never fired a shot until the 28th of February 1994 when it took down four Bosnian-Serb military aircraft in support of the implementation of a "no-fly zone" over Bosnia.[28]

In 1992, NATO assisted the UN with various minor operations, including the enforcement of a naval embargo,[29] a no-fly zone over Bosnia-Herzegovina[30] and close air support to the United Nations Protection Force (UNPROFOR).[31] The – then still young – relationship between the UN and NATO led sometimes to unworkable situations. Illustrative was the so-called "dual key" arrangement for approval for air strikes in support of UNPROFOR. Close air support could only be provided when both organizations – NATO and the UN – agreed.[32] The result was that many air strikes were delayed due to different perceptions between the two organizations. By the end of 1995, the crisis in Yugoslavia had developed into a massacre where more than 250.000 people already were killed.

NATO took decisive action after the genocide of Srebrenica.[33] When the UN withdrew its forces to safe areas, NATO unilaterally started air strikes for eleven days on Bosnian-Serb military facilities,[34] without the previously mentioned

28 Operation "Deny Flight", 12 April 1993 until 20 December 1995.

29 Operation "Maritime Monitor", started 16 July 1992 based on UNSCR 713 and 715, later replaced by Operation Maritime Guard from 22 November 1992.

30 Operation "Sky Monitor", started 16 October 1992 and was based on UNSCR 781 (1992).

31 United Nations Security Council resolution 836 (1993), 4 June 1993.

32 The dual-key arrangement was caused by the fact that NATO did not want to act as a subsidiary of the UN. Both organizations kept their authority very close. Although the North Atlantic Treaty makes no reference to article 52 of the UN Charter nor does NATO consider itself as a regional organization, the UN considers NATO as being such. NATO officials have been reluctant to consider NATO as a regional organization out of concern that such categorisation would imply additional obligations in the UN context. See NATO Review, no. 3, autumn 1999, pp. 24–27. The UN is disinclined to name regional organisations it mandates that have mainly military functions. The only time the UN mentions NATO is in para. 4 annex 2 to the UNSCR 1244 (1999).

33 From 13 until 22 July 1995 more than 8.000 Bosnians were killed and 25.000 to 30.000 were made refugee.

34 Operation "Deliberate Force". While the strikes were executed over a period of 11 days (29 August 1995 until 14 September 1995), the operation started from 30 August 1995 until 20 September 1995.

UN-NATO dual-key authorization.[35] The air strikes had a significant contribution in ending the hostilities and concluding the Dayton Peace Accords,[36] but also resulted in the collapse of the UN-NATO operational relationship. NATO would not let the UN dictate its rules of engagement of the operation or veto its action anymore. The relationship between the two organizations became more of a coordinating – rather than joint decision-making arrangement.[37] The fact that the UN would not exercise joint command and control over NATO's operations anymore is relevant in respect to questions of attribution of wrongful conduct, which will be analysed more closely in Chapter 7 of this book. NATO's preferred model for cooperation with the UN henceforth became a strict separation of military and civilian responsibilities.[38]

The 1991 Strategic Concept did not explicitly include the type of operations that the Alliance was conducting in the Balkans. The fact that, by 1992, the Alliance was conducting "out-of-area, non-article 5 crisis response operations" pressed the NATO member States to adjust the Strategic Concept to the new situation. On 24 April 1999, the NAC approved a revised Strategic Concept that, among other changes, explicitly introduced crisis-management operations or so-called "non-article 5 crisis response operations".[39] As the name "non-article 5" suggests, the task does not find reference in the provisions of the 1949 Washington Treaty.

---

35 Gazzini, T. (2006) *The changing rules on the use of force in international law*, United Kingdom: Manchester University Press, p. 70 *"The changes in the procedural arrangements, and in particular the abandonment of the so-called dual-key procedure, finally deprived the United Nations of any form of effective control and meant that the operation could not have been revised, suspended or terminated without the NAC consent".*

36 The General Framework Agreement for Peace, signed on the 14 December 1995 between the Presidents of Bosnia, Serbia and Croatia.

37 Blermann, R., *NATO's Troubled Relations with Partner Organizations: A Resource-Dependence Explanation* in S. Mayer (ed.), *NATO's Post-Cold War Politics: The Changing Provision of Security*, p. 215.

38 Harsch, M.F. (2015) *The power of dependence: NATO-UN cooperation in crisis management*, United Kingdom: Oxford University Press, p. 54.

39 The Alliance's Strategic Concept, approved by the Heads of State and Government participating in the meeting of the North Atlantic Council in Washington D.C., 24 April 1999, para 41 *"They must also be prepared to contribute to conflict prevention and to conduct non-Article 5 crisis response operations"* and para 20 *"These risks include uncertainty and instability in and around the Euro-Atlantic area and the possibility of regional crises at the periphery of the Alliance, which could evolve rapidly."*

There has been academic[40] and political debate[41] whether the new tasks in the 1999 Strategic Concept constituted an amendment of the 1949 Washington Treaty and whether the Strategic Concept required parliamentary approval.[42] The view held here is that the 1949 Washington Treaty is open-worded, allowing the NAC to adapt the organization to the new security environment and to introduce new functions in accordance with its aims. The Washinton Treaty is a starting point from where through decisions of the NAC the organization

---

40 Simma, B. (1999) *'NATO, the UN and the use of force: Legal aspects'*, European Journal of International Law, 10(1), pp. 1–22. doi: 10.1093/ejil/10.1.1, p. 18. Gazzini, T. (2001) *'NATO coercive military activities in the Yugoslav crisis (1992–1999)'*, European Journal of International Law, 12(3), pp. 391–436. doi: 10.1093/ejil/12.3.391, pp. 413–414. Gazzini argues that the text of the 1999 Strategic Concept is vague and does not create any legally binding obligation. Therefore, a formal amendment of the Washington Treaty was not required. Gazzini continuous that even if the 1999 Strategic Concept would have gone beyond the Washington Treaty, *"nothing would have prevented NATO member States from performing activities entirely outside those included in the 1949 Treaty* [...] *provided that the relevant NAC"* Gazzini, T. (2001) *'NATO coercive military activities in the Yugoslav crisis (1992–1999)'*, European Journal of International Law, 12(3), pp. 391–436. doi: 10.1093/ejil/12.3.391, pp. 413–414. The view that decisions of the NAC are a collective expression of the member States' will and hence are never indicative of a *volonté distincte* of the organization is too strict. The fact that decisions taken by the member States jointly through their representation in such organs does not mean that the organization is subject to the will of the member States. In support of this view are Seyersted and Amerasinghe, Seyersted, F. (1964a) *'International Personality of Intergovernmental Organizations. Do Their Capacities Really Depend upon Their Constitutions'*, Indian Journal of International Law, 4(4), p. 53, Amerasinghe, C.F. (2005) *Principles of the institutional law of international organizations* (Cambridge studies in international and comparative law series). United Kingdom: Cambridge University Press, p. 83. As will be examined in Chapter 5, the NAC is left sufficient room to not to be considered the authority of any single (member) State or other international organization. (Cambridge studies in international and comparative law series). United Kingdom: Cambridge University Press, p. 83. As will be examined in Chapter 5, the NAC is left sufficient room to not to be considered the authority of any single (member) State or other international organization.

41 The US Senate argued whether the 1999 Strategic Concept requires ratification by the Senate as it contained new commitments for the US, US Congressional Record, 25 May 1999, p. 10701.

42 German Federal Constitutional Court, 19 June 2001, PDS parliamentary group v. Federal Government. PDS argued that the 1999 Strategic Concept constituted an amendment to the 1949 Washington Treaty and required the prior approval by the German parliament.

grows.[43] In the words of the German Constitutional Court, the changes made by the NAC are *"understood as a further development and a concretisation of the open wording of the NATO Treaty"*.[44] It is relevant, however, to note that the Strategic Concept did not introduce new changes. Rather, the 1999 Strategic Concept *"summarizes and formalizes a string of ministerial communiqués and lesser decisions that have emerged since the last Strategic Concept"*.[45]

The 1999 Strategic Concept did not answer some of the poignant questions that remained after the operations in the Balkans. One of those questions was whether Operation Allied Force set a precedent for NATO to operate without an explicit UN mandate.[46] Several scholars view that the military intervention did not have a legal basis in international law and hence violated the provisions of the UN Charter on the prohibition of inter-State use of force. Operation Allied Force resulted in a claim submitted by the former Yugoslav Republic against the members of the Alliance for, *inter alia,* an alleged breach of the obligation not to intervene in the internal affairs of another State, contained in Article 2(4) of the UN Charter.[47] An important observation for this book is that the respondent NATO member States argued that if there was a case of a breach of the UN Charter, the breach should be attributed to NATO and not to the individual member States.[48] This observation will be further examined in Chapter 5 regarding the practice of member States regarding the international legal personality of the Alliance. Irrespective of whether Operation Allied Force constituted a breach of an obligation of the UN Charter, many of the member States agreed that NATO's legitimacy of using force in

43 Klabbers, J., (2008), *'The paradox of international institutional law',* International Organizations Law Review, 5 doi: 10.1163/157237408X326138, p. 14.

44 German Federal Constitutional Court, 19 June 2001, PDS Parliamentary Group v. Federal Government, para. 16.

45 Ringmose, J., Ryinning, S., *"Come home NATO? The Atlantic Alliance's new Strategic Concept",* Danish Institute of International Law.

46 The *Deutscher Bundestag, Plenarprotokoll* 13/248/, 16 October 1998, at 23129, *"The decision of NATO* [on air strikes against the FRY] *must not become a precedent. As far as the Security Council monopoly on force* [Gewaltmonopol] *is concerned, we must avoid getting on a slippery slope",* quoted by Simma, B. (1999) *'NATO, the UN and the use of force: Legal aspects',* European Journal of International Law, 10(1), pp. 1–22. doi: 10.1093/ejil/10.1.1, p. 13.

47 International Court of Justice, *Legality of the use of force* (*Yugoslavia v. Spain*), Application instituting proceedings, 29 April 1999, p. 3.

48 International Court of Justice, *Legality of the use of force,* International Court of Justice, *Legality of Use of Force* (Serbia and Montenegro v. Portugal), Preliminary objections of the Portuguese Republic, 5 July 2000, Chapter II, para 40.

non-article 5 operations should stem from an explicit mandate from the UN Security Council.[49]

The 1999 Strategic Concept left the possibility open for NATO to act globally and did not restrict it to the Euro-Atlantic region. The Concept refers to threats *"affecting"* the Euro-Atlantic area. For this reason, the Alliance is determined *"to shape its security environment and enhance the peace and stability in the Euro-Atlantic area"* and must *"also take account of the global context"*. The risks include – for instance – terrorism, sabotage and organised crime.

The events on 11 September 2001 proved the prediction in the 1999 Strategic Concept correct. This time the Alliance acted with more coherence than in the 1990s during the Yugoslav crisis. The Al Qaida terrorist attacks of 11 September 2001 on US' territory destroyed several landmark buildings, among those the Twin Towers in New York. Within hours after the terrorist attacks, the North Atlantic Council unanimously condemned the attacks, pledged its assistance and support, and determined that the attack consisted of an action covered by Article 5 of the Treaty.[50] The debate on whether NATO would or would not operate out of its Euro-Atlantic area ended, in the words of the French Ambassador to NATO: *"with the collapse of the twin towers"*. The expectation was that NATO would be an integral part of the military response in Afghanistan. However, the US preferred to pursue its right to self-defence only with a select group of capable allies.[51] Ultimately, NATO did become involved in Afghanistan but not as a result of the invocation of Article 5. In August 2003, NATO took the lead over the peace support operation "International Security Assistance Force (ISAF)".[52]

---

49 Simma, B. (1999) *'NATO, the UN and the use of force: Legal aspects'*, European Journal of International Law, 10(1), pp. 1–22. doi: 10.1093/ejil/10.1.1, pp. 1–22; I. Brownlie, Chr. Chinkin, V. Lowe 49 International and Comparative Law Quarterly 876–943, 2000, L. Henkin, R. Wedgwood, J. Charney, Chr. Chinkin, R. Falk, Th. Franck and W.M. Reisman, *Editorial Comments: NATO's Kosovo Intervention*, 93 American Journal of International Law, pp. 824–878 (1999). In contrast, C. Greenwood argues that NATO did not act in violation of *jus ad bellum, Evidence to the House of Commons Foreign Affairs Committee,* Foreign Affairs Committee Report, 1999–2000, HC Paper 28-II, p. 137.

50 Statement by the North Atlantic Council, Press release PR/CP (2001)/122, 11 September 2001.

51 One US official stated: "I think it's safe to say that we won't be asking SACEUR to put together a battle plan for Afghanistan", J. Dempsey, *et al.*, 'White House Avoids Seeking NATO-Wide Aid', *Financial Times*, 27 September 2001. Cited in P.H. Gordon, "NATO After 11 September," *Survival*, Vol. 43, No. 4, Winter 2001–2002, p. 92.

52 The International Security Assistance Force, UN Security Council resolution 1386 (2003), 20 December 2001.

The "11 September" attacks had an impact on NATO in several areas. NATO's enlargement plans have usually been met with strong opposition from Russia, especially when in 1999 NATO enlarged with Poland, Hungary and the Czech Republic. The common interests to combat terrorism led Russia to reconsider its opposition to enlargement.[53] In 2004, NATO expanded to 26 members, with the accession of seven Eastern-European countries; the largest expansion round ever.[54] It also set out a transformation of NATO, envisaging a new role on counter-terrorism and the defence against weapons of mass destruction.

The threat that terrorism posed to the Alliance deserved a new Strategic Concept, but the relationships within NATO were not conducive for such revisions.[55] As late as 2009, a Group of Experts prepared recommendations for the formulations of the Concept of 2010.[56] The Strategic Concept 2010 outlines three tasks for the Alliance: Collective Defence, Crisis Management and Cooperative Security. All three tasks have a global and expeditionary dimension. These first two tasks are relevant to this book, because it aims at examining the responsibility of NATO during its military operations, which are either collective self-defence operations or crisis response operations. The 1999 Strategic Concept formalised NATO non-article 5 crisis response operations and, with the advent of the 2010 Strategic Concept, the member States agree that the interests of NATO to conduct military operations are global as long as there is a threat against the *security* of the member States. Whereas the 1991 and 1999 Concepts related to threats and attacks against '*the territory of the* Alliance', these references have been completely removed in the 2010 Concept.[57]

The traumatic experience of NATO in conducting crisis management operations in Kosovo and Afghanistan has not led to a decision to abandon the task of non-article 5 crisis response operations. On the contrary, the 2010 Strategic Concept elevated crisis management to a core task, next to collective security and cooperation. Lessons learned from past operations were also drawn in the Strategic Concept; NATO now commits to a more comprehensive approach in crisis management operations, integrating politics, security, development, rule of law, human rights and humanitarian dimensions in cooperation with humanitarian actors, the UN, EU and other players in international missions.

---

53 Jones, G., 'Putin Softens Opposition to NATO Expansion', *Reuters*, 3 October 2001.

54 Bulgaria, Estonia, Latvia, Lithuania, Romania, Slovakia and Slovenia joined the Alliance.

55 Danish Institute for International Studies, DIIS Report 2011:06, "*After the Strategic Concept, towards a NATO version 3.0*", p. 13.

56 Group of Experts' report *NATO 2020: Assured Security: Dynamic Engagement*.

57 Danish Institute for International Studies, DIIS Report 2011:06, "*After the Strategic Concept, towards a NATO version 3.0*", p. 15.

The tension in the consensual decision-making process by NATO's did not diminish. The increased number of operations and the expansion of member States to 28 called for greater commitment of the members when embarking on new missions. The Group of Experts for the 2010 Strategic Concept recommended changes for streamlining the decision-making process, including proposals to give the Secretary General or NATO military leaders more authority to respond to emergency situations and to consider that only fundamental decisions should be submitted for decision by the NAC.[58]

These tools and processes moved the planning and execution of operations from national autonomy to more institutionally-driven. NATO itself now generates necessary incentives for member States to agree on collective action and comply with the common policies, making the Alliance more than the sum of its parts.[59] Clearly, member States can have political reservations to a particular mission and even opt out in contributing forces. This happened in the case of Operation Unified Protector, where Germany abstained on the vote on a UN Security Council mandate and withdraw its forces from the NATO Airborne Warning and Control System (AWACS) and the Standing NATO Maritime Group 1 (SNMG-1).[60] At the same time, Germany approved the NAC decision to initiate the operation and supported the mission to launch a successful mission. This built-in flexibility in NATO's planning and execution of operations shows the evolving distinct role between NATO and its member States, which indicates that the organization might have international legal personality. This feature will be further examined in Chapter 5.

3.4 Conclusions

This chapter provided in an overview of the key moments in the development of NATO. The Alliance was created in 1949, primarily, as a trans-Atlantic collective defense mechanism. Through its sixty-five years of existence, NATO adapted its strategy and institutional structure. NATO's strategy changed from focusing only on collective self-defence to include non-article 5 crisis response

58 Danish Institute for International Studies, DIIS Report 2011:06, *"After the Strategic Concept, towards a NATO version 3.0"*, pp. 34–35.

59 Tuschhoff, Chr., *The Impact of NATO's Defence Planning and Force Generation on Member States*, in Mayer, S. (ed.) (2014) *NATO's post-cold war politics: The changing provision of security*, United Kingdom: Palgrave Macmillan, Chapter 11.

60 Brockmeier, S., *Germany and the Intervention in Libya*, International Institute for International Studies, Survival, Vol. 55, No. 6, December 2013 – January 2014, p. 63.

operations.[61] The Alliance' institutional structure has been adapted to cope with the new strategy and be flexible and responsive to a wide range of contingencies. NATO has played an autonomous role in the process of adjusting NATO's policies, institutional structure and strategy.[62]

Two conclusions can be drawn here, which are of relevance to the topic of responsibility of NATO during its military operations.

First, the key moments in the development of NATO show that the Organization changed in scope and character of its activities through political processes without involving any formal changes in its legal character. This conclusion is drawn from the nature of the documents that have transformed and enlarge the Alliance. All of the documents are not legal, but military and political in nature. The member States did not make any formal amendments to NATO's constituent document, i.e. the 1949 Washington Treaty. Moreover, during NATO's existence, member States did not express any intention to strengthen the attributes of its legal personality. Therefore, any conclusion on whether NATO has international legal personality should come from a *de facto* analysis – through observing its activities and objectives of the Organization. This chapter briefly touched upon some of the aspects that allude to such an international legal personality, which will be further elaborated upon in Chapter 5 on the international legal personality of NATO.

Second, without adopting any formal amendments of the Washington Treaty, NATO underwent substantial transformation into an organization with much broader activities both in type and scope, through the adopted political documents and decision-making. This raises the questions whether these informal changes of its constituent treaty have created international legal obligations for NATO and had impact on the development of its international legal personality. Both questions are of relevance for international responsibility of NATO for an unlawful conduct.

61 With the current Strategic Concept of 2010, priority is given to collective defence again. Strategic Concept for the Defence and Security of the Members of the North Atlantic Treaty Organization, adopted by the Heads of State and Government at the NATO Summit in Lisbon, 19–20 November 2010.

62 Reinalda, B. and Verbeek, B. (eds.) (1998) *Autonomous policy making by international organizations*, New York: Taylor & Francis, p. 122.

CHAPTER 4

Current Institutional Framework of NATO and NATO's Decision Making Process

4.1 Introduction

This chapter describes the current institutional framework of NATO and the decision making process for its operations. This will provide further understanding of the powers of NATO and the relationship between NATO and the member States, which is relevant for the question of attribution of conduct of personnel to NATO, troop contributing nations or other international organizations such as the UN. Moreover, the overview provides in insight on whether NATO is an entity separate from its member States, i.e. whether it meets the indicia of an international organization with international legal personality. The conclusions in this chapter will be used further on in Chapters 5 and 7.

Paragraph 4.2 gives a brief outline of the various organs of the Alliance, their composition, tasks and their position within the NATO structure. The intention of providing this outline is to facilitate understanding of the political-military structure and how hierarchically NATO is organised.

Paragraph 4.3 examines the relationship between NATO and its member States and NATO's decision-making process. Since the North Atlantic Council (NAC), in which all the member States participate, is the highest political decision-making organ of NATO, it is appropriate to examine both the relationship between NATO and States as well as NATO's decision-making process. It is important to discuss the decision-making process in the NAC to establish to whom a wrongful act can be attributed: to NATO, to its member States or to both. It can also assist in establishing in which situations – i.e. under which conditions – NATO member States and / or NATO as an international organization will be held responsible. This paragraph will, additionally, examine the relationship between NATO and non-NATO member States, for the same reasons as indicated above and because non-member States regularly participate in NATO-led operations.

The outline is followed by an analysis of the relationship between NATO and the UN. The choice to limit the analysis to the relationship between NATO and the UN is made in order to avoid an overly generic or exhaustive study on relationships between NATO and other international organizations or such organizations in general. Moreover, the relationship with the UN is the

 | DOI 10.1163/9789004354647_005

more straightforward choice to examine as the member States made explicit reference in the Washington Treaty to the context and position NATO takes within the UN system. The context is established by referring to Article 51 of the UN Charter – the right to take collective action against an armed attack – which forms the basis for the establishment of NATO. The Washington Treaty also acknowledges the primary role of the UN Security Council in the maintenance and restoration of international peace and security. Moreover, since NATO relies for its non-article 5 crisis response operations – which consist of the majority of NATO-led operations – on a mandate or authorization from the UN Security Council, the relationship between NATO and the UN is of relevance here. Finally, from a practical point of view, the UN is likely one of the most important partners of NATO.

4.2 Current Institutional Framework of NATO

4.2.1 *Introduction*

NATO consists of two main types of institutional structures: a civilian structure and a military structure. The civilian structure is responsible for policy- and decision-making which provides for the functioning of the Organization both internally and externally.

The military structure is involved in the planning and execution of military operations. All NATO operations are decided upon by the civilian structure and carried out by military structure. It means that both parts of NATO participate in the initiation, planning and execution of NATO operations.

4.2.2 *The Civilian Structure*

a The North Atlantic Council

The Washington Treaty stands out for its brevity, with a mere 14 articles and does expand a great deal on the structure, tasks and responsibilities of the Alliance. The treaty establishes only one organ, the North Atlantic Council (NAC), and attributes the necessary powers to implement the treaty.[1] The NAC is the highest decision-making organ in the Organization. The Council is composed of the representatives of all Member States, which holds regular meetings at the level of Foreign- or Defence Ministers (Ministerials), Heads of States

1 Article 9, North Atlantic Treaty 1949, 34 UNTS 243, 24 August 1949, *"The Parties hereby establish a Council, on which each of them shall be represented to consider matters concerning the implementation of this Treaty".*

(Summits) or Permanent Representatives. As such, the NAC is the most important organ for the member States to express their views and to take collective decisions on political issues of the Alliance. This feature is of relevance to determine whether NATO has international legal personality. An indication that an international organization has international legal personality is – according to the theory of 'objective legal personality' which is further described in Chapter 5 – that an organization is not subject to the authority of any other State or organised community. Since the NAC is not subject to the authority of another legal entity other than the participating States, the assumption is that NATO has international legal personality.[2]

The Washington Treaty does not prescribe the way the Council should take its decisions, but the NAC adopted consensus as the standard. This translates to decisions being adopted without a formal voting procedure, provided that no member raises any formal objection.[3] The decision-making process of NATO is described more elaborately when this book examines the relationship between the member States and NATO in paragraph 4.3. It is relevant to note here that decision-making through consensus is both seen as an argument in favour[4] and against[5] the existence of international legal personality of the Alliance. Arguments against such personality put emphasis on the fact that NAC decisions are collective decisions made by its member States, which assumes that the NAC expresses the will of the member States, rather than the Organization. On the other hand, member States have a right to express objections that they may have and block any decision, making the NAC's decisions entirely reliant on the common agreement of all member States, rather than that of one State. The introduction of the "silence procedure" and opting-out mechanism enhances the autonomy of the Organization – referred to later in this chapter – and alludes to the possibility that NATO may have a *volonté distincte* from its member States. A *volonté distincte*, or 'separate will', may indicate under certain legal theories that the Organization has international legal personality. It is held here that the consensus rule on itself is not an indicator of

2 Seyersted, F. (1964b) *'Objective International Legal Personality of Intergovernmental Organizations: Do Their Capacities Really Depend upon the Conditions Establishing Them'*, Nordisk Tidsskrift for International Ret, 1 (34), p. 47.

3 *NATO Handbook*, 2001.

4 Rosen, N. (2013) *'How Are Multinational NATO Operations Responsible for International Humanitarian Law Operations'*, The Fletcher Forum of World Affairs, 37(3), p. 165.

5 Gazzini, T. (2006) *The changing rules on the use of force in international law*. United Kingdom: Manchester University Press.

either the existence or non-existence of international legal personality. Rather, a more distinguishing factor is to examine in how far the member States retain control in the decision-making process taken by the NAC. A conclusion on the existence of international legal personality of the Alliance will be given in Chapter 5.

The Washington Treaty does not prescribe the span of topics which the NAC can decide upon. The Council's authority is generally confined to the aim of NATO, which is to *"safeguard the freedom, common heritage and civilization of their peoples"* and to *"promote stability and well-being in the North-Atlantic Area"*. In that respect, the Washington Treaty leaves ample room for interpretation and discretion in decision-making.[6]

The founders have left to the discretion of the Council to *"set up such subsidiary bodies as may be necessary."*[7] The NAC created a variety of subsidiary bodies, of which the most important here are the Secretary General, the Military Committee and the various organs of the NATO Command Structure.

b The Secretary General

The Secretary General leads a unified international secretariat to assist the plenary organ – the NAC – and to serve as the Chairman of the Council.[8] As such, he is the chief executive of NATO and responsible for promoting and directing the process of consultation and decision-making within the Alliance.[9]

6 The US Deputy Secretary of State Talbott stated for instance that the Washington Treaty does not impose arbitrary geographical or functional limits, in Simma, B. (1999) *'NATO, the UN and the use of force: Legal aspects'*, European Journal of International Law, 10(1), pp. 1–22. doi: 10.1093/ejil/10.1.1, p. 15. Moreover, even if the NAC would take on topics that are beyond those that were explicitly conferred to in the Washington Treaty, it has always acts – primarily through the NAC – with the consent, acquiescence or approval of the members. Various authors, such as Klabbers, Engström and Kennedy, have argued that if the member States consent in these powers by demonstrating approval or acquiescence, these powers are implied to achieve the purposes for which the Alliance was set up. Klabbers, J. (2001) *'The Life and Times of International Organizations'*, Nordic Journal for International Law, 70; Engström, V., *Understanding Powers of International Organizations,* 2009, pp. 53–73; D. Kennedy, *The sources of international law,* American University International Law Review, Vol. 2:1, 1987, p. 4. Contrary: Kaniel, M. (1996) *The exclusive treaty-making power of the European community: Up to the period of the single European act,* The Netherlands: Wolters Kluwer Law & Business, p. 101.

7 Article 9, North Atlantic Treaty 1949, 34 UNTS 243, 24 August 1949.

8 Final Communiqué of the Ninth Session of the North Atlantic Council ("The Lisbon Decisions" on the reorganization of the Alliance and the appointment of a Secretary General), 25 February 1952.

9 NATO Legal Deskbook, 16 January 2008, *draft.*

The Secretary General is supported by the International Staff, forming the so-called "civilian structure".

The Secretary General is also the representative for external relations. He maintains relationships on the level of Ministers of Foreign Affairs, - Defense and Heads of State during the operations.[10] The Secretary General is usually the signatory for international agreements binding the Alliance, e.g. the exchange of letters with the Afghan authorities relating to the Status of ISAF Personnel in Afghanistan is signed on the side of the Alliance by the Secretary General.[11]

4.2.3 *The Military Structure*

NATO's military structure consists of the Military Committee, supported by its International Military Staff, and the NATO Command Structure.

a The Military Committee

The Military Committee (MC) is composed of the highest national military representatives from each Member State, assisting the Council with military expertise[12] and works under the overall political authority of the NAC.[13] It assists and advises the NAC on military matters and provides military guidance to the NATO Strategic Commanders of the NATO Command Structure. The MC takes its decisions by consensus; this way full commitment is achieved in both the military as well as the political requirements and objectives of the mission.

The MC plays an important role in the drafting of NATO strategic concepts and advises the Council of the military situation in countries were NATO is conducting operations. The role of the Chairman of the MC is to represent and defend the consensus-based advice to the NAC. The Military Committee is supported by the International Military Staff.

The Committee is an essential link between the political and military structure of NATO. The Military Committee provides the NAC with military advice agreed by all Chiefs of Defence. The consensus among the highest military

10 E.g. Letter of the Afghan Minister of Defence to the Secretary General, dated 30 August 2008.

11 Exchange of letters between the NATO Secretary General and the Afghan Minister of Foreign Affairs, 5 September 2004 and 22 November 2004.

12 Excluding Iceland, which – due to the lack of military forces – sends a civilian representative.

13 The Defence Planning Committee was dissolved in June 2010 during the third NATO Committee Review. Its responsibilities are absorbed by the North Atlantic Council.

authorities of NATO represents a firm commitment that the operation is militarily achievable with the forces available from the nations.

b The NATO Command Structure

The NATO Command Structure consists of two Strategic Commands, Allied Command Operations and Allied Command Transformation. In 1950, the NAC created the Supreme Allied Commander Europe (SACEUR)[14] and gave it the responsibility to *"organize* [national units assigned to him] *into an effective integrated defence force".*[15] Currently, SACEUR is responsible for the planning and commanding all NATO-led operations. He is bound by the political constraints given by the NAC, who maintains political oversight of operations. The command structure enables NATO to plan and execute operations while maintaining strategic military and political coherence throughout the chain of command.

SACEUR has at his disposition various subordinate commands which makes up Allied Command Operations, or ACO. ACO includes two Joint Force Commands (JFC Brunssum and JFC Naples), each of which is capable to plan, conduct and sustain a major joint operation[16] at the operational level. There are also three other specialised commands (Air Command, Land Command and Maritime Command) directly under SACEUR's command, which provide support to the Joint Force Command, but are also able to plan, conduct and sustain a smaller joint operation by themselves and report directly to SACEUR.

Supreme Allied Command Transformation has the lead role for the transformation of NATO's military structure, forces, capabilities and doctrines in order to improve the military effectiveness of the Alliance. SACT does not have a specific role in commanding operations and will not be further examined in detail as it is not of particular relevance to NATO's responsibilities during its operations.

In NATO-led operations, SACEUR will appoint one of its subordinate headquarters to plan and execute the mission (figure 2). One of the Joint Force Commands, or – in case of a smaller mission, the Maritime-, Land- or Air Command – can establish a headquarters in the mission area that will be responsible for running of day-to-day operations. SACEUR will retain Operational

14 Final Communiqué, 18–19 December 1950.

15 Final Communiqué, 18–19 December 1950.

16 NATO, Ministerial Guidance MG06, quoted in Danish Institute for International Studies, *NATO's New Strategic Concept: A Comprehensive Assessment*, 2011:02.

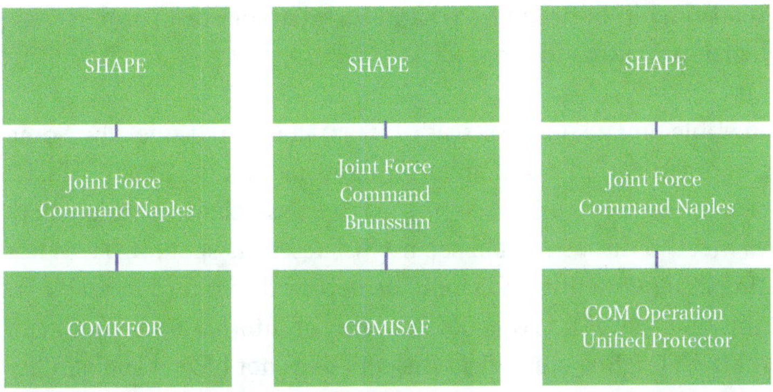

FIGURE 2 *Command and control of KFOR, ISAF and Operation Unified Protector.*

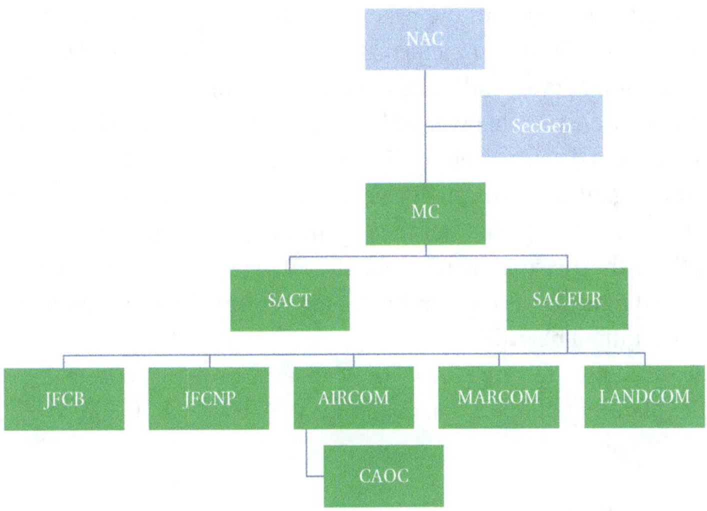

FIGURE 3 *NATO's civil (blue) and military (green) structure.*

Command (i.e. the authority to assign missions or tasks, to deploy units and to reassign forces)[17] over the mission, while delegating Operational Control (i.e. the authority to direct forces assigned so that the commander may accomplish specific missions or tasks which are usually limited by function, time, or location) to the subordinate headquarters (figure 3).[18]

17 AAP-6, *NATO Glossary of Terms and Definitions*, 2010.

18 Source: www.nato.int. JFCBS (Joint Force Command Brunssum), JFCNP (Joint Force Command Naples), aircom (Air Command), MARCOM (Maritime Command), landcom (Land Command), CAOC (Combined Air Operations Command). ACT's subordinate commands are not depicted here, neither are the signal battalions.

4.3 The Relationship between NATO and Its Member States and the Decision-making Process

There is considerable debate on the status of NATO in international law. Some view NATO as an organization independent from its members, capable of having a will of its own.[19] Other studies see NATO as a trans-Atlantic forum where member States meet to discuss global security issues.[20] As such, NATO is not capable of acting independently and would be deprived of international legal personality. Consequently, if NATO is not a subject of international law, it can not bear international rights and obligations and does not have responsibility under international law.

Those studies which hold the view that NATO is a forum or a mere Alliance of like-minded States rather than an independent international organization, base their arguments primarily on the process in which member States take decisions in the North Atlantic Council (NAC). NATO takes decisions by consensus of all the member States and therefore there is no real autonomy of the organization. The consensus rule by itself is not an indicator of international legal personality, as was discussed above. The measure by which the member States control the organization through this decision-making procedure is a better indicator for estalishing whether the organization has international legal personality.[21] For this reason, the relationship between NATO and its member States and the degree in which member States control decisions made by NATO is further examined below.

This chapter will focus on three areas, the consensus-rule in NATO's decision making, the planning of operations and the contribution of forces to the Alliance.

4.3.1 *Consensus-rule*

NATO decisions are made by consensus, after discussion and consultation among member countries.[22] A decision reached by consensus is an agreement reached by common consent.

19 Zwanenburg, M.C. (2005) *Accountability of peace support operations*, Netherlands: Martinus Nijhoff Publishers.

20 Verhoeven, J. (2000) *Droit international public*. Larcier, p. 613. T. Gazzini, *Personality of International Organizations*, in Klabbers, J. and Wallendahl, A. (eds.) (2012) *Research handbook on the law of international organizations*, United Kingdom: Edward Elgar Publishing.

21 White, P.N.D., Collins, R. and White, N.D. (eds.) (2010) *International organizations and the idea of autonomy: Institutional independence in the international legal order*, United Kingdom: Routledge, p. 68.

22 http://www.nato.int/cps/en/natolive/topics_49178.htm.

It is important to differentiate between decision-making based on consensus and unanimity. Unanimity requires an actively stated vote in favour of a measure, which the Alliance does not seek. Actually, there is no voting at all in NATO's decision-making process. Instead, decisions are taken when there is an absence of objection by any member State. Member States can express their objections either privately with the Secretary General, raise them during NAC meetings, or even go public with their disagreement.[23] Of course, each choice comes at a political cost. Hence, the role of the Secretary General is essential to maintain the cohesion of the Alliance. To this end, the Secretary General may employ a tactic called the "silence-procedure". This procedure allows States to reach consensus on those topics that are politically sensitive for some of the member States. It entails that a decision will be automatically passed by the NAC after a stated time-period set by the Secretary General, unless a member State objects by sending a formal letter to the Secretary General thereby breaking the silence.[24] In some cases, the political cost for an opposing member State's representative of openly being identified as blocking the decision may outweigh the benefit of seeing the proposed action stopped. In those cases, a member State may prefer not to block the decision, but rather mitigate its concerns through caveats for its forces or even to choose not to participate fully in the operation.

The silence-procedure has proven useful in situations where domestic opposition exists in the member States for a certain military intervention. In Operation Allied Force, public disagreement would have placed NATO member States in a conflict before world media and would play in favour for President Milosevic. The silence procedure allowed Member States not needing to take a public position and permitted NATO to move forward.[25] Similarly, the silence procedure provided Germany – which faced public opposition regarding a military intervention in Libya – in an opportunity to avoid to take publicly a position regarding the decision in favour of NATO's Operation Unified Protector.[26]

23 Hendrickson, R.C. (2006) *Diplomacy and war at NATO: The secretary general and military action after the cold war*, United States: University of Missouri Press, p. 107.

24 Gallis, P. (2003) *CRS report for congress NATO's decision-making procedure background*, available at: https://fas.org/man/crs/RS21510.pdf (Accessed: 14 May 2016). Hendrickson, R.C. (2006) *Diplomacy and war at NATO: The secretary general and military action after the cold war*, United States: University of Missouri Press, p. 107, 2006.

25 Hendrickson, R.C. (2006) Diplomacy and war at NATO: *The secretary general and military action after the cold war*, United States: University of Missouri Press, p. 108, 2006.

26 As a member of the UN Security Council, in the period 2011–2012, Germany abstained from voting for the UN Security Council resolution 1973(2011) to authorize a mandate to protect civilians under the threat of attack in Libya. While Germany did not contribute

The silence procedure shows that the Alliance can continue to move forward even with the dissociation of one or more of the member States. The decision making procedure is not – by itself – an argument that NATO lacks autonomy and, hence, international legal personality. As stated above, the autonomy depends on the degree of control that the member States exercise over the organization. The consensus procedure illustrates that there is no requirement for member States to exercise such control and thereby allowing the Organization to enjoy a certain degree of autonomy. Member States are also free to choose which operations they prefer to participate in. In case a member State has concerns regarding a specific mission, it may decide not to participate in the mission with military forces and materiel, while at the same time choose not to block any decision relating to the operation.

In this regard it is also worth mentioning that in some situations, the Troop Contributing Nations' involvement in the decision making process is limited to the decision whether or not to participate with military forces, without having any role in the formulation of the political aspects of a mission.

States which are not members of NATO may contribute with military forces to a NATO-led mission. NATO relies extensively on the contribution of forces from so-called "Non-NATO Contributing Nations (NNCN)". These are States which are not parties to the Washington Treaty and are not members of NATO, but are willing to contribute forces to a NATO-led operation. From the earliest operations, NNCN have contributed to NATO operations in a substantial manner, notably Russia as the single largest contributor. As of September 2008, approximately 62,500 personnel were deployed in 5 NATO-led operations of which 4,300 personnel were provided by 16 NNCN.[27] The Political Military Framework regulates the participation of NNCN in NATO operations. The process starts with an expression of interest by the NNCN in contributing to a specific NATO-led operation. Participation is dependent upon NAC approval, and, once approved, NNCN enter into technical agreements with NATO to work out security, technical and financial issues.[28] NNCN will be consulted on all aspects

---

any troops to the operation, it did not withdraw German officers serving at the Joint Headquarters Naples responsible for the planning of the operation. Germany also allowed allies to use German territory as a logistical base for the operation. This issue is elaborated further in this chapter when examining the force generation process. Mayer, S. (ed.) (2014) *NATO's post-cold war politics: The changing provision of security*, United Kingdom: Palgrave Macmillan.

27 NATO Parliamentary Assembly, *159 DSCFC 08 E Rev 1 – Contributions of Non-NATO member to NATO operations*, http://www.nato-pa.int/default.asp ?SHORTCUT=1475.

28 Participation of partnership for peace countries and other partner nations in NATO operations are regulated by specific agreements, such as the Enhanced and More Operational

of the operation, but do not have decision making power on, for instance, the concept of the operation, rules of engagement and periodic mission reviews.[29] NNCN do not have any political influence on the mission as they do not take part in the decision making process at the NAC, but to allow SACEUR to have Operational Command and Control over their military forces.

Even though the NAC enlarged the influence of NNCN in the operations they choose to participate in and are consulted and offered the opportunity to put forward views on all relevant issues of the operations, NATO, still retains full political decision-making authority.[30] This shows that NATO as an international organization can act, to a certain extent, independently from States participating in the operation, in particular with respect to NNCN.

4.3.2 *Planning Process of NATO Operations*

A second area where the particular nature of the relationship between NATO and the member States becomes apparent is during the operational planning process.

It would be fair to conclude that NATO was effectively an instrument of the member States until the early 1990s. During the Cold War-period, the planning of operations was limited to the development of several regional Standing Defence Plans against one identified potential aggressor. These plans were pre-approved by the NAC. The Defence Planning Committee[31] set so-called "Force Goals" to which member States commit their forces for a period of 6 years. Member States annually reported on how they intended to meet these requirements.[32] Overall, the decisions were taken at the capitals without much need of NATO's involvement other than being a forum where discussions could take place.

NATO relied on the same planning processes that existed during the Cold War for its first "non-article 5" operations in the early 1990s. And in fact, there

---

Partnership (EMOP), Political-Military Framework for NATO-led PfP operations, and other documents. Decision-making, however, remains the sole prerogative of the NAC.

29 NATO, *Political Military Framework for Partner involvement in NATO-led Operations*, Annex to PO(2011)0141, 13 April 2011.

30 NAC, *Political military framework for partner involvement in NATO-led operations*, Annex to PO(2011)0141, 13 April 2011.

31 The Defence Planning Committee was the former senior decision-making body on matters relating to the integrated military structure of the Alliance. It has been dissolved in 2010 and its responsibilities have been absorbed by the NAC.

32 Wendt, J.C. and Brown, N. (1986) *Improving the NATO Force Planning Process*, available at: https://www.rand.org/content/dam/rand/pubs/reports/2009/R3383.pdf (Accessed: 16 May 2016), p. 3.

was no real need to change the planning processes, as the first operations were fairly straightforward. They consisted of monitoring of an arms embargo (e.g. operation Maritime Monitor) or a no-fly zone (e.g. operation Sky Monitor). Neither, the IFOR, SFOR and KFOR required much involvement of NATO in the planning of the operation, as most of the forces were provided by a lead- or framework nation, which would take the responsibility for organizing the forces necessary in a specific sector. For instance, in implementing the Dayton Peace Agreement, Bosnia-Herzegovina was divided into 3 regions for which each a lead nation was assigned to carry out the operation.[33]

The planning of ISAF and NATO Training Mission in Iraq (NTM-I) operations was much more complex. These operations took place much farther away from NATO's borders adding complexity in logistical planning and defence expenditure. They also took place in much less benign environments. Moreover, both operations went beyond the monitoring of a cease-fire and included tasks such as counter-insurgency activities, reconstruction of civil infrastructure and mentoring of government officials.

The increased complexity of the operations required a more sophisticated planning process than the pre-delegation model that was used in previous operations. In the current planning process, when tasked by the NAC, SACEUR will conduct a formal assessment of the identified crisis and will give considerations on the use of the NATO military instrument to assist with a situation resolution. The NAC may then task SACEUR to develop military response options. Subsequently, the NAC may decide whether SACEUR should provide a concept of operations within the political direction given by the Council.[34] The member States rely heavily on the planning done by SACEUR's staff, as its integrated system analysis, planning and assessment tools,[35] congregated databases on capabilities and availability of member States' forces[36] and doctrine[37] provide planning capabilities that are not easily replicated in the national Ministries of Defense.

The planning process does not alter the national autonomy of the member States or their 'veto' power at the NAC. The member States retain their

33 Multinational Division (MND) South-East, led by France, MND South-West, led by the UK and MND North, led by the US.

34 NATO, *NATO's Assessment of a crisis and development of response strategies. http://www.nato.int/cps/en/natohq/official_texts_75565.htm?*

35 E.g. Tools for Operational Planning Functional Area Service (TOPFAS), Effective Visible Execution (EVE), Allied Deployment and Movement System (ADAMS), Coalition Reception, Staging and Onward Movement (CORSOM).

36 E.g. Logistics Functional Area Services (LOGFAS).

37 COPD, the Comprehensive Operations Planning Directive, version 2, 2013.

authority to disapprove certain proposals and to halt or change a given course of action. However, the incremental decision-making process and the unique planning capabilities of NATO make it more difficult for member States to refuse participation on general grounds and discourages uncooperative behaviour.[38] This observation leads to the conclusion that even though the member States retain sovereign control over NATO's actions, the degree of control is limited on general political aspects of a mission and not on the specifics of each aspect of the operation.

4.3.3 *The Command and Control Relationship*

The third and the last area that is examined here with respect to the relationship between NATO and its member States is the command and control relationship.

NATO does not have military forces permanently assigned to the Organization. When a mission is deemed necessary, NATO will request nations to contribute the required forces and materiel to the mission. Nations will inform NATO on their contributions and transfer part of their authority over their forces to Alliance.[39] Authority is then delegated throughout the organization at various levels.

The degree of authority that each of the levels exercises is defined by the 'command and control' structure set in place.[40] 'Command' is the authority to direct, coordinate or control armed forces to achieve particular objectives. 'Control' is the authority to organise, direct and coordinate the activities of the forces assigned to implement orders and directives.

NATO differentiates between three levels of command and control, ranging from (a) Full Command, (b) Operational Command and Control and (c) Tactical Command and Control.

States normally retain "Full Command", which is the authority that covers every aspect of military and administration. It is very uncommon for States to transfer Full Command to NATO or any other international organization or State. Full Command includes the authority to decide to participate in a certain mission and to withdraw from participation in accordance with the terms agreed to. It also includes the authority to take administrative and disciplinary

38 Mayer, S. (ed.) (2014) *NATO's post-cold war politics: The changing provision of security*, United Kingdom: Palgrave Macmillan, p. 203.

39 Similar to UN operations. D. Fleck, *Legal Aspects of the Transfer of Authority in UN Peace Operations*, 42 Netherlands Yearbook of International Law 2011, p. 39.

40 Capstone Doctrine, Allied Joint Publication 01(D), Chapter 6 Command and Control of Operations.

measures against personnel of its own armed forces.[41] As described in Chapter 2, the Commander of the Kosovo Force (COMKFOR) did not have the authority to take disciplinary measures against personnel that violated his order not to frequent prostitutes in Kosovo or to be engaged in the act of human trafficking. COMKFOR was dependent on the sending States to ensure that such regulations are enforceable through national disciplinary sanctions.[42]

States that contribute forces to NATO operations normally will transfer "Operational Command and Control" to the Alliance. Operational Command is the authority to assign missions or tasks, to deploy units and to reassign forces.[43] It is the authority needed to effectuate the overall strategic objectives of the whole operation. Operational Control is the authority to direct forces assigned so that the commander may accomplish specific missions or tasks which are usually limited by function, time, or location. This includes the authority to issue binding directives for forces assigned to his command. For example, as illustrated in Chapter 2, the tactical directive issued by COMISAF that restrained the use of force by troops assigned to him is an example of operational control. COMKFOR similarly had the authority to limit the frequenting certain bars and locales by KFOR personnel is the exercise of operational control.

'Tactical Command' is also transferred by TCNs to SACEUR. SACEUR usually delegates tactical command to subordinate command. Tactical Command is the authority to assign tasks to forces for the accomplishment of the mission, and Tactical Control is the detailed and local direction and control of movements or manoeuvres necessary to accomplish missions or tasks assigned.

TCNs will ordinarily transfer Operational Command and Control to NATO, while retaining Full Command – including Administrative Control – over their forces. The transfer follows a formal procedure, which entails the TCN sending SACEUR a 'transfer of authority message'. This message describes which units are placed under command of NATO and which level of authority is being transferred. After the transfer of command to NATO, the nations are not able to exercise control over their forces anymore, except by re-assuming command and thereby effectively taking their forces out from the mission. States may,

41 This authority is also referred to as Administrative Control (ADCON) and defined as the direction or exercise of authority over subordinate or other organizations in respect to administrative matters such as personnel management, supply, services, and other matters not included in the operational missions of the subordinate or other organizations, AAP-6(200), *NATO Glossary of Terms and Definitions*.

42 Amnesty International (2004) 'So does it mean that we have the rights?' Protecting the human rights of women and girls trafficked for forced prostitution in Kosovo. Available at: http://reliefweb.int/report/serbia/so-does-it-mean-we-have-rights-protecting.

43 AAP-6, *NATO Glossary of Terms and Definitions*, 2010.

however, issue limitations and restriction on the use of their forces, i.e. 'national caveats' and 'red-card holdership'.[44]

In few instances, TCNs have re-assumed command over their forces during a NATO operation. As described in Chapter 2 of this book, Canada reassumed command over its forces during ISAF, when it assessed that the transfer of detainees captured by Canadian forces to the government of Afghanistan would pose them to the risk of being tortured.

The transfer of authority over forces from States to NATO has relevant consequences to the question of responsibility for wrongful conduct during NATO operations, in particular to the aspect of attribution. Attribution of a wrongful act to NATO depends on whether NATO has international legal personality and whether the wrongful act was under the effective control of NATO. These issues are examined more elaborately in Chapters 5 and 7 of this book. It is relevant to note here that when TCNs place their forces at the disposal of NATO, they transfer the authority to assign missions or tasks, to deploy units and to reassign forces. This means that NATO exercises effective control over these forces with respect to mission-related tasks. This effective control, however, may be undermined by the issuance of national caveats, limitations or interference by the TCN involved or when the TCN decides to re-assume command over its forces.

NATO's command and control relationship also illustrate the relationship that the Alliance has with its member States and other TCNs. Nations transfer the authority over their forces to NATO, which indicates that the Alliance has a large degree of autonomy, even if nations still retain the possibility to re-assume command over thëir forces and the fact that they can impose limitations and restrictions on the use of the forces.

4.4 The Relationship between NATO and the UN

NATO's constituent document refers in several places to the UN, the UN Security Council and the UN Charter, showing the commitment of the founding members to the principles of the United Nations. Certain founding States even suggested to define NATO as a 'regional arrangement' in reference to Chapter VIII of the UN Charter.[45] Under Chapter VIII of the UN Charter,

44 Chapter 7 will go into further detail on the consequences that national caveats may have on the attribution of wrongful conduct to NATO.

45 Article 52, Charter of the United Nations, 1945, 1 UNTS XVI, 24 October 1945, 6 June 1945. France made this suggestion during the negotiations on the establishment of NATO,

the UN Security Council may utilise such arrangements or agencies for enforcement action under its authority. This suggestion was, however, opposed[46] as it could be interpreted as making NATO's enforcement measures subject to a veto in the UN Security Council, rendering NATO's existence absurd.[47] Any reference to Chapter VIII of the UN Charter was therefore intentionally omitted, leaving only Article 51 of the UN Charter as a basis for military action(s) of NATO under Article 5 of the Washington Treaty. NATO was not considered to become an organization that would be used to implement measures taken by the UN Security Council in accordance with Chapter VII of the UN Charter.

The perception that NATO could not be a vehicle for the UN Security Council to implement its mandates, changed after the fall of the Soviet Union, when an institutionalised relationship between NATO and the UN started to emerge. The United Nations was involved in peacekeeping operations since 1956[48] and saw an enormous increase in missions from 1989.[49] These operations were entirely conducted under UN command and control, without participation of any other international organization. Member States would be requested to provide troops and materiel to a UN-led mission. The personnel were placed at the disposal of the UN, which were characteristically identified as "blue-helmets".

With the increased demand for missions, the UN turned to lead nations and international organizations to take over some of the burden to plan and lead peacekeeping and peace-enforcements missions. NATO became an important partner for the UN as the UN lacked the resources to implement its peace enforcement measures. NATO, on its turn, found the participation in the UN missions important as it was trying to redefine its tasks and activities and to transform its structure to meet the security challenges which occurred in the post-Cold War period.

An important aspect defining the UN-NATO relationship in the context of peace operations is the detailed guidance given by the UN Security Council

Leurdijk, D.A., *The UN and NATO: The logic of primacy,* in M. Charles (ed.), *The United Nations and Regional Security: Europe and Beyond,* 2003, p. 57.

46 Leurdijk, D.A., *The UN and NATO: The logic of primacy,* in Charles, M. (ed.), *The United Nations and Regional Security: Europe and Beyond,* 2003, p. 57.

47 Oertel, J. (no date) *The United Nations and NATO, paper prepared for the ACUNS 21st Annual Meeting,* Bonn, Germany, 5–7 June, p. 2.

48 While the first UN mission was the United Nations Truce Supervision Organizations (UNTSO), 29 May 1948, the first 'peacekeeping' mission was the United Nations Emergency Force, established on 7 November 1956.

49 Between 1948 and 1988, the UN mandated 15 peacekeeping operations. Between 1989 and 2002 it increased to 39, Mays, A.T., *Historical Dictionary of Multinational Peacekeeping, 2004,* p. xlvii.

regarding the mandate and the objectives to be achieved of a specific peace operation. The UN Security Council can authorise member States or international organizations[50] to implement a specific mandate. In earlier UN Security Council resolutions, this mandate contained detailed guidance on how the objectives of the operation were to be achieved. For instance, UNSCR 1244(1999) listed eight specific areas for which the NATO-led Kosovo Force was made responsible.[51] More recent UN Security Council resolutions leave a fair amount

50 IFOR, UNSCR 1031(1995), 15 December 1995, para. 14, *"Authorizes the Member States acting through or in cooperation with the organization referred to in Annex 1-A of the Peace Agreement to establish a multinational implementation force (IFOR) under unified command and control in order to fulfil the role specified in Annex 1-A and Annex 2 of the Peace Agreement";*

SFOR, UNSCR 1088(1995), 12 December 1996, para. 18, *"Authorizes the Member States acting through or in cooperation with the organization referred to in Annex 1-A of the Peace Agreement to establish for a planned period of 18 months a multinational stabilization force (SFOR) as the legal successor to IFOR under unified command and control in order to fulfil the role specified in Annex 1-A and Annex 2 of the Peace Agreement;"*

KFOR, UNSCR 1244(1999), 10 June 1999, para. 7, *"Authorizes Member States and relevant international organizations to establish the international security presence in Kosovo* [...]" para 7.

ISAF, UNSCR 1386(2001), 20 December 2001, para. 3, *"Authorizes Member States participating in the International Security Assistance Force to take all necessary measures to fulfil its mandate".*

51 KFOR, UNSCR 1244(1999), 10 June 1999, para. 9, "*Decides that the responsibilities of the international security presence to be deployed and acting in Kosovo will include:*

a) Deterring renewed hostilities, maintaining and where necessary enforcing a ceasefire, and ensuring the withdrawal and preventing the return into Kosovo of Federal and Republic military, police and paramilitary forces, except as provided in point 6 of annex 2;
b) Demilitarizing the Kosovo Liberation Army (KLA) and other armed Kosovo Albanian groups as required in paragraph 15 below;
c) Establishing a secure environment in which refugees and displaced persons can return home in safety, the international civil presence can operate, a transitional administration can be established, and humanitarian aid can be delivered;
d) Ensuring public safety and order until the international civil presence can take responsibility for this task;
e) Supervising demining until the international civil presence can, as appropriate, take over responsibility for this task;
f) Supporting, as appropriate, and coordinating closely with the work of the international civil presence;
g) Conducting border monitoring duties as required;
h) Ensuring the protection and freedom of movement of itself, the international civil presence, and other international organizations;".

of discretionary power to the mandated entity to decide on how it will attain the objectives, basically authorizing to "take all necessary measures" to fulfil the mandate.[52] The Security Council does not impose a specific command relationship or hierarchy between the UN and the mandated entity. However, in certain situations it requires States or international organization to coordinate with the UN Secretary General on the measures taken to implement the mandate or to report on the progress of the operation periodically.[53]

NATO and the UN cooperated quite successfully during operations in the Balkans. Initially, NATO enforced UN Security Council's embargo on weapons in the Adriatic Sea[54] and a no-fly zone over Bosnia-Herzegovina.[55] The cooperation intensified when the Alliance provided air support to the United Nations Protection Force, or UNPROFOR.[56] Close air support provided by NATO was made conditional on the approval by the UN, which strained the relationship between the two organizations. Politically divergent views between the UN and NATO on the air support to UNPROFOR resulted in a time lag in the taking of decisions or resulted in no decisions at all. The observed difficulties led to future operations being more independent from each other. For instance, KFOR was placed outside UNMiK's command and had a separate mandate.[57]

52 ISAF, UNSCR 1386(2001), 20 December 2001, para. 3, *"Authorizes Member States participating in the International Security Assistance Force to take all necessary measures to fulfil its mandate"*.

53 Operation Unified Protector, UNSCR 1973(2011), 17 March 2011, para. 4, *"requests the Member States concerned to inform the Secretary General immediately of the measures they take pursuant to the authorization conferred by this paragraph which shall be immediately report to the Security Council"*, para 11, *"Decides that the Member States concerned shall inform the Secretary General and the Secretary General of the League of Arab States immediately of measures taken in exercise of the authority conferred by paragraph 8 and above, including to supply a concept of operations"*.

ISAF, UNSCR 1386(2001), 20 December 2001, para. 9. *"Requests the leadership of the International Security Assistance Force to provide periodic reports on progress towards the implementation of its mandate through the Secretary General"*.

54 Operation Maritime Monitor, 16 July 1992–22 November 1992, followed by Operation Maritime Guard, 22 November 1992–15 June 1993 and Operation Sharp Guard, 15 June 1993–19 June 1996 (terminated 2 October 1996) under UN Security Council resolution 713(1991) 25 September 1991 and 757(1992) 30 May 1992.

55 Operation Sky Monitor, 15 October 1992–12 April 1993, followed by Operation Deny Flight, 12 April 1993–21 December 1995 under UN Security Council resolution 781(1992), 9 October 1992.

56 United Nations Protection Force, UN Security Council resolution 743(1992), 21 February 1992. Operation Deny Flight included close air support to UNPROFOR.

57 United Nations Security Council resolution 1244(1999), 10 June 1999.

Subsequent operations also showed that NATO operations and UN operations in the same area have distinct mandates, tasks and command structure. In Iraq, the NATO Training Mission-Iraq (NTM-I) is separated from the UN Assistance Mission for Iraq (UNAMI) and in Afghanistan, the United Nations Assistance Mission in Afghanistan – a peacekeeping mission focusing on recovery and reconstruction[58] – was separate from ISAF's more stand-alone character with its own mandate and its own command structure.[59]

In 2005, the Alliance proposed a framework agreement with the UN to create a more structured relationship between the two organizations.[60] In September 2008, this proposal resulted in a Joint Declaration between the UN and NATO on their mutual cooperation, in particular in the field of information sharing and operational coordination and support.[61] Paragraph 4 of the Declaration stipulates that:

> Understanding that this framework should be flexible and evolving over time, we agree to further develop the cooperation between our organizations on issues of common interest, in, but not limited to, communication and information-sharing, including on issues pertaining to the protection of civilian populations; capacity-building, training and exercises; lessons learned, planning and support for contingencies; and operational coordination and support.

In conclusion, The UN Security Council is the only institution to authorise the use of force to maintain or restore international peace and security. A UN Security Council resolution is the legal basis for NATO to conduct non-article 5 crisis response operations, that involve the use of force. UN Security Council resolutions will continue to govern NATO's non-article 5 operations, but the Alliance remains independent from the United Nations in aspects of command and control in NATO operations. The Security Council will not have any authority regarding the command and control of forces in NATO-led operations. The UN can not assign missions or tasks to NATO personnel, to deploy units or to reassign the forces. This authority will be vested in the commander that has

58 UNAMI, United Nations Security Council resolution 1500(2003), 14 August 2003, NTM-I, United Nations Security Council resolution 1546(2004), 8 June 2004.

59 ISAF, United Nations Security Council resolution 1386(2001), 20 December 2001, UNAMA, United Nations Security Council resolution 1401(2002), 28 March 2002.

60 http://www.nato.int/docu/update/2005/09-september/e0919b.htm.

61 Joint Declaration by the UN Secretary General and NATO's Secretary General, 23 September 2008.

Operational Command, which is SACEUR. This aspect is relevant to the question of responsibility of NATO for violations of international law and will be further examined in Chapter 7.

4.5 Conclusions

This chapter has described the institutional framework of NATO. Member States are represented in the North Atlantic Council (NAC), which is the highest political organ of the Alliance. Decisions on NATO operations are taken by the Council through consensus. The Secretary General of the Alliance is responsible for steering this process of consultation and has several tools at its disposal to achieve consensus, in particular the so-called 'silence procedure'. Consensus and the silence procedure show that NATO enjoys a degree of autonomy from its member States, as the Alliance can function even without full agreement of all of the members.

The NAC, its supporting International Staff and the civilian agencies constitute the civilian structure of the Alliance. The military structure consists of the Military Committee, supported by the International Military Staff, the two Supreme Commands and international military headquarters subordinate to them. Supreme Allied Commander Europe commands NATO operations. SACEUR has "operational command and control" over the military forces assigned to him by the Troop Contributing Nations, which could either be member States or States that are not member to NATO (Non-NATO Contributing Nations, or NNCN). Two aspects are relevant to note here. First, States that participate in NATO-led operations transfer a significant degree of control over military forces to NATO. Chapter 7 will examine in more detail whether the degree of control transferred to NATO by States equates to 'effective control'. If NATO does have effective control over conduct of forces placed at its disposal, the conduct can be attributed to NATO. Secondly, it is relevant to note that the participation of NNCN in NATO-led operations show that NATO is a separate entity from its member States. NNCN do not take part in the decision-making process at the political level and neither have operational command and control over their forces once they are placed under the authority of SACEUR. This illustrates that NATO can act separately from its member States and enjoys a high degree of autonomy. This feature – further examined in Chapter 5 – speaks in favour of the existence of international legal personality of NATO.

Finally, the relationship between NATO and the UN has been examined. The UN Security Council has the primary responsibility for the maintenance of international peace and security. Only the UN Security Council can authorise the use of force to maintain or restore international peace and security. As such, NATO non-article 5 crisis response operations that involve the use of force require authorization from the UN Security Council.

The UN has no control over the conduct of military personnel placed at the disposal of the Alliance. TCNs do not transfer any authority over their forces to the UN. Other than authorizing the NATO non-article 5 crisis response operations, the UN is not involved in the operation. The role of the UN in NATO operations is further examined in Chapter 7, but on the foregoing, a preliminary conclusion can be made that the UN does not exercise 'effective control' over military personnel in NATO operations.

CHAPTER 5

The International Legal Personality of NATO

5.1 Introduction

International legal personality is a concept of international law used to distinguish between entities that are relevant to the international legal system and those which are excluded from it.[1] Entities that have international legal personality are subjects of international law and have rights and obligations under international law. Only subjects of international law can be held responsible for violations of breaches of international obligations. Without international legal personality an international organization cannot be held responsible under international law.[2] For this reason, it is essential to determine whether NATO has international legal personality.

The existence of NATO's international legal personality has been debated in legal literature. Some authors deny NATO of having such status in international law.[3] Gazzini, for example, states that "[f]*or the time being, NATO remains an institutional union acting through common organs.*"[4] Others allocate a more relative international legal personality to NATO.[5] Schermers and Blokker argue that closed organizations, such as NATO, have legal personality only with those

1 Portmann, R. (2013) *Legal personality in international law*, United Kingdom: Cambridge University Press, p. 1.

2 The ILC's Articles on the Responsibility of International Organizations explicitly limits responsibility under international law to those international organizations *"possessing their own international legal personality"*., ILC, Article 2, *Draft Articles on the Responsibility of International Organizations*, 2011. ILC, *First report on responsibility of international organizations*, A/CN.4/532, 26 March 2003, para. 15 *"When considering a definition of international organizations that is functional to the purposes of the draft articles on responsibility of international organizations, one has to start from the premise that responsibility under international law arise only for a subject of international law".*

3 Seidl-Hohenveldern, I., *Liability of Member States for Acts or Omissions of an International Organization*, in S. Schlemmer-Schulte & K-Y Tung (eds.), Liber Amicorum Ibrahim F.I. Shihata: International Finance and Development Law, 2001, p. 91.

4 Gazzini, T. (2001) '*NATO coercive military activities in the Yugoslav crisis (1992–1999)*', European Journal of International Law, 12(3), pp. 391–436. doi: 10.1093/ejil/12.3.391, p. 425.

5 Larsen states that NATO's legal personality vis-à-vis non-member States and individuals is unresolved, Larsen, K.M., *The Human Rights Treaty Obligations of Peacekeepers*, 2012, p. 99.

 | DOI 10.1163/9789004354647_006

who have recognised them explicitly.[6] Most authors, including Zwanenburg,[7] Pellet,[8] Reichard[9] and Cohen-Jonathan,[10] consider that NATO does have international legal personality. Their arguments, as well as those arguments against the existence of NATO's international legal personality will be examined in this chapter.

The starting point for determining the *indicia* or characteristics of international organization that possess international legal personality is the Advisory Opinion of the International Court of Justice in "*Reparation for injuries suffered in the service of the United Nations*". Paragraph 5.2 examines the ICJ's Opinion and related literature to establish the indicia of international legal personality and how they are applied to international organizations.

Paragraph 5.3 will determine whether the indicia are present at NATO in order to reach a conclusion whether NATO has international legal personality. The observations made in Chapter 3 on the key moments in the development of NATO are relevant here, as they explain that NATO has developed from an institutional union[11] to an international organization separate from its member States. Also, reference is made to Chapter 4 which has examined the tasks and powers of the various organs of NATO and illustrate the autonomy of NATO in relation to the member States.

Paragraphs 5.4 and 5.5 examine whether jurisprudence and State practice confirm the existence of international legal personality of NATO. A direct affirmation of the international legal personality in international jurisprudence, as the ICJ did with respect to the international personality of the United Nations in its Advisory Opinion in the *Reparations* case, would resolve the question whether NATO has such status in international law. Unfortunately, such explicit confirmation is not (yet) available, but there are some decisions that indirectly touch upon the subject, in particular before the International

---

6 Schermers, H.G. and Blokker, N.M. (2011) *International institutional law: Unity within diversity, The* Netherlands: Brill, 990–991.

7 Zwanenburg, M.C. (2005) *Accountability of peace support operations*, The Netherlands: Martinus Nijhoff Publishers, p. 66.

8 Pellet, A., *L'imputabilité d'éventuels actes illicites – Responsabilité de l'OTAN ou des Etats membres*, inTomuschat, C. (ed.) (2001) *Kosovo and the international community: A legal assessment*, The Netherlands: Martinus Nijhoff, p. 198.

9 Reichard, M. (2004) *'Some Legal Issues Concerning the EU-NATO Berlin Plus Arrangement'*, Nordic Journal of International Law, (73), p. 52.

10 Cohen-Jonathan, G. (2000) *'Cour européenne des droits de l'homme et droit international général',* Annuaire français de Droit International, (46), p. 631.

11 Gazzini, T. (2001) 'NATO coercive military activities in the Yugoslav crisis (1992–1999)', European Journal of International Law, 12(3), pp. 391–436. doi: 10.1093/ejil/12.3.391, p. 425.

Criminal Tribunal for the Former Yugoslavia (ICTY). Paragraph 5.5 analyses the practice of States and international organizations with respect to the international legal personality of the Alliance. The practice of States and international organizations is relevant to examine, as the extent and the consequences of international legal personality depend on the acceptance by other international actors to engage with NATO.[12]

Lastly, paragraph 5.6 will end the chapter with a conclusion on the existence of NATO's international legal personality.

5.2 Indicia of the Existence of International Legal Personality

Whether an international organization could be a subject of international law was examined for the first time in 1949 when the ICJ gave an advisory opinion on the question whether the UN could bring an international claim against a non-member State to obtain reparation for damages caused to the UN or to the victim.[13] Prior to that opinion, scholars had been sceptical to the idea that international organizations could be bearers of international rights and duties.[14]

Explicit reference to the international legal personality of the UN was carefully avoided in the UN Charter as it was considered a politically sensitive topic. Instead, the Commission dealing with this topic at the time considered that it would be *"superfluous to make this the subject of a text. In effect, it will be determined implicitly from the provisions of the Charter taken as a whole."*[15]

In its Advisory Opinion, the ICJ examined the powers of the UN that indicate the existence of international legal personality. The Court noted that the founders had equipped the Organization with organs with special and broad ranging tasks, such as the maintenance of international peace and security. The Court went on to point out that the Charter defined the relationship between the Organization and its members; *"by requiring them to give it every assistance in any action undertaken by it, and to accept and carry out the decisions of the*

12 Larsen, K.M. (2014) *The human rights treaty obligations of Peacekeepers*, United Kingdom: Cambridge University Press, pp. 98–99.

13 International Court of Justice, *Reparations for Injuries suffered in the Service of the United Nations*, (1949), ICJ Reports 1949, 174.

14 Klabbers, J. (2009) *An introduction to international institutional law*, United Kingdom: Cambridge University Press, p. 42. Malanczuk, P. (2011) *Akehurst's modern introduction to international law*, 7th edn. London: Taylor & Francis, p. 92.

15 Documents of the United Nations Conference on International Organization, San Francisco (1945), Vol. XIII (Commission IV, Judicial Organization), p. 710.

Security Council; by authorizing the General Assembly to make recommendations to the Members; by giving the Organization legal capacity and privileges and immunities in the territories of each of its Members; and by providing for the conclusion of agreements between the Organization and its Members."[16] Based on these considerations, the ICJ determined that the UN had international legal personality.

The ICJ remained vague on exactly how the UN had acquired those powers. The Opinion contained a circular argument by stating that the UN had the power to bring a claim against its own members, if it had international legal personality, while the presence of international legal personality was proven by the fact that it had these powers since they could *"only be explained on the basis of the possession of a large measure of international legal personality".*

This ambiguity gave rise to two main theories on how international legal personality originates: the subjective and the objective theory.[17] The subjective theory revolves around the – implicit or explicit[18] – intention or "will" of its founders to endow the organization with such capacity. The will of the founders can be expressed in the constituent document of the international organization, by explicitly stating that the organization has international legal personality. More often, however, founding member States do not include such explicit reference. The existence of international legal personality may then be inferred – according to the subjective theory – from the powers that the founding members have endowed the organization that indicate international legal personality. In either case, whether explicit or implicit, international legal personality is the product of the intention of the founders.

However, the theory has some limited practical use, in particular when non-members do not recognise the organization having such a status in international law. If non-members refuse to enter into obligations with the international organization, there is little support to maintain that the organization has legal personality, even if this was the "will" of the founders. Another problem with the subjective theory is that it presumes that the organization will function as intended by its founders. In certain cases,

---

16 International Court of Justice, *Reparations for Injuries suffered in the Service of the United Nations,* (1949), *ICJ Reports 1949*, 174, p. 8 and 9.

17 Gazzini, T., *Personality of international organizations*, in Klabbers, J. and Wallendahl, A. (eds.) (2012) *Research handbook on the law of international organizations*, United Kingdom: Edward Elgar Publishing, pp. 33–56.

18 The trend to avoid mentioning international legal personality in the constituent documents seems to reverse. The Rome Statute of the International Criminal Court contains in article 4 explicit reference to the personality of the Court. The same applies to the Shanghai Cooperation Organisation and the International Seabed Authority.

the constituent document refers to international legal personality, such as Article 4(1) of the Statute of the International Criminal Court,[19] but the organization has not acted (yet) upon the international level, which leaves the question open whether the organization is a subject of international law.

The objective theory puts the emphasis on the second part of the ICJ's argumentation, where it suggests that the UN has acquired international legal personality, simply because it possessed certain attributes. The powers of the organization are not derived from the constitution, but from common law, which is developed in practice as customary international law.[20] The existence of international legal personality is – according to the objective theory – not dependent on the intentions that the founders might have had with the organization. Rather, legal personality exists whenever the organization has met certain factual characteristics.[21] The most important characteristic, according to Seyersted, is that the organization must possess a distinct will of its own.[22] The drawback of this theory is that it remains inconclusive on how the organization can have a distinct will – or *volonté distincte* – if the organization is not empowered to take decision binding its membership by a mere majority. Unanimous decision making, after all, can always be traced back to its member States.[23]

19 Article 4(1) *Rome Statute of the International Criminal Court*, 2002, 2187 UNTS 90, 1 July 2002, *"The Court shall have international legal personality. It shall also have such legal capacity as may be necessary for the exercise of its functions and the fulfilment of its purposes."*

20 Seyersted, F. (1964a) *'International Personality of Intergovernmental Organizations. Do Their Capacities Really Depend upon Their Constitutions'*, Indian Journal of International Law, 4(4), p. 53.

21 Seyersted, F. (2008) *Common law of international organizations*, The Netherlands: Martinus Nijhoff, p. 43.

22 The concept of *volonté distincte* is largely encapsulated by the concept of international legal personality but the two terms are conflated to a significant degree. While the existence of a separate will is embodied in the concept of international legal personality, the *extent* of that will is to be found in the nature of the elements which presume international legal personality, *"for instance in the presence of majority voting in the organs; width and purposes; the intrusiveness of powers; the nature of decision-making; and the depth of membership."* White, N.D. (2005) *The law of international Organisations*, United Kingdom: Manchester University Press, p. 30.

23 Klabbers, J. (2009) *An introduction to international institutional law*, United Kingdom: Cambridge University Press p. 48.

The practical differences between two theories on international personality may be of minor importance.[24] Both the intention of the founding members (*"the Organization was intended to exercise and enjoy* [...]*"*) and the practice of the organization ("[it] *is in fact exercising and enjoying, functions and rights"*) are relevant and cannot be seen completely separate from each other.[25] A pragmatic approach is quoted by Klabbers as the "presumptive personality".[26] If an organization performs acts that can only be explained on the basis of international legal personality, it must be presumed to have such personality. The theory is supported by the passage in the ICJ *Reparation* case stating: *"that fifty States, representing the vast majority of the members of the international community, had the power, in conformity with international law, to bring into being an entity possessing international legal personality, and not merely personality recognized by them alone, together with the capacity to bring claims"*,[27] leaving unspecified whether the members actually wanted to create an entity with international legal personality.[28] The founders may have endowed the organization with certain powers to perform acts, which would explain the existence of international legal personality, it is not the only decisive factor.

There are several indicia of international legal personality. The list of indicia is not exhaustive, which means that there may be other indicia that could lead to the presumption that an organization has international legal personality. Neither does an international organization need to mark all of the indicia to be presumed as having legal personality.

The indicia are generally recognised by academic literature as including: (1) the power to bring and (2) receive international claims,[29] (3) the power to conclude international agreements[30] and (4) the enjoyment of immunities

24 Zwanenburg, M.C. (2005) *Accountability of peace support operations*, The Netherlands: Martinus Nijhoff Publishers, p. 66. Muller, A.S. (1995) *International organizations and their host states: Aspects of their legal relationship*, The Netherlands: Brill, p. 75.

25 Schermers, H.G. and Blokker, N.M. (2003) *International institutional law: Unity within diversity*, The Netherlands: Brill, p. 1568.

26 Klabbers, J. (2002) *An introduction to international institutional law*, United Kingdom: Cambridge University Press, p. 55.

27 International Court of Justice, *Reparations for Injuries suffered in the Service of the United Nations*, (1949), ICJ Reports 1949, 174, p. 185.

28 Klabbers, J. (2002) *An introduction to international institutional law*, United Kingdom: Cambridge University Press, p. 56.

29 Klabbers, J. (2002) *An introduction to international institutional law*, United Kingdom: Cambridge University Press, pp. 38–40.

30 Klabbers, J. (2002) *An introduction to international institutional law*, United Kingdom: Cambridge University Press, pp. 40–41.

and privileges.[31] Other indicia that are mentioned in legal literature are status under municipal law; express or implied recognition; jurisdiction over organs; accreditation of missions or representatives.[32]

It is important to emphasise here that it is not necessary that an international organization meets all indicia in order to ascertain that it has international legal personality. The indicia are derived from the functions and powers that States have, who are the *primus inter pares* of subjects of international law. If international organizations are empowered to conclude treaties, bring and receive claims, enjoy immunities, exchange diplomats and mobilise forces, as States do, then how would they not be considered as having international legal personality.[33] This does not mean that international organizations and States are the same. The ICJ noted that the UN is not the same as a State, nor that its personality and rights and duties are the same as those of a State.[34] International organizations may possess only certain powers that States may have and still be considered subjects of international law.

Some authors include in this list of indicia that the organization needs to be a permanent association of states, or other organizations, with lawful objects, equipped with organs. This seems to refer to elements of the definition of an international organization, rather than an indicator of international legal personality.[35] NATO is a permanent association of States with the lawful aim to safeguard the freedom, common heritage and civilisation of their peoples.[36] It can therefore be concluded that NATO fulfils this criterion, but it is doubtful whether these are indicators of legal personality as almost every international organization is an association of States or other organizations with lawful objects and equipped with organs.

The next paragraph will examine whether NATO has the indicia of international legal personality as mentioned earlier. By applying the theory of

31 Klabbers, J. (2002) *An introduction to international institutional law*, United Kingdom: Cambridge University Press, pp. 41–43.

32 Meijknecht, A.K. and Meijknecht, A. (2001) *Towards international personality Vol. 10: The positions of minorities and Indigenious peoples in international law*, Antwerp: Intersentia Uitgevers N V, p. 35.

33 H.G. Schermers, N.M. Blokker, *International Institutional Law*, 195, para. 1566.

34 International Court of Justice, *Reparations for Injuries suffered in the Service of the United Nations*, (1949), ICJ Reports 1949, 174, pp. 179–180.

35 Crawford, J., *Brownlie's Principles of Public International Law*, 2008, p. 169, Amerasinghe, C.F., *Principles of the Institutional Law of International Organizations*, 2005, p. 82.

36 North Atlantic Treaty, preamble, 4 April 1949 and Strategic Concept for the Defence and Security of the Members of the North Atlantic Treaty Organization, 19–20 November 2010.

presumptive personality, it can be held that NATO possesses international legal personality.

5.3 The International Legal Personality of NATO

The international legal personality of NATO has been a frequent topic in legal literature. Various authors have examined whether NATO has international legal personality, but only to a marginal extent and often coming to complete opposite conclusions. The divergence in opinions may be explained by the period of which that scholars have looked at the Alliance. In its earlier years, NATO may not have exercised its powers and shown the characteristics of international legal personality. After the transformation described in Chapters 3 and 4 in the period after the Cold War, NATO developed itself into a considerable more independent and autonomous organization.

There is no explicit answer given by the founders of the Alliance, whether the organization should have international legal personality. NATO's constituent document does not give a clear indication whether the founding members had the intention to give the organization status under international law. The Washington Treaty does not contain any explicit reference to international legal personality of the Alliance. The "Agreement on the status of the North Atlantic Treaty Organization, National Representatives and International Staff" (Ottawa Agreement) includes a provision that the Alliance possesses juridical personality and has the capacity to conclude contracts, acquire and dispose of movable and immovable property and to institute legal proceedings.[37] This, however, refers to the legal personality of NATO within the domestic systems of its member States and not to a personality on the international level. Similarly, the "Protocol on the Status of International Military Headquarters Set Up Pursuant to the North Atlantic Treaty" (Paris Protocol) ensures that the two Supreme Headquarters of NATO have legal personality within the legal domestic framework of its member States, but it does not refer to an international legal personality.[38]

The founding fathers have endowed the Alliance with certain powers that would explain the existence of international legal personality. The Paris Protocol and Ottawa Agreement give the Alliance the power to conclude international

37 Article IV, Agreement on the Status of the North Atlantic Treaty Organization, National Representatives and International Staff, 1951, 200 UNTS 3, 20 September 1951.

38 Article X, Protocol on the Status of International Military Headquarters Set Up Pursuant to the North Atlantic Treaty, 28 August 1952.

agreements.[39] NATO has entered into various international agreements with its member States hosting its headquarters on their territory.[40] The Alliance has also concluded international agreements with non-Member States. In broad terms, NATO entered into international agreements for cooperation

39 Art. XVI Protocol on the Status of International Military Headquarters Set Up Pursuant to the North Atlantic Treaty, 28 August 1952, Art. XXV, Agreement on the Status of the North Atlantic Treaty Organization, National Representatives and International Staff, 1951, 200 UNTS 3, 20 September 1951.

40 E.g. The agreement concerning the application of Part IV of the Agreement on the Status of the North Atlantic Treaty Organisation, National Representatives and International Staff, signed at Ottawa on 20 September 1951, to the officials of NATO civilian bodies located on the territory of the United States of America, 3 March 1981. United States of America and Headquarters of the Supreme Allied Commander Atlantic under the North Atlantic Treaty, *Agreement (with exchange of letters) regarding the Headquarters of the Supreme Allied Commander Atlantic*, 22 October 1954. Treaty between the Kingdom of Spain and the North Atlantic Treaty Organization represented by the Supreme Headquarters Allied Powers Europe on the special conditions applicable to the establishment and operation on Spanish territory of international military headquarters, 28 February 2000. Notawisseling houdende een verdrag tussen het Koninkrijk der Nederlanden en de Noord Atlantische Verdragsorganisatie (NAVO) betreffende de privileges en immuniteiten van het personeel van de NATO Consultation, Command and Control Agency (nc3A) en hun gezinsleden, 29 September 2009. United States of America and the North Atlantic Treaty Organization, *Agreement concerning the application of Part IV of the Agreement on the Status of the North Atlantic Treaty Organization, national representatives and international staff, signed in Ottawa on 20 September 1951, to the officials of NATO civilian bodies located on the territory of the United States of America*, 3 March 1981. Exchange of letters on the status of the deployable CIS module in Haderslev in the future NATO Command Structure, 10 February 2012. Also; Exchange of letters on the status of the deployable CIS module in Izmir in the future NATO Command Structure, 2 February 2012; Exchange of letters on the status of the Combined Air Operations Centre in Torrejon in the future NATO Command Structure, 30 January 2012; Exchange of letters on the status of the NATO Signal Battalion in Bydgoszcz in the future NATO Command Structure, 6 February 2012; Exchange of letters on the status of the NATO Signal Battalion, the Deployable Communication and Information System Modules and their Support Units in Wesel and Elmpt and the Combined Air Operations Centre in Uedem in the future NATO Command Structure, 26 September 2012; Exchange of letters on the status of the NATO Signal Battalion and four of its Deployable CIS modules in Grazzanise and the Deployable Air Command and Control Centre in Poggio Renatico in the future NATO Command Structure, 16 February 2012; Exchange of letters on the status of Allied Joint Force Command Headquarters moving to Lago Patria and the future Joint Force Headquarters Naples in Lago Patria in the future NATO Command Structure, 26 March 2012, Exchange of letters on the status of the International Submarine Escape and Rescue Liaison Office (Ismerlo) in the future NATO Command Structure, February 2012.

in the defence field[41] and mission-related Status of Forces Agreements.[42] For instance, NATO has extended the existent Status of Forces Agreement with the government of Afghanistan through an exchange of letters between the NATO Secretary General and the Afghan Minister of Foreign Affairs, to the NATO-led ISAF operation.[43] For its subsequent mission in Afghanistan (Resolute Support), NATO concluded a bilateral Status of Forces Agreement with the Afghan

---

41 An example of the former category is the NATO-Russia agreement of 1997, which sets out a framework for cooperation between the two parties Founding Act on Mutual Relations, Cooperation and Security between NATO and the Russian Federation, Paris, 27 May 1997. The agreement led to the establishment of a new organ, the NATO-Russia Council. Other various agreements between NATO and third parties have been concluded to enhance cooperation in one way or another. There is the NATO-Ukraine agreement (Charter on a Distinctive Partnership between the North Atlantic Treaty Organization and Ukraine, 9 July 1997). The Charter is supplemented by the "Declaration to Complement the Charter on a Distinctive Partnership between NATO and Ukraine", 21 August 2009. The Charter establishes a new decision body called the "NATO-Ukraine Commission", responsible for developing the NATO-Ukraine relationship and for directing cooperative activities and providing a forum for consultation between the Allies and Ukraine on security issues of common concern the coordination and consultation of activities. Another example of an agreement with non-member States are the so-called "Partnership for Peace" agreements. This agreement sets out an individual partnership and cooperation programme agreed between the participating State and NATO. The members take part in the Euro-Atlantic Partnership Council, which is a multilateral forum for dialogue and consultation on political and security-related issues among Allies and Partner countries. The EAPC consists of 28 NATO members and 22 Partner Countries. The framework arrangements have led on their turn to various implementing agreements between NATO and the host nation to regulate specifics on tax privileges, immunities and other aspects relating to the status of NATO personnel. The Mediterranean Dialogue is formally not an agreement but a decision by the NAC to cooperate with non-nato countries in the Mediterranean region. The countries involve Algeria, Egypt, Israel, Jordan, Mauritania, Morocco and Tunisia. The countries and NATO focus on agreed priority areas enumerated in the Mediterranean Dialogue Work Programme. NATO's Istanbul Cooperation Initiative (ICI) was launched at the Summit meeting of 2004. The ICI consists of 4 countries; Bahrain, Kuwait, Qatar and the United Arab Emirates.

42 IFOR: Agreement on the Military Aspects of the Peace Settlement Appendix B to Annex 1 A of the General Framework Agreement, between the Republic of Bosnia and Herzegovina and the North Atlantic Treaty Organization, 30 November 1995.

NTM-I: Exchange of letters between the National Security Advisor of the government of Iraq and NATO's Secretary General, 21/23 December 2008.

Pakistan Earthquake Relief operation: Exchange of Letters between the Government of Pakistan and NATO, 4 November 2006.

43 Exchange of letters between the NATO Secretary General and the Afghan Minister of Foreign Affairs, 5 September 2004 and 22 November 2004.

government on 30 September 2014.[44] NATO has also entered into agreements with other international organizations, such as the EU,[45] UN[46] and, more recently, Interpol.[47]

Solely on the fact that NATO has been given the power to conclude international agreements and that the organization indeed exercised such powers, leads to the plausible conclusion that NATO possesses international legal personality.[48] But NATO meets even more indicia of legal personality, further confirming the existence of such status.

Immunity is another indication of international legal personality. It is traditionally seen as a prerequisite for an international organization to enable them to carry out their tasks in an independent fashion.[49] Often, constitutional documents contain a clause providing for privileges and immunities in the member States.[50] The Ottawa Agreement accords immunity to NATO and certain categories of personnel, including national representatives and officials of the organization.[51] The immunity has also been tested on occasion, most recently

44 Referred to in UNSCR 2189(2014), 12 December 2014, *"Noting the signing of the Security and Defence Cooperation Agreement between the United States of America and the Islamic Republic of Afghanistan (Bilateral Security Agreement) on 30 September 2014, and welcoming the signing of the Status of Forces Agreement between the Islamic Republic of Afghanistan and NATO on 30 September 2014 and as ratified by the Parliament of Afghanistan on 27 November 2014, Noting that the bilateral agreement between NATO and Afghanistan and the invitation of the Government of Afghanistan to NATO to establish Resolute Support Mission provide a sound legal basis for Resolute Support Mission."*

45 The Berlin Plus Agreements are a package of agreements concluded on 16 December 2002. See also www.nato.int/shape/news/2003/shape_eu/se030822a.htm.

46 Joint Declaration by the UN Secretary General and NATO's Secretary General, 23 September 2008.

47 This is an initiative launched by Interpol in 2012 to share counter-piracy information between NATO and Interpol. Interpol has developed a database to analyze Somali piracy networks and streamline intelligence, which information is intended to be shared with the Alliance. Interpol Press release, *"Interpol and NATO cooperation set to boost global efforts against maritime piracy"*, www.interpol.int, 6 October 2012.

48 Voetelink, J., *Status of Forces: Criminal Jurisdiction over Military Personnel Abroad*, 2015, p. 177.

49 Reinisch, A., *Privileges and Immunities*, in Klabbers, J. and Wallendahl, A. (eds.) (2012) *Research handbook on the law of international organizations*, United Kingdom: Edward Elgar Publishing, p. 132.

50 White, N.D. (2005) *The law of international Organisations*, United Kingdom: Manchester University Press, p. 42.

51 Respectively article V, XII and articles XVIII and XXI Agreement on the Status of the North Atlantic Treaty Organization, National Representatives and International Staff signed in Ottawa, 20 September 1951.

when a Belgian court dismissed a claim for compensation for damages submitted by an Egyptian citizen in Libya caused by NATO during Operation Unified Protector, due to the immunity of NATO HQ in Brussels.[52]

NATO's International Military Headquarters and its personnel enjoy a slightly less favourable status. Immunity is limited to the official documents and archives of the International Military Headquarters.[53] Jurisdiction over the personnel of the International Military Headquarters is regulated by Article IV of the Paris Protocol in conjunction with the NATO SOFA.[54] Personnel working in the International Military Headquarters do not enjoy immunity in the host State. Instead, in most cases concurrent jurisdiction of both the host State and sending State exist.

The 1951 Ottawa Agreement and 1952 Paris Protocol are geographically limited to the trans-Atlantic region,[55] but even beyond NATO's geographical area, the Alliance enjoys certain privileges and immunities via the conclusion of bilateral agreements.[56] As a standard practice, NATO missions enjoy immunity in the host States through the conclusion of SOFAs with the receiving State. For instance, the privileges and immunities for the IFOR-, and later SFOR-mission,

52 Tribunal of First Instance of Brussels, *El Hamidi & Chlih v. NATO*, R.G. no. 11/9647/A, 21 October 2012.

53 Article XII, Protocol on the Status of International Military Headquarters set up pursuant to the North Atlantic Treaty, 28 August 1952 (Paris Protocol).

54 Agreement between the Parties to the North Atlantic Treaty regarding the Status of their Forces, 19 June 1951 (NATO SOFA).

55 Agreement on the Status of the North Atlantic Treaty Organization, National Representatives and International Staff, 1951, 200 UNTS 3, 20 September 1951, refers to privileges and immunities to the territory of the member States. The preamble of the Protocol on the Status of International Military Headquarters Set up Pursuant to the North Atlantic Treaty limits the applicability to the *"North Atlantic Treaty area"*. The North Atlantic Treaty Area is delimited by the territory in Europe and North America as well as islands under the jurisdiction of any party in the North Atlantic area north of the Tropic of Cancer (Appendix 3 to the North Atlantic Treaty). This would exclude for instance Greece and Turkey, but were included through a modification done by article 2, subparas. i. and ii. of the 22 October 1951 Accession Protocol.

56 The status of NATO international military headquarters and personnel in the territory of States participating in the Partnership for Peace (PfP) programme is regulated in a protocol to the Ottawa Agreement adopted in 1995 which extends the provisions of the Ottawa Agreement to PfP countries. Further Additional Protocol to the Agreement among the States Parties to the North Atlantic Treaty and the other States participating in the Partnership for Peace regarding the Status of their Forces, 19 December 1995.

are stipulated in the General Framework Agreement for Peace.[57] The KFOR mission has been granted absolute immunity, while its personnel have immunity from Kosovar courts.[58] Similarly, ISAF and its personnel enjoy immunity in Afghanistan through the conclusion of the Military Technical Agreement and subsequent exchange of letters between NATO and Afghanistan.[59] Immunity in the host State, however, does not preclude criminal prosecution in other States. However, there are no known instances where NATO personnel have been prosecuted for criminal acts by third states. In one instance, NATO's Secretary General, SACEUR and other high ranking military leaders were prosecuted and convicted *in absentia* by a district Court in Belgrade, but this has to be regarded as a more political symbolic prosecution than a proper example of criminal jurisdiction exercised by a third State.[60]

The Ottawa Agreement regarding NATO HQ and civilian agencies[61] as well as the Paris Protocol regarding international military headquarters[62] state that the Alliance can bring and receive claims. The provisions, however, refer to the legal standing before domestic courts of the member States, which is not in itself an indication of *international* legal personality of the organization. Until now, NATO has not received from or brought international claims against any State, including NATO member States. In fact, there has been an occasion where the Alliance could have received a claim from China regarding the bombing of her Embassy during Operation Allied Force. Instead, the United States of America chose to take responsibility for the mistake in targeting and

---

57 Art. 2, Appendix B to Annex 1A of the General Framework Agreement for Peace, 21 November 1995.

58 UNMiK Regulation UNMiK/REG/2000/47, 18 August 2000.

59 Military Technical Agreement between the International Security Assistance Force (ISAF) and the Interim Administration of Afghanistan ('Interim Administration'), 4 January 2002; Exchange of letters between the Secretary General of NATO and the Afghan Minister of Foreign Affairs, 22 November 2004. It is important to note that, although reference is made to the UN Convention on the Privileges and Immunities of the United Nations of 13 February 1946, the immunities of ISAF troops is expanded to absolute immunity from jurisdiction of the host State – not only functional – in favour of the jurisdiction of the sending State. Almost all SOFAS – including UN mission SOFAS – expand the immunity of military personnel to such extent that the sending State has exclusive jurisdiction over its forces.

60 Laursen, A., *NATO, the War over Kosovo, and the ICTY Investigation,* American University International Law Review, Vol. 17, Issue 4, 2002, p. 770.

61 Art. IV, Agreement on the Status of the North Atlantic Treaty Organization, National Representatives and International Staff, 1951, 200 UNTS 3, 20 September 1951.

62 Article XI, Protocol on the Status of International Military Headquarters Set Up Pursuant to the North Atlantic Treaty, 28 August 1952.

compensated China for the damage and injury caused. No other examples are known where a claim has been brought against NATO by a State or other international entity, nor are there instances known where NATO has brought a claim against other international subjects.

In summary, NATO has concluded a variety of international agreements, enjoys immunity and privileges in the national jurisdictions of its member States as well as in certain third States with whom it has concluded Status of Forces Agreements. This capacity and performance of acts on the international level can only be explained on the basis of international legal personality. The fact that the Alliance has not brought or received international claims yet, does not negate the existence of international legal personality. There is general consensus in academic literature that it is not required that an international organization fulfils all the indicia of international legal personality in order to conclude that it has such status. It would be almost impossible for an international organization to meet all indicia that pertain to statehood.[63] International legal personality is presumed once it performs acts that can only be explained on the basis of international legal personality, which – in the case of NATO – must be presumed.

This presumption may be rebutted with evidence of e.g. contrary practice. The following two paragraphs will examine whether the existence of international legal personality of NATO is supported by the jurisprudence of (international) tribunals and courts and by the practice of States and other international organizations.

5.4 Jurisprudence of International Courts and Tribunals

There is no jurisprudence of international courts or tribunals that confirms the existence of NATO's international legal personality. There are cases in which claims were brought against individual member States of NATO, but not against NATO itself. This is due to the fact that NATO has no *locus standi* before any international court. It is an understandable choice to submit applications against (a) NATO member State(s), so to avoid the risk that the case would be declared inadmissible. NATO is not a party to international agreements that have judicial remedies included,[64] and since NATO is immune from legal

63 Fastenrath, U., Simma, B., *From Bilateralism to Community Interest: Essays in Honour of Judge Bruno Simma*, 2011, p. 41.

64 Article 59 ECHR states: (*1*) *This Convention shall be open to the signatories of the member of the Council of Europe. It shall be ratified. Ratifications shall be deposited with the*

process the organization is excluded to become a party in a contentious case.[65] This is illustrated in cases before the International Court of Justice and before the European Court of Human Rights (ECtHR) relating to the bombing of the Federal Republic of Yugoslavia in 1999. NATO does not have *locus standi* before the ICJ and – therefore – the Federal Republic of Yugoslavia (subsequently Serbia and Montenegro) *"had to go to great lengths in arguing that the bombing* [during Operation Allied Force against Serbia in 1999] *was the responsibility of every single NATO member State"*[66] Serbia maintained that the NATO-led Operation Allied Force was a violation of several international obligations binding upon the defendant States, in particular the violation of the obligation not to use force against another State and not to intervene in the internal affairs of another State, as contained in Article 2(4) of the United Nations Charter. Yugoslavia filed individual, but identical, complaints against Belgium, Canada, France, Germany, Italy, The Netherlands, Portugal, Spain, the United Kingdom and the United States of America. Equally, before the ECtHR, Banković *et al*, who were victims and relatives of victims of a NATO airstrike on 23 April 1999 on the main State Radio and Television station (Radio Televizije Srbije (RTS)), turned to the individual member States of NATO instead of NATO itself.[67]

The issue of international legal personality of NATO has been touched upon indirectly by the International Criminal Tribunal for the former Yugoslavia (ICTY). Article 29 of the ICTY Statute states that *"States shall co-operate with the International Criminal Tribunal in the investigation and prosecution of persons accused of committing serious violations of international humanitarian law.* [...]". In *Simić et al.*,[68] the Trial Chamber concluded that this obligation also applied to SFOR as an international organization.[69] According to Larsen, the only deduction possible is that the ICTY considers NATO to possess international

Secretary General of the Council of Europe. (2) The European Union may accede to this Convention. [...]".

65 Art. 34, ICJ Statute, *"Only States may be parties in cases before the Court".*

66 Schmalenbach, K., *Dispute Settlement,* in Klabbers, J. and Wallendahl, A. (eds.) (2012) *Research handbook on the law of international organizations*, United Kingdom: Edward Elgar Publishing, p. 257.

67 European Court of Human Rights, *Vlastimir and Borka Bankovic and others v. Belgium, the Czech Republic, Denmark, France, Germany, Greece, Hungary, Iceland, Italy, Luxembourg, the Netherlands, Norway, Poland, Portugal, Spain, Turkey and the United Kingdom,* Application no. 52207/99, 12 December 2001.

68 ICTY, Trial Chamber, Decision (Defence motion for judicial assistance to be provided by SFOR and others), it-95-9, *Simić and others,* 18 October 2000, para. 48.

69 Larsen, K.M., *The Human Rights Treaty Obligations for Peacekeepers,* 2014, p. 96.

legal personality separate from that of its member States, otherwise the order would have been addressed to the individual member States.[70]

5.5 State Practice and Practice of International Organizations

There is considerable practice of States and international organizations that relate to the existence of international legal personality of NATO. States and international organizations have argued that the Alliance possesses international legal personality. This paragraph provides an overview of their views and considerations.

The Alliance' members have – at a time convenient for them – either acknowledged or denied that the Alliance has legal personality.[71] The prevalent opinion of the members is that NATO possesses international legal personality. In the *Use of Force* cases before the ICJ, the defendant States maintained that NATO is an international organization with international legal personality and that the actions regarding the use of force against the former Yugoslavia are attributable to NATO, instead of the individual nations. The Netherlands submitted that Operational Allied Force[72] and KFOR[73] are "NATO operations" initiated by the NAC and that its actions are attributable to the Alliance. Portugal and France, similarly, submitted that NATO is an international organization with legal personality and consequently bears responsibility for actions taken during the operation.[74] Portugal stated that NATO is an international organization with international legal personality and, consequently *"assumes full responsibility under international law for its actions in Kosovo, and not its*

70 Larsen, K.M., *The Human Rights Treaty Obligations for Peacekeepers*, 2014, p. 96.

71 Gaja, G., Second report on responsibility of international organizations, 3 May – 4 June and 5 July – 6 August 2004, A/CN.4/541, at 3–4, para. 7.

72 ICJ, Case Concerning Legality of Use of Force (Yugoslavia v. Netherlands), Preliminary objections of the Kingdom of The Netherlands, para. 7.2.5, 5 July 2000.

73 ICJ, Case Concerning Legality of Use of Force (Yugoslavia v. Netherlands), Preliminary objections of the Kingdom of The Netherlands, para. 7.2.7, 5 July 2000.

74 ICJ, Legality of the use of force, Preliminary objections of the Portuguese Republic, p. 38, 5 July 2000. ICJ, *Legality of Use of Force*, Preliminary objections of the French Republic, 5 July 2000, Chapter II, para 40, *"The establishment of the North Atlantic Council* [...] *brought into being a genuine international organization* [...] *having organs, given special tasks and enjoying legal capacity and privileges and immunities. All of these are elements which led the* [ICJ] *in its Advisory Opinion of 11 April 1949 concerning Reparation for Injuries Suffered in the Service of the United Nations to conclude, in the case of the United Nations, that the Organization was an "international person".*

member States."[75] According to Portugal, the Former Republic of Yugoslavia should have directed its claims against NATO. France, similarly, objected to the claims being directed to the member States instead of NATO and argued that the Former Republic of Yugoslavia proposition *"fails to allow for the fact of international legal personality, which precludes a State being held liable for an organization's acts simply because the State is a member"*.[76]

In the *Bankovic* case, NATO member States argued that the European Court of Human Rights could not decide on the merits of the case as it would be determining the rights and obligations of the United States of America and Canada and of NATO itself, thereby implying that NATO has the capacity to carry international obligations and hence has international legal personality.[77] France raised the issue that *"the bombardment was not imputable to the respondent States but to NATO, an organisation with an international legal personality separate of the respondent States"*.[78]

Some authors argue that the compensation paid by the US to China for the damage and injury caused by the bombing of the Chinese Embassy in Serbia during the NATO operation Allied Force show that – at least – the US denies the existence of international legal personality of NATO.[79] This conclusion may not be entirely accurate. In 2011 the former Chinese president Jiang Zemin admitted in an unpublished memoir that Serbian military intelligence units were hiding inside the Chinese embassy in Belgrade when NATO bombed it in 1999. The diplomatic bargain appeared to be that the United States of America saved China's face by apologizing for a "mistake" and the Chinese allowed the street rage to cool off without serious violence. In the view of the US, the actions,

---

75 ICJ. Legality of the use of force, Preliminary objections of the Kingdom of Portugal, para. 136, 5 July 2000.

76 Legality of the use of force, Preliminary objections of the Republic of France, para. 23, 5 July 2000.

77 ECtHR, *Bankovic, Stojadinovic, Stoimenovski, Joksimovic and Sukovic v. Belgium, The Czech Republic, Denmark, France, Germany, Greece, Hungary, Iceland, Italy, Luxembourg, The Netherlands, Norway, Poland, Portugal, Spain, Turkey and The United Kingdom*, Decision of the Grand Chamber to the admissibility of Application no. 52207/99, ECHR 2001-xii, para 31.

78 ECtHR, *Bankovic, Stojadinovic, Stoimenovski, Joksimovic and Sukovic v. Belgium, The Czech Republic, Denmark, France, Germany, Greece, Hungary, Iceland, Italy, Luxembourg, The Netherlands, Norway, Poland, Portugal, Spain, Turkey and The United Kingdom*, Decision of the Grand Chamber to the admissibility of Application no. 52207/99, ECHR 2001-XII, para 32.

79 Gazzini, T. (2001) '*NATO coercive military activities in the Yugoslav crisis (1992–1999)*', European Journal of International Law, 12(3), pp. 391–436. doi: 10.1093/ejil/12.3.391, p. 425.

including the intelligence that identified the target and the use of US aircraft, were attributable to the US, rather than to NATO. Whether the assessment of the US is correct or whether there were other political motives for the US to compensate China is not relevant to examine here further. What is important is that the compensation paid by the US is not by itself an indication that the US denies the existence of international legal personality of the Alliance.

International organizations have also been confronted with the question of international legal personality of NATO. NATO launched Operation Unified Protector in 2011 to implement UN Security Council resolution 1970(2011)[80] and 1973(2011)[81] to implement an arms embargo, a no-fly zone as well as to protect the civilian population from attacks from both rebel- and Libyan military forces. In certain instances, air strikes were carried out in densely populated areas with higher risks of civilian casualties and collateral damage. While the vast majority of NATO airstrikes did not result in civilian casualties or collateral damage to civilian objects, certain human rights organizations and the UN Human Rights Council claimed that airstrikes conducted on targets in Tripoli, Zlitan, Majer, Sirte, Bani Walid, Surman, Gurdabiya resulted in excessive incidental damage and injury.[82] The UN Human Rights Council established an International Commission of Inquiry and NATO exchanged several letters regarding incidents that have occurred during Operation Unified Protector. The fact that the International Commission of Inquiry addressed NATO – instead of the individual troop contributing nations – alludes to the assumption that NATO has a separate legal status from its member States under international law.[83]

NATO itself initially maintained that it has international legal personality. NATO's Secretary General has on various occasions alluded to the existence of an international legal personality of NATO.[84] Furthermore, in the submittal of

80 UN Security Council Resolution 1970(2011), 26 February 2011.

81 UN Security Council Resolutino 1973(2011), 17 March 2011.

82 Amnesty International, *The Forgotten Victims of NATO Strikes,* March 2012, p. 9. Human Rights Watch, *Unacknowledged Deaths, Civilian Casualties in NATO's Air Campaign in Libya,* 2012, p. 32. United Nations Human Rights Council, *Report of the International Commission of Inquiry on Libya,* A/hrc/19/68, 2 March 2012.

83 UN Human Rights Council, *Report of the International Commission of Inquiry on Libya,* A/HRC/19/68, 2 March 2012.

84 NATO Secretary General, *Strategic Airlift Capability* (SAC) – *Initiative Adoption of the NAMO charter,* 20 June 2007, *"It is accordingly agreed that only the member States of NAMO shall jointly and directly assume responsibility vis-à-vis NATO, and shall bear any resulting cost and liability for the implementation of the Airlift Management Programme, notwithstanding the fact that NAMO will be established, by the Council, pursuant to Article 9 of the North Atlantic Treaty and within the meaning of the Ottawa Agreement and will share in*

NATO's observations on the ILC's work on the responsibility of international organizations, the Alliance mentions that NATO does have legal personality.[85] On other occasions, NATO has been ambivalent to accept the existence of international legal personality. A NATO legal adviser to the Secretary General held an ambiguous opinion on whether NATO is a subject of international law, maintaining that "[...] *it is the individual member States who have legal obligations. States' own legal officials must ensure their participating forces' compliance with international law."* This statement renounces the existence of NATO's legal personality.[86] The same legal office, however, on another occasion has confirmed that NATO is a subject of international law and has international legal personality.[87]

5.6 Conclusions

This chapter examined the existence of international legal personality of NATO. Legal personality is relevant to the responsibility of NATO and its personnel during military operations. Without international legal personality, NATO cannot be responsible.

Unfortunately, there is little jurisprudence on the concept of international legal personality. In 1949, the ICJ formed an Opinion on the personality of the UN, but remained vague on how this was determined. This resulted in various theories on how legal personality is acquired. The two mainstream theories in academic literature are the 'subjective theory' and 'objective theory', which both give explanations on how international legal personality can be determined to exist, but also have received criticism. The practical approach

---

the international legal personality of NATO as well as the juridical personality possessed by NATO by virtue of Article IV of the Ottawa Agreement."

85 UN General Assembly, International Law Commission, *Responsibility of International Organizations, Comments and observation received from international organizations,* UN Doc A/cn.4/637, *"The following comments relate to the structure of the organization, its decision-making procedures and its practice with respect to claims. NATO is an international organization within the meaning of draft article 2(a) of the draft articles, and as such a subject of international law. It possesses international legal personality as well as treaty-making power."* Para. 2, p. 11.

86 Amnesty International, NATO/Federal Republic of Yugoslavia "Collateral damage" or unlawful killings? Violations of the Laws of War by NATO during Operation Allied Force, p. 13, 5 June 2000.

87 B. DeVidts, *Speaking notes on "aspects related to the Legal Status of the North Atlantic Treaty Organisation"*, 22 November 2004 (CJ(2004)0910), copy on file with the author.

of Klabbers' 'presumptive personality' reconciles to some degree both theories.[88] This theory presumes the existence of international legal personality of an international organization if it performs acts that can only be explained on the basis of international legal personality. This chapter has examined NATO's legal personality on the basis of the two mainstream theories, but also inclined towards the 'presumptive theory' to give a practical answer.

Some authors doubt whether the Alliance has legal personality.[89] These authors argue that NATO has not acted on the international level. The often-used example in this respect is the compensation by the US (in lieu to NATO) to China for the damages suffered during NATO's intervention in Kosovo. Other arguments denying the international legal personality of NATO is the fact that NATO takes its decision by consensus, leading to believe that the Alliance does not have any "will" of its own. These doubts would be to some degree valid, if the focus was on the earlier years of the NATO. During the Cold War – and probably during its first non-article 5 operation as well – it may have been difficult to consider that the Alliance has international legal personality. NATO's static defence operations against the former Soviet Union did not require an autonomous role separate from its member States. The member States were fully capable to independently devise military plans and coordinate these with each other. The establishment of SACEUR in 1952, which integrated military forces, marked the beginning of a transformation, but NATO started to evolve into an organization with legal personality only after the Cold War.

Since then, the Alliance has gone through a significant transformation, as described in Chapters 3 and 4. The Organization has concluded international agreements with States and other international organizations. NATO and its personnel enjoy privileges and immunities in its member States, but also in Afghanistan, Iraq, in the States of the former Yugoslavia and in various other mission areas. It should not be ruled out that the Alliance might bring and receive international claims in the future if the exercise of the jurisdiction by the courts would be made possible.

It is not required that an international organization show all the *indicia* of international legal personality. If this were the case, barely any international

---

88 Klabbers, J. (2002) *An introduction to international institutional law,* United Kingdom: Cambridge University Press, p. 55.

89 Gazzini, T. (2001) '*NATO coercive military activities in the Yugoslav crisis (1992–1999)*', European Journal of International Law, 12(3), pp. 391–436. doi: 10.1093/ejil/12.3.391, p. 425. To a lesser extent: K.M. Larsen *The Human Rights Treaty Obligations of Peacekeepers,* 2012, p. 99 and Schermers, H.G. and Blokker, N.M. (2011) *International institutional law: Unity within diversity,* The Netherlands: Brill, 990–991.

organization would have such status in international law. NATO is presumed to have international legal personality on the basis of the fact that it has concluded international agreements and that the organization and its personnel enjoy privileges and immunities. This presumption may be rebutted if there is evidence to the contrary.

Practice of States and international organizations, as well as the jurisprudence of international courts and tribunals, confirm the presumption that NATO has international legal personality.

The military intervention in the former Yugoslavia gave rise to several claims for damages resulting from NATO military operations. Yugoslavia filed complaints against several member States of NATO, while individuals turned their claims for damages to individual member States of NATO instead to NATO itself.[90] The respondent States in both cases argued that the claims should have been filed against NATO – on the basis of that it had international legal personality – instead of the individual nations. These early cases are not indicative of either the existence or non-existence of international legal personality, but of the absence of NATO's *locus standi* in the courts. Claimants may have chosen to start their proceedings against individual States, so to avoid their claim being regarded non-admissible.

International courts and tribunals have confirmed NATO's legal personality. Both the ICTY and the ICC came to this conclusion in relation to NATO operations in respectively the Balkans and Libya. International organizations, including the UN, have addressed NATO in relation to alleged breaches of international obligations binding upon the organization. The UN International Commission of Inquiry, notably, addressed NATO – and not individual member States – with respect to airstrikes in Libya that may have caused incidental loss of civilian life and damage to civilian infrastructure.[91] Finally, States have confirmed NATO's legal personality in the ILC's commentary to the Articles on Responsibility of International Organizations, where they stated that *"NATO is an international organization within the meaning of draft article 2(a) of the draft articles, and as such a subject of international law. It possesses international legal personality as well as treaty-making power".*[92]

90 European Court of Human Rights, *Vlastimir and Borka Bankovic and others v. Belgium, the Czech Republic, Denmark, France, Germany, Greece, Hungary, Iceland, Italy, Luxembourg, the Netherlands, Norway, Poland, Portugal, Spain, Turkey and the United Kingdom*, Application no. 52207/99, 12 December 2001.

91 UN Human Rights Council, *Report of the International Commission of Inquiry on Libya*, A/HRC/19/68, 2 March 2012.

92 UN General Assembly, International Law Commission, *Responsibility of International Organizations, Comments and observation received from international organizations*, UN Doc A/CN.4/637, para. 2, p. 11.

The scepticism regarding the international legal personality of NATO diminished gradually from the 1990s. Academic writers, States and international organization increasingly argue in favour of the Alliance' status under international law. Even NATO itself had to become convinced of its own personality. The out-of-area operations required the conclusion of Status of Force Agreements (SOFAS) with third States. NATO aptly took the initiative and concluded SOFAS with Bosnia-Herzegovina, Afghanistan, Libya and other countries, thereby affirming its status in international law.

In conclusion, NATO certainly meets several indicia of international legal personality as is evidenced by its performance of actions on the international level, notably treaty-making power and privileges and immunities. The existence of international legal personality is – in a way – also confirmed by the practice of States and other international organizations. Recent academic literature furthermore supports this conclusion.

The consequences of NATO's international legal personality include that the organization can bear international rights and obligations and, under specific circumstances, can be held responsible for breaches of those obligations. Another consequence is that certain conduct can be attributed to NATO as an organization. A practical recommendation would be that Troop Contributing Nations do not need to issue national caveats for their contribution to NATO operations, since it is the Alliance that will be held responsible and not the individual member States. Certainly, member States could circumvent their obligations by taking advantage of the organization's competence with respect to that obligation.[93] There is a difference between deliberately evading responsibility and the issue of caveats. Similarly, there would neither by a need to conclude bilateral transfer agreements regarding the treatment of detainees. Instead, NATO may conclude a single overarching agreement with the host nation in order to ensure abidance to its international obligations for the same reason above.

The following question would then be: to which international obligations is the Alliance bound? The next chapter will examine this aspect.

93 Ryngaert, C., *Member State Responsibility fort he Acts of International Organizations*, Utrecht Law Review, Vol. 7, Issues 1, 2011, p. 144.

CHAPTER 6

Binding International Obligations Relevant to NATO's Operations

6.1 Introduction

Chapter 5 concluded that NATO must be considered to be an international organization with international legal personality. A consequence of international legal personality is that the organization can bear international rights and obligations. This chapter will examine which binding international obligations exist in so far as they are relevant to NATO's operations. An analysis of binding international obligations is important to the topic of this book, since a breach of such an obligation entails a wrongful act, which, as a general principle of international law, gives rise to the responsibility of NATO.[1]

In general, international organizations are bound by a variety of international norms originating from various sources, such as general international law, their constitutions or international agreements.[2] There are five categories of international obligations that can be distinguished by their sources or origin.[3] While other categorizations may equally be valid, the only intention here is to give an overview of existing international obligations that might be binding upon NATO. Distinguishing between categories of obligations based on their origin or source, i.e. the character of the primary rule containing the obligation, seems to be the most obvious choice. The sources are: (1) NATO's constitutional documents, (2) the UN Charter and UN Security Council resolutions, (3) international conventional law, in particular international humanitarian law (IHL) and international human rights law (IHRL), (4) international

---

1 Ago, R., *Second Report on State Responsibility, by Roberto Ago, Special Rapporteur* – the origin of international responsibility, A/CN.4/233, p. 179. There was no reason for the International Law Commission to adopt a different approach with regard to international organizations. In the Draft Articles on the Responsibility of International Organizations the ILC has used the same wording. Gaja, M., Special Rapporteur, *First Report on Responsibility of International Organizations*, A/CN.4/532, 26 March 2003, p. 19.

2 ICJ, Advisory opinion on the *interpretation of the agreement of 25 March 1951 between the WHO and Egypt*, 20 December 1980, ICJ Reports 1980, para 37.

3 Economides, C.P., *Content of the Obligation: Obligations of Means and Obligations of Result*, in Crawford, J., Pellet, A., Olleson, S. (eds.), *The Law of International Responsibility*, 2010, p. 372.

 | DOI 10.1163/9789004354647_007

customary law, again with a particular focus on IHL and IHRL and (5) rules of internal and external law of NATO. Paragraphs 6.2 to 6.6 will respectively examine the obligations under each of these categories.

Obligations that pertain primarily to garrison support activities are not considered here for the reasons mentioned earlier in the introductory chapter of this book. Examples of such unrelated obligations are the obligation to request diplomatic clearance for overflight of State aircraft under the Chicago Convention[4] or obligations to refrain from releasing pollutants into water resources under customary international environmental laws.

After an examination of the international obligations binding upon NATO in paragraphs 6.2 to 6.6, paragraph 6.7 will provide final observations and conclusions.

6.2 International Obligations under NATO's Constitutional Documents

The Washington Treaty establishes NATO as an international organization. As such, this treaty could be considered the only constituent treaty of the Alliance. Other agreements, like the NATO Status of Forces Agreement, the Ottawa Agreement and the Paris Protocol regulate important aspects of the organizations, but are not per sé constituent documents of the Alliance. These aspects include the status, privileges and immunities of the NATO Headquarters in Brussels and other civilian headquarters, including their personnel, regulated by the Ottawa Agreement. Similarly, the Paris Protocol regulates the same issues for NATO International Military Headquarters and their personnel. The NATO SOFA, finally, regulates the status of forces and civilian component stationed in another NATO member State. For reasons of inclusiveness, his book has grouped all of these agreements within the definition of constituent documents of NATO.

The Washington Treaty – partially due to its relative conciseness – does not contain a wealth of international obligations. The prevalent obligation is the reference to the UN Charter. The Washington Treaty states that the (member) States will settle disputes by peaceful means and refrain in its *"international relations from the threat or use of force in any manner inconsistent with the purposes of the United Nations"*.[5] The UN Charter prohibits the threat or use of

4 Convention on International Civil Aviation, 7 December 1944.

5 Articles 1 and 5 of the North Atlantic Treaty 1949, 34 UNTS 243, 24 August 1949.

force against the territorial integrity or political independence of any State.[6] The only two exceptions to this rule are the right of (collective) self-defence against an armed attack by another State and the use of force in accordance with the authorization of the UN Security Council.[7] The member States require of the Alliance that – in the exercise of collective self-defence of Article 5 of the Washington Treaty – it will do such within the limits of Article 51 of the UN Charter and that it will terminate an action taken on this basis when the UN Security Council has taken the measures necessary to restore and maintain international peace and security.

As stated in Chapter 3 of this research, when NATO transformed from a pure collective self-defence organization to include collective security tasks, it broadened its tasks well beyond Article 5. Through the adoption of the Strategic Concept of 1999, NATO now undertakes non-article 5 crisis-response operations. These operations – by reference to the UN Charter in the Washington Treaty – are equally undertaken in accordance with the UN Charter and specifically Article 42.[8]

However, it is important to emphasise that the source of the obligation to adhere to the UN Charter is the Washington Treaty. An action that entails a violation of the principles of the UN Charter results in a violation of the Washington Treaty and will trigger – under certain conditions – the responsibility of NATO. This paragraph does not examine whether NATO is bound directly to the UN Charter or to those norms of the UN Charter which are customary in nature. Paragraphs 6.3 and 6.5 which follow below, will analyse respectively whether NATO is bound to the UN Charter directly and to international customary law. This paragraph deals only with the international obligations binding upon NATO under its constitutional documents.

6 Article 2 paragraph 4 of the UN Charter: *"All Members shall refrain in their international relations from the threat or use of force against the territorial integrity or political independence of any State, or in any other manner inconsistent with the Purposes of the United Nations."*

7 Article 42 of the UN Charter: *"Should the Security Council consider that measures provided for in Article 41 would be inadequate or have proved to be inadequate, it may take such action by air, sea, or land forces as may be necessary to maintain or restore international peace and security. Such action may include demonstrations, blockade, and other operations by air, sea, or land forces of Members of the United Nations."*

8 1999 Strategic Concept Paragraph 10: *"To achieve its essential purpose, as an Alliance of nations committed to the Washington Treaty and the United Nations Charter, the Alliance performs the following fundamental security tasks* [...]*".* Paragraph 11 continues: *"In fulfilling its purpose and fundamental security tasks, the Alliance will continue to respect the legitimate security interests of others, and seek the peaceful resolution of disputes as set out in the Charter of the United Nations."*

It seems that in the past, NATO violated the self-imposed obligation to adhere to the principles of the UN Charter in one particular instance. Operation Allied Force conducted in the Federal Republic of Yugoslavia (Serbia and Montenegro) did not have a clear UN Security Council's mandate, which would be required as the legal basis to use force in Kosovo. According to NATO, the operation was conducted in response to a humanitarian crisis that was ongoing by halting Serbian attacks on civilians in Kosovo in 1999. Some of the NAC members asserted that each Ally was responsible for justifying their own participation, but stated that the military intervention in Kosovo did not establish any precedent. This language stresses the binding obligations of NATO under the Washington Treaty to adhere to the provisions of the UN Charter.[9]

Other important documents of NATO, such as the NATO SOFA, Paris Protocol and Ottawa Agreement, create obligations for the Alliance as well. The NATO SOFA contains obligations with respect to the exercise of jurisdiction by the member States of the Alliance. Article VII of the NATO SOFA regulates the exercise of jurisdiction by either the host- or sending State over members of a force or civilian component and their dependents. The sending State has the primary right to exercise jurisdiction in certain specific cases, for instance when an offence has been committed by a member of the force against the person of another member of the force of the sending State.[10] In one situation, the primary right to exercise jurisdiction has been the subject of dispute between two NATO member States.[11] In a case where the Dutch military police arrested a US service member – Staff Sergeant Short – for the murder of his wife, the US requested the extradition of Short in order to exercise criminal jurisdiction. On the basis of the NATO SOFA, the US would have the primary right to exercise jurisdiction, however, this right was denied by the Dutch authorities, based on the argument that the surrender to the US would violate human rights obligations to which the Netherlands is bound, as the suspect would likely face capital punishment. The Supreme Court of the Netherlands acknowledged the conflict between international human rights obligations and the obligation enshrined in the NATO SOFA. The Court finally decided in favour of the human rights obligations, and consequently required the Dutch

9 D.S. Yost, *"NATO's 1999 Strategic Concept",* Security Strategies: NATO, the United States and the European Union, NATO Defense College, 2005, pp. 24–26.

10 Agreement between the Parties to the North Atlantic Treaty regarding the Status of their Forces, 19 June 1951, Art. VII, para 3(a)(i).

11 Hoge Raad der Nederlanden, *Short v. Kingdom of The Netherlands*, ECLI:NL:HR1990:AD7494, 30 March 1990.

government to violate the provision of the NATO SOFA and not to allow the US to exercise its primary right to exercise jurisdiction.[12]

From the wording of the obligation to allow the sending State to exercise jurisdiction, it is apparent that the obligation rests upon the member States, not upon NATO itself. As such, the NATO SOFA doesn't create a direct binding international obligation for NATO. Nevertheless, NATO would be affected by a breach by one of the member States, as it would undermine the very nature of the Alliance. NATO has an indirect obligation to protect the interests of its members as well as of the organization itself and to intervene whenever the provisions of the NATO SOFA are violated. A breach of the NATO SOFA would result not only in an action taken by the State whose rights are violated but also by the other NATO members and by NATO itself. However, it would go too far to conclude that the NATO SOFA creates international legal obligation(s) for NATO as its primary addressee of the obligations contained therein are explicitly States.

The Paris Protocol imposes several international obligations upon NATO. Article II obliges International Military Headquarters (IMHQs) to respect the laws of the host nation.[13] Article VI of the Paris Protocol imposes the obligation upon the IMHQ to waive claims against the member States, if damage was caused by member States' employees or military property to the IMHQ.[14]

The Ottawa Agreement establishes the immunity of NATO's civilian headquarters – a feature that is not mentioned in the Paris Protocol for NATO's military headquarters.[15] Personnel serving at international civilian headquarters[16] equally enjoy immunity from jurisdiction of the host State in so far the as is necessary for the exercise of their functions.[17] Article XXII of the Ottawa Agreement stipulates that immunity needs to be waived if it would impede the course of justice and can be waived without prejudice to the interests of the Organization.[18] The immunity is apparently of relative little importance for this thesis on the responsibility of NATO as it's operations take place outside the territory of the member States. The Ottawa Agreement

12 Fleck, D. (ed.), *The Handbook of the Law of Visiting Forces*, 2001, p. 126. Agreement between the Parties to the North Atlantic Treaty regarding the Status of their Forces, 19 June 1951, Art. VII, para 3(a)(i).

13 Article IV Paris Protocol jo. article II NATO SOFA.

14 Article VI Paris Protocol jo. article VIII NATO SOFA.

15 Article V Ottawa Agreement.

16 International staff and experts on mission. Representatives of member States enjoy absolute immunity, article XIII Ottawa Agreement.

17 Article XII, XIII, XIV Ottawa Agreement.

18 Article XXII Ottawa Agreement.

and Paris Protocol only apply within the NATO area. However, many of the strategic and political decisions are taken at NATO Headquarters in Brussels, Belgium or at one of the operational headquarters leading the operation. Therefore, the immunity of, and the exercise of jurisdiction over, NATO personnel is relevant here to mention.

Article XXII does not impose an international obligation to waive immunity, even though the formulation *"the duty to waive immunity"* seems to imply such. In deciding about the waiver of immunity, the Alliance should determine whether the immunity impedes the course of justice, balanced against the interests of the organization. As contrary it may seem, international crimes may be committed within the context of official activities and, as such, the perpetrator may enjoy immunity from criminal jurisdiction.[19] In those cases NATO may consider whether the immunity would impede the course of justice and waive immunity when required and if it would not prejudice the interests of NATO. As the Alliance has expressed in various policy documents and status agreements that its personnel shall conduct its operations with full respect for the principles and rules of international law, it would not be consistent with this posture not to waive immunity in case of crimes committed by NATO personnel.

In summary, NATO's constituent documents do not include a wealth of international obligations. The Washington Treaty obliges the Alliance to adhere to the principles of the UN Charter. The NATO SOFA, Paris Protocol and Ottawa Agreement contain obligations resting upon member States with respect to the exercise of jurisdiction over NATO personnel. There is only one specific obligation binding upon the Alliance, which is the obligation to waive immunity over NATO personnel employed at NATO international civilian headquarters, if the immunity impedes the course of justice.

6.3 International Obligations under the UN Charter

Treaties do not create obligations or rights for third States or third international organizations without the consent of that State or of that international organization.[20] For this reason, the Charter of the United Nations cannot create

19 Akande, D., Shah, S., *Immunities of State Officials, International Crimes, and Foreign Domestic Courts,* 21 European Journal of International Law, no. 4, 2011.

20 Art. 34, Vienna Convention on the Law of Treaties between States and International Organizations or between International Organizations, 21 March 1986.

binding obligations for NATO, as the Alliance is not a party to the Charter.[21] Neither is NATO bound to resolutions adopted by the UN Security Council. Morover, most UN Security Council resolutions relating to NATO-led operations do not address the Alliance directly, rather the troop contributing nations participating in the missions.[22] Where the Security Council does address NATO, it often does not impose any international obligations.[23] Three UN Security Council resolutions, UNSCR 827(1993, UNSCR 1244(1999) and UNSCR 1851(2008), address NATO directly and seemingly impose international obligations upon it. This perception, however, is incorrect.

UN Security Council resolution 1244(1999) demands *"full cooperation by all concerned, including the international security presence, with the International Tribunal for the Former Yugoslavia"*.[24] The international security presence in the former Yugoslavia is NATO's Implementation Force (IFOR) and subsequent Stabilisation Force (SFOR). This obligation stems from the earlier UN Security Council resolution 827(1993), which imposes the obligation upon States to cooperate fully with the International Criminal Tribunal for the Former Yugoslavia.[25] Clearly, Resolution 827(1993) addresses States and not international organizations, such as NATO. But the obligation has led to several requests to the Tribunal to order SFOR (NATO) to provide documents and witnesses for use in evidentiary hearings. The ICTY did not have the opportunity to examine whether NATO could be obliged to disclose this information, as the applicant withdrew its request.[26] In *Ojdanić*, the Tribunal was presented with another opportunity to examine the extent of the obligation for NATO to cooperate. The Appeals Chamber examined this request and concluded that NATO is an

21 Whether or not NATO is bound by the prohibition of the threat or use of armed force as embodied in article 2 of the UN Charter on the basis that this provision has raised to a customary status is a different question and is examined elsewhere in this book.

22 E.g. ISAF: para. 4, UNSCR 1510(2003),13 October 2003, *"Authorizes the Member States participating in the International Security Assistance Force to take all necessary measures to fulfil its mandate."* Operation Unified Protector: para. 4, UNSCR 1973(2011), 17 March 2011," Authorizes *Member States that have notified the Secretary General, acting nationally or through regional organizations or arrangements, and acting in cooperation with the Secretary General, to take all necessary measures, notwithstanding paragraph 9 of resolution 1970 (2011), to protect civilians* [...]".

23 E.g. Operation Resolute Support, UNSCR 2189(2014), 12 December 2014.

24 UNSCR 1244(1999), 10 June 1999, para. 14.

25 UNSCR 827(1993), 25 May 1993, para. 4.

26 ICTY, Trial, Simić, Case no. it-95-9-PT, Decision on Motion for Judicial Assistance to be Provided by NATO and Others, 18 October 2000, para. 54.

international organization, presumably with international legal personality.[27] However, since NATO is not a party to the UN Charter it was beyond the reach of the Tribunal's authority to order the Alliance to disclose information.[28] UNSCR 1244(1999) included a similar obligation to cooperate with the Tribunal and even went further to include "all concerned" instead of referring to States.[29] Nevertheless, this does not change the conclusion that NATO cannot formally be bound to UN Security Council resolutions.

Debate also existed on whether NATO was obliged in operations IFOR and SFOR to search and arrest war criminals in the former Yugoslavia on the basis of UN Security Council resolution 827(1993). The resolution addressed States to execute arrest warrants and to cooperate with the International Criminal Tribunal for the former Yugoslavia.[30] Even though the obligations rested upon the States contributing forces and not NATO, certain scholars argued that the multinational force was required to implement the UN Security Council resolutions.[31] It is questionable whether IFOR and SFOR were under such obligation. UNSCR 827(1993) addresses States, not NATO. Moreover, the Dayton Peace Agreement specifically puts the obligation on the Republic of Bosnia and Herzegovina, the Federation of Bosnia and Herzegovina and the Republika Srpska to comply with *"any order or request from the International Tribunal for the Former Yugoslavia for the arrest, detention, surrender of [...] who*

27 ICTY, Appeal, Milutinović et al., Case no. IT-05-87-PT, Decision on the Second Application of Dragoljub Ojdanić for Binding Orders Pursuant to Rule 54*bis*, 17 November 2005, paras. 48–49.

28 ICTY, Appeal, Milutinović et al., Case no. IT-05-87-PT, Decision on the Second Application of Dragoljub Ojdanić for Binding Orders Pursuant to Rule 54*bis*, 17 November 2005, paras. 36–37. J. d'Aspremont (ed.), *Participants in the International Legal System*, 2011, p. 194.

29 UNSCR 1244(1999), 10 June 1999, para. 4: *"Demands full cooperation by all concerned, including the international security presence, with the International Tribunal fort he Former Yugoslavia."*

30 United Security Council resolution 827(1993), 25 May 1993, para. 4; *"Decides that all States shall cooperate fully with the International Tribunal and its organs in accordance with the present resolution and the Statute of the International Tribunal and that consequently all States shall take any measure necessary under their domestic law to implement the provisions of the present resolution and the Statute, including the obligation of States to comply with requests for assistance or orders issued by a Trial Chamber under Article 29 of the Statute".*

31 Joines, J.R.W.D., *The Implications of the Peace Agreement for the International Criminal Tribunal for the Former Yugoslavia*, 7 EJIL (1996), N. Figà-Talamanca, *The Role of NATO in the Peace Agreement for Bosnia and Herzegovina*, 7 EJIL (1996) 171.

are accused of violations within the jurisdiction of the Tribunal".[32] If one of the Parties would not comply with this obligation, NATO (IFOR) has the authority to take such actions as required, e.g. the detention of war criminals.[33] However, no obligation rests upon the organization to do so. In 1996, NATO concluded a Memorandum of Understanding (MOU) with the ICTY on the procedures for cooperation between IFOR and the ICTY, but it did not create any legal obligation on the part of NATO.[34] Therefore, the States participating in IFOR and SFOR did not have any obligation to search and arrest indicted war criminals, nor did there rest such obligation on IFOR and SFOR forces. In any case, the obligation certainly did not rest on NATO itself, as NATO was not explicitly addressed in the resolution.[35]

There has also been discussion whether KFOR is bound by IHRL through a UN Security Council's mandate. UN Security Council resolution 1244(1999) includes the responsibility of the international civil presence in Kosovo to protect and promote human rights.[36] The resolution does not oblige KFOR explicitly to adhere to international human rights standards when conducting its mission, neither its mandate included protection and promotion of human rights. Certain authors argue that since KFOR was deployed in support of UNMiK, it was bound to support the protection and promotion of human rights as well.[37] The construction that KFOR, in support of UNMiK, was bound to comply with these norms is somewhat far-sought. KFOR and UNMiK were completely separated in command, authority and mandate. KFOR's mandate seemed to override applicable domestic law and no other authority was placed

---

32 Articles IX(g) and X Annex 1A, *Military Aspects of the Peace Settlement and Appendices to Annex* 1A to The General Framework Agreement for Peace in Bosnia and Herzegovina, 14 December 1995.

33 Article 1(2)(b), Annex 1A, *Military Aspects of the Peace Settlement and Appendices to Annex* 1A to The General Framework Agreement for Peace in Bosnia and Herzegovina, 14 December 1995.

34 Memorandum of Understanding between the International Criminal Tribunal for the Former Yugoslavia and The Supreme Headquarters Allied Powers Europe Concerning Practical Arrangements for the Detention and Transfer to the Tribunal of Persons Indicted for War Crimes by the Tribunal, 9 May 1996.

35 Gaeta, P., *Is NATO Authorized or Obliged to Arrest Persons Indicted by the International Criminal Tribunal for the Former Yugoslavia?* European Journal of International Law 9 (1998).

36 United Nations Security Council resolution 1244(1999), 10 June 1999, para 11(j).

37 Cerone, J., *Outlining KFOR Accountability in Post-Conflict Kosovo,* American Society of International Law, October 2000. J. Cerone, *Minding the Gap: Outlining KFOR Accountability in Post-Conflict Kosovo,* 12, European Journal of International Law, no. 3, 2001.

above KFOR other than NATO. The scepticism that an obligation for NATO to abide by human rights law could be construed through the UN Security Council resolution 1244(1999) is shared by other authors.[38]

In that respect, the Security Council resolution 1244(1999) is different from, for example, the UN Security Council resolution 1851(2008) on the establishment of an anti-piracy mission in the Horn of Africa, which requires States *and regional organizations* to adhere to applicable IHL and IHRL standards.[39] This Resolution, however, does not contain any additional obligation for NATO than those that may or may not exist under international IHL or IHRL, which will be examined in paragraph 6.4 and 6.5.

The abovementioned examples show that the UN Security Council has not formulated any obligations addressed to NATO. It is also unlikely that it will do that in the future as the Security Council is not able to bind a non-party to the UN Charter.

Even though NATO is not bound by the UN Charter or its decisions, all of its 29 member States are. All NATO Member States are party to the UN Charter and therefore bound by its provisions. With respect to the binding nature of UN Security Council resolutions, Article 25 of the UN Charter obliges member States to *"accept and to carry out the decisions of the Security Council in accordance with the present Charter"*. Additionally, Article 103 of the UN Charter provides a primacy of the Charter in case of a potential conflict between obligations of the UN member States under the Charter and their obligations under any other international agreement.

The question then arises whether NATO is bound – indirectly – by the UN Charter because of the fact that its member States are party to it. The European Court of Justice (ECJ) considered this question with regard to the obligation of the European Commission to respect obligations binding upon its member States.[40] In the *Kadi* case, the Court of First Instance held that the UN Charter imposes binding obligations on its member States, which must therefore take all measures necessary to ensure that the UN Security Council resolution is put

38 Pacquée, D., Dewulf, S., *International Territorial Administrations and the Rule of Law: The Case of Kosovo,* Essex Human Rights Review Vol. 4 No. 1, February 2007, p. 5.

39 UN Security Council resolution 1851(2008), 16 December 2008, para. 6; "[...] *decides that* [...] *States and regional organizations cooperating in the fight against piracy and armed robbery at sea off the coast of Somalia* [...] *may undertake all necessary measures that are appropriate* [...], *provided, however, that any measures undertaken pursuant to the authority of this paragraph shall be undertaken consistent with applicable humanitarian and human rights law*".

40 ECJ (Grand Chamber), European Commission et al v. Yassin Abdullah Kadi, Appeal, Joined Cases 584/10, C-593/10, C-595/10, 18 July 2013.

into effect.[41] The EC itself is not directly bound to the UN Charter and is therefore not required, as an obligation under public international law, to accept and carry out the Resolution.[42]

Nevertheless, the member States were bound by the obligations of the UN Charter prior to the creation of the EC, and by concluding a treaty between them they could not transfer more powers to the EC or withdraw from obligations under the Charter.[43] In so far as under the EC Treaty the Community had assumed powers previously exercised by Member States in the area governed by the Charter of the United Nations, the provisions of that Charter have the effect of binding the Community.[44] Therefore, the Court argued, when the EC implements the UN Security Council resolution, the *"Community is to take due account of the terms and objectives of the resolution concerned and of the relevant obligations under the Charter of the United Nations".*[45]

In other words, NATO is not directly bound to the Charter of the United Nations, nor do the UN Security Council resolutions impose any international obligations for the Alliance. However, since the members of NATO are bound to the UN Charter, the Alliance would need to take due account of the terms and objectives of the UN Security Council resolutions and of the relevant obligations under the Charter. Hence, it is concluded that the UN Charter and UN Security Council resolutions are indirectly binding upon NATO.

6.4 International Obligations under Conventional Law

6.4.1 *Conventional International Humanitarian Law and International Human Rights Law*

International Humanitarian Law (IHL) and International Human Rights Law (IHRL) are terms that encapsulate both international treaties and customary

---

41 Court of First Instance, Kadi v Council of the European Union and Commission of the European Communities, Judgment, Case T-315/01, 21 September 2005, para. 189.

42 Court of First Instance, Kadi v Council of the European Union and Commission of the European Communities, Judgment, Case T-315/01, 21 September 2005, para. 192.

43 Court of First Instance, Kadi v Council of the European Union and Commission of the European Communities, Judgment, Case T-315/01, 21 September 2005, para. 193–195.

44 Court of First Instance, Kadi v Council of the European Union and Commission of the European Communities, Judgment, Case T-315/01, 21 September 2005, para. 203.

45 ECJ (Grand Chamber), Kadi v Council of the European Union and Commission of the European Communities, Judgment, action for annulment, appeal, Case C-402/05 P, [2008] ECR I-6351, [2009] AC 1225, 3 September 2008, para. 296.

rules. IHL treaties includes the four 1949 Geneva Conventions,[46] the 1977 Additional Protocols[47] and various specialised agreements such as the 1980 Convention on Certain Conventional Weapons and its five Protocols, the 1993 Chemical Weapons Convention and the 1997 Ottawa Convention Banning Anti-Personnel Landmines.

Regional Human Rights Conventions include the 1950 European Convention for the Protection of Human Rights and Fundamental Freedoms (ECHR),[48] the 1969 American Convention on Human Rights (ACHR)[49] and the 1986 African Charter on Human and People's Rights (ACHPR)[50] Universal conventions include the 1966 International Covenant on Civil and Political Rights (ICCPR)[51] and the 1984 Convention against Torture and Other Cruel, Inhuman or Degrading Treatment or Punishment (CAT).[52]

IHL and IHRL treaties often doe not provide the possibility for accession by international organizations. The ECHR refers to "High Contracting Parties",[53] while the ICCPR refers to "The States Parties to the present Covenant".[54] The terminology does not need to be an absolute obstacle for international organizations to accede to these treaties. It would be possible for international organizations to accede to these conventions if adequate legal documents are

---

46 Geneva Convention for the Amelioration of the Condition of the Wounded and Sick in Armed Forces in the Field, opened for signature 12 August 1949, (Geneva Convention I); Geneva Convention of the Amelioration of the Condition of the Wounded, Sick and Shipwrecked Members of Armed Forces at Sea 12 August 1949 (Geneva Convention II); Geneva Convention Relative to the Treatment of Prisoners of War, 12 August 1949 (Geneva Convention III); *Geneva Convention Relative to the Protection of Civilian Persons in Time of War* (Geneva Convention IV), 1949, 75 UNTS 287, 12 August 1949, (Geneva Convention IV).

47 *Protocol Additional to the Geneva Conventions of 12 August 1949, and relating to the Protection of Victims of International Armed Conflicts*, 1977, 1125 UNTS 3, 8 June 1977, (Additional Protocol I); Protocol Additional to the Geneva Conventions of 12 August 1949, and relating to the Protection of Victims of Non-International Armed Conflicts, 1977, 1125 UNTS 609, 8 June 1977 (Additional Protocol II).

48 European Convention for the Protection of Human Rights and Fundamental Freedoms, 4 November 1950.

49 American Convention on Human Rights, 22 November 1969.

50 African Charter on Human and People's Rights, entered into force 21 October 1986.

51 International Covenant on Civil and Political Rights, 16 December 1966.

52 Convention against Torture and Other Cruel, Inhuman or Degrading Treatment or Punishment, entered into force 26 June 1987.

53 Art. 1, European Convention for the Protection of Human Rights and Fundamental Freedoms, 4 November 1950.

54 Preamble, International Covenant on Civil and Political Rights, 16 December 1966.

adopted. For instance, the States Party to the ECHR, by adopting Article 17 of Protocol No. 14 to the Convention for the Protection of Human Rights and Fundamental Freedoms, amending the control system of the Convention, made it possible for the EU to accede to the ECHR.[55] However, practice shows that international organizations have not shown readiness to find the ways to accede to IHL and IHRL conventions.[56] Even if it would be possible, NATO has not shown any preparedness to enter in any IHL or IHRL agreement.[57]

It is therefore concluded that NATO is not formally bound by those human rights or international humanitarian law treaties. However, in as far as the provision of international humantarian law or human rights law are also customary law, or even *jus cogens*, NATO is bound by it. The international obligations under international customary law is examined in paragraph 6.5.

6.4.2 *Mission-SOFAs between NATO and the Host State*

NATO can enter into international agreements with States or other international organizations. These international agreements may contain international obligations binding upon NATO. This paragraph will examine binding obligations contained in mission Status of Forces Agreement (mission-SOFAs).

Mission-SOFAs regulate more or less the same topics in every operation, regardless the international organization that is conducting the operation. The EU[58] and the UN[59] utilise a model-SOFA, which forms the blueprint for international agreements between their organization and the host nation. NATO does not have a model-SOFA, but its mission-SOFAs have a certain degree of similarity. The Alliance has concluded several mission SOFAs, for instance,

---

55 Protocol No. 14 to the Convention fort he Protection of Human Rights and Fundamental Freedoms, Amending the Control System of the Convention, 13 May 2004, entered into force 1 June 2010.

56 With regard to the EU: Naert, F., *International Law Aspects of the EU's Security and Defence Policy*, 2010, p. 527. Regarding the UN: Zwanenburg, M.C. (2005) *Accountability of peace support operations*, Netherlands: Martinus Nijhoff Publishers, p. 141.

57 Letter of M.S. Johnson, Jr., the Legal Advisor to the Supreme Allied Commander in Europe (SACEUR) to Amnesty International, 12 March 1996. According to Johnson, IFOR should not be equated to a State in terms of international obligations, thereby likely referring to the obstacle for IFOR or NATO to accede to IHL instruments.

58 Council of the European Union, *Draft Model Agreement on the status of the European Union-led forces between the European Union and a Host State*, 11894/07, 20 July 2007.

59 United Nations General Assembly, Model Status-of-Forces-Agreement for Peace-keeping Operations, A/45/594, 9 October 1990.

for its operations IFOR/SFOR and ISAF/Resolute Support.[60] NATO did not need to conclude a mission-SOFA for ISAF as this was already in place, prior to the change of command over the ISAF mission to NATO in 2005. In 2003, ISAF was conducted by a coalition of States, which concluded in January 2002 the necessary Status of Forces arrangements with the interim government of Afghanistan.[61] The Alliance did expand the existing SOFA through an exchange of letters with the Interim Government of Afghanistan, to include NATO forces and contractors.[62] In 2014, NATO entered into a bilateral SOFA with Afghanistan for its follow-up mission Operation Resolute Support.[63]

A recurring theme in NATO mission-SOFAs is the obligation of mission personnel to respect host nation laws, which correlates with the functional immunity from host nation jurisdiction accorded to personnel.[64] Whether or not the term involves the duty to obey local laws or a duty to "merely" take them

---

60 The legal status of the KFOR mission is regulated by the Military Technical Agreement between the International Security Force ("KFOR") and the Governments of the Federal Republic of Yugoslavia and the Republic of Serbia, 9 June 1999. Since UN Security Council 1244(1999) mandated unmiK to administer the territory of Kosovo, a mission SOFA with the host nation was not a preferred option and would impinge on the competence of the UN-led mission. Instead UNMiK issued regulation 2000/47, which constitutes in fact a mission-SOFA.

61 Military Technical Agreement between the International Security Assistance Force (ISAF) and the Interim Administration of Afghanistan ('Interim Administration'), 4 January 2002.

62 Exchange of letters between the Secretary General of NATO and the Afghan Minister of Foreign Affairs, dated 5 September 2004 and 22 November 2004.

63 Status of Forces Agreement between the Afghan government and NATO, signed 30 September 2014.

64 UN: United Nations General Assembly, Model Status-of-Forces-Agreement for Peacekeeping Operations, A/45/594, 9 October 1990, para IV(6), "[...] *The United Nations peacekeeping operation and its members shall respect all local laws and regulations*". EU: Council of the European Union, Draft Model Agreement on the status of the European Union-led forces between the European Union and a Host State, 11894/07, 20 July 2007, article 2(1), "*EUFOR and EUFOR personnel shall respect the laws and regulations of the Host State and shall refrain from any action or activity incompatible with the objectives of the mission.*" NATO, e.g. Annex A to the Military Technical Agreement between the International Security Assistance Force (ISAF) and the Interim Administration of Afghanistan ('Interim Administration'), 4 January 2002, para. 2, "*All ISAF and supporting personnel, including liaison personnel, enjoying privileges and immunities under the Arrangement will respect the laws of Afghanistan, insofar as it is compatible with the UNSCR (1386) and will refrain from activities not compatible with the nature of the mission.*"

into consideration has been a subject of many legal discussions.[65] The view held here is that the duty to respect does not imply that NATO is bound by the legislation of the host State. Rather, a violation of domestic laws by mission personnel would constitute a breach of the duty laid down in the mission SOFA. NATO formulates the obligation to respect local laws the same way as other international organizations engaged in peace support operations. For instance the SOFA with Bosnia Herzegovina regulating the status of SFOR and its personnel states that mission personnel shall *"respect the laws of the Republic of Bosnia and Herzegovina insofar as it is compatible with the entrusted tasks/ mandate and shall refrain from activities not compatible with the nature of the Operation.*[66] If, for instance, a member of the mission would deliberately deposit waste outside the military compound in violation of domestic environmental laws, this would entail a breach – not of the host nation laws – but of obligation under the mission-SOFA as well as the obligation to compensate the host nation for the damages caused.

In conclusion, NATO mission-SOFAs are a relevant source of international obligations binding upon NATO, in particular where the international agreement refers to the obligation to respect domestic laws of the host Nation.

6.4.3 *Memoranda of Understanding between NATO and TCNs*

Memoranda of understanding (MOUs) are a common used type of agreement in military operations that regulate a variety of topics, ranging from logistic support, financial regulations, command and control and many other issues. MOUs have been concluded between the international organization conducting the operation and the Troop Contributing Nations (TCNs) as well as between the international organization and the host nation.

Each international organization uses its own format of an MOU. When States contribute forces to an UN-led mission, the "Revised Draft Model Memorandum of Understanding between the United Nations and Troop Contributing Countries" stipulates the delineation of responsibilities between the UN and

65 Lazereff, S., *Status of Military Forces under Current International Law,* 1971, pp. 100–101. Batstone, R., Respect for the Law of the Receiving State in Fleck, D. (ed.) (2001) *The handbook of the law of visiting forces*, United Kingdom: Oxford University Press, p. 61, Sari, A., *Status of Forces and Status of Mission Agreements under the ESDP: The EU's Evolving Practice,* 19 European Journal of International Law 1, 2008, pp. 67–100.

66 General Framework Agreement for Peace, 10 November 1995, Appendix B to Annex 1A *"Agreement between the Republic of Bosnia Herzegovina and the North Atlantic Treaty Organization (NATO) Concerning the Status of NATO and its Personnel".*

the TCN.[67] The MOU regulates the command and control relationship of the UN and TCN over the contributed forces and, by concluding the MOU, the TCN agrees to respect the local laws of the host nation, the standards of conduct of the UN and to respect a number of IHL conventions.[68] The UN sees the conclusions of these MOU as an efficient tool to ensure responsibility for conduct of forces contributed by TCNs. The UN used the MOU to implement various measures in order to prevent (further) incidents regarding sexual exploitation and abuse by UN peacekeepers and to ensure accountability of personnel for criminal behaviour. The UN considers the MOU a binding agreement between the UN and troop contributing country. It is questionable though how such an agreement can create international obligations, when the intention of an MOU is to create only a political commitment. The linguistic features of MOUs avoid creating a legally binding document.

NATO does not consider that MOUs are legally binding documents. NATO and its member States actively try to avoid terms in the MOU that may reflect such a possible legally binding nature.[69]

NATO concluded MOUs with troop contributing nations to regulate financial and logistical aspects of a mission.[70] NATO may also conclude MOUs with the host nation to stipulate the conditions of support delivered by the host nation to the mission. More recently, MOUs have covered a variety of other topics as well. The topics included issues such as the gathering of intelligence in the host nation or the sharing of information between the host nation and

---

67 UN, Model MOU, Letter Dated 11 January 2006 from the Chairman of the 2004 Working Group on Contingent-Owned Equipment to the Chairman of the Fifth Committee, UN Doc A/C.5/60/26, 11 January 2006 annex *"Manual on Policies and Procedures concerning the Reimbursement and Control of Contingent-Owned Equipment of Troop/Police Contributors Participating in Peacekeeping Missions".* Revised Draft Model MOU, Report of the Special Committee on Peacekeeping Operations and Its Working Group on the 2007 Resumed Session, UN Doc A/61/19 (Pt III), 12 June 2007 annex *"Revised Draft Model Memorandum of Understanding".*

68 Article 28 of the Model MOU: The UN peacekeeping mission *"shall observe and respect the principles and spirit of the general international convention applicable to the conduct of military personnel. The international convention referred to above include the four Geneva Conventions of 12 August 1949 and their Additional Protocols of 8 June 1977 and the* UNESCO *Convention of 14 May 1954 on the Protection of Cultural Property in the event of armed conflict.* [TCNS] *shall therefore ensure that the members of its national contingent serving with* {the UN peacekeeping operation] *be fully acquainted with the principles and spirit of these Conventions".*

69 NATO Legal Deskbook, Second Edition, 2010, pp. 127–128.

70 AJP-4.9, Modes of Multinational Logistic Support, November 2005.

NATO. One particular practice that emerged that is relevant to the topic of responsibility of NATO during its operations, is the conclusion of an MOU with the host nation to receive diplomatic assurances on the treatment of detainees that are transferred by the mission to the host nation. As described in Chapter 2 on the detention operations by Canada in ISAF, several TCNs have concluded such MOUs with the Afghan government. The majority of writers argue that such diplomatic assurances contained in MOUs are not legally binding and hence to not absolve the transferring State from its obligations under IHRL.[71]

NATO did not conclude a single overarching MOU with the government of Afghanistan, because each TCN has different international obligations under IHRL. There was insufficient common ground that could enable NATO to come to a single MOU with Afghanistan. As a result, bilateral MOUs between TCNs and Afghanistan were concluded, which led to differences in the handling of detainees and, at times, constituted a hindrance to effective military cooperation.[72] Even though NATO tried to conclude an overarching MOU, the political differences between the nations impeded this initiative.

In conclusion, MOUs are politically binding documents, but do not contain any legally binding international obligations for NATO. For this reason, MOUs are not a relevant source of international obligations to NATO even if the content of such documents contain references to international human rights law and international humanitarian law.

6.5 International Obligations under Customary Law

This paragraph will examine whether the Alliance is bound to the rules of customary international law. In general, international organizations that have international legal personality are bound by international customary law insofar the organization is able, by its nature and powers, to apply these rules.[73] The fact that an international organization partakes as a subject of international law in international relations means that the organization is, *ipso facto,*

71 Kleffner, J.K., Operational Detention, in T. Gill, D. Fleck (eds.), *The Handbook of the International Law of Military Operations*, 2010, p. 469. UNHCR, *Note on Diplomatic Assurances and International Refugee Protection,* Aug 2006, http://www.refworld.org/pdfid/44dc81164.pdf. Human Rights Watch, "Diplomatic Assurances" against Torture, http://www.hrw.org/sites/default/files/related_material/ecaqna1106web.pdf.

72 Hartmann, J., *The Copenhagen Process: Principles and Guidelines,* EJIL Talk, 3 November 2012.

73 Schermers, H.G. and Blokker, N.M. (1995) *International institutional law: Unity within diversity,* The Netherlands: Brill, pp. 824–825.

bound by the relevant rules of customary international law. In other words, with powers to act on the international level comes responsibility to abide by international law. Denying the existence of such obligations would be denying the existence of legal personality.[74]

On the basis of this premise, it is held that NATO is bound by customary international law. NATO itself has not expressly acknowledged the applicability of international customary law to its operations. The strongest wording it has used is that NATO *respects* international customary law as a matter of principle, not as a matter of a binding international obligation resting upon the Alliance.[75] NATO's point of view that it is not bound to international customary law is predominantly grounded in the belief that NATO is not able, by its nature and powers, to apply these rules of customary IHL and IHRL. NATO lacks the disciplinary and criminal powers that States possess over their armed forces, which would preclude them to implement and enforce these provisions.[76] However, the absence of criminal and disciplinary powers would not need to stand in the way to consider that NATO is bound by the customary norms of laws of armed conflict. The lack of such powers does not relate to the binding nature of international obligations found in customary international law *per sé*, rather to the extent of binding obligations under international customary law.[77]

6.5.1 *International Obligations under Customary IHL*

In their ICRC study *Customary International Humanitarian Law,* Henckaerts and Doswald-Beck inventoried the norms of IHL that have gained customary

74 ICJ, Advisory Opinion, *Interpretation of the Agreement of 25 March 1951 between the WHO and Egypt,* 20 December 1980, pp. 89–90.

75 Matthee, M., Toebes, B., Brus, M. (eds.), *Armed Conflict and International Law: In Search of the Human Face,* 2013, p. 21.

76 See also the argument of the UN that it cannot comply with the provisions of IHL as it lacks the competence to conduct prosecution of peacekeepers, Naert, F., *International Law Aspects of the EU's Security and Defence Policy,* 2010, pp. 533–534. Scholars have rejected this argument as the UN could have the competence to conduct prosecution of peacekeepers, through e.g. the establishment of an international tribunal that could prosecute UN peacekeepers if it wishes so.

77 The lack of disciplinary powers and criminal jurisdiction may be of importance to the question of 'effective control', but not to the question of the binding nature of international customary norms of NATO. Effective control is required to attribute wrongful conduct of personnel that is placed at the disposal of an international organisation. This aspect will be examined in Chapter 7 of this thesis.

status.[78] The authors identified 161 rules of customary international humanitarian law. The majority of rules of the 1949 Geneva Conventions, including common Article 3, are considered to be customary law, as well as the 1907 Hague Regulations.[79] Other treaties, such as the 1977 Additional Protocols, also contain provisions of a customary nature.

This paragraph does not intend to replicate the work of the ICRC by identifying here relevant customary norms of IHL to NATO operations. Rather, the intent is to analyse whether customary IHL is a relevant source of international obligations binding to NATO. There are two questions which need to be answered to reach any conclusions on this aspect. First: Is international customary IHL applicable to international organizations, as these norms are addressed to States primarily? Second: Since IHL only applies to participants to an armed conflict, can NATO be seen as such? This paragraph will analyse these two questions in order to come to a conclusion whether the Alliance is bound, and to what extent it is bound, to customary IHL.

a The Addressee of the Norms of IHL

The IHL treaties were designed with States as the addressees in mind, which is apparent from the form and content of the 1949 Geneva Conventions and the 1907 Hague Regulations. The Conventions speak of "the territory of the High Contracting Parties"[80] and use terms as "States" and "Governments".[81]

This raises the question whether international humanitarian law can be applicable – by analogy and where appropriate – to international organisations.[82] International organisations do not resemble to States. They do not have a territory, nor is the concept of sovereignty meaningful to them. These attributes are closely connected to the norms of international humanitarian law.

Nevertheless, some authors argue that the application of international humanitarian law to international organisations seems to be "*less revolutionary*

78 Henckaerts, J-M., Doswald-Beck, L. (eds.), *Customary International Humanitarian Law*, 2005.

79 Henckaerts, J-M., Doswald-Beck, L. (eds.), *Customary International Humanitarian Law*, 2005.

80 Common Article 2 of the 1949 Geneva Conventions, "[...] *The Convention shall also apply to all cases of partial or total occupation of the present Convention.* [...]".

81 E.g. Article 4 and 6, 1907 Hague Regulations, "*Prisoners of war are in the power o the hostile Government* [...]", "*The State may utilize the labour of prisoners of war according to their rank and aptitude* [...]."

82 Shraga, D., *The United Nations as an Actor Bound by International Humanitarian Law*, 5 International Peacekeeping 64, 1998, p. 65.

than the application of many other international rules".[83] The norms are applicable to non-state actors, such as armed opposition groups, as well. Zwanenburg[84] and Zegveld[85] even suggest that some international organisations could fit the definition of "organised armed groups".[86] The essential criterion of organised armed groups is the existence of a responsible command, which certain international organisations, and certainly NATO, have. Zwanenburg does not suggest that NATO should be equated to an organised armed group. Instead, since IHL can be applicable to non-State actors, the view that international organisations could be bound by this body of law is not that far sought than thought at first glance.[87]

In essence, the question whether the norms can be applicable to international organisations is not ruled out simply because the addressee of the norms are States. The norms can be equally applicable to international organisations, such as NATO, as they are able to abide by these norms and are capable of (partially) implementing them. The manner and degree in which NATO is able to implement norms of customary International Humanitarian Law is discussed further on.

b The Qualification of an Armed Conflict in Which NATO Participates

An international armed conflict is an armed conflict between two States. An armed conflict between an international organisation and a State would be defined as non-international, as the latter is not a State. However, this literal interpretation is not the prevailing view. International organisations are, like States, subjects of international law and, if two subjects of international law come into armed conflict with another, the conflict is considered international because it is regulated by the same international regime.[88]

---

83 Zwanenburg, M.C. (2005) *Accountability of peace support operations*, Netherlands: Martinus Nijhoff Publishers, p. 165.

84 Zwanenburg, M.C. (2005) *Accountability of peace support operations*, Netherlands: Martinus Nijhoff Publishers, p. 165.

85 Zegveld, L., *Accountability of armed opposition groups in international law,* Cambridge studies in international and comparative law, 2002.

86 ICTY, Trial Chamber, Judgment, *Prosecutor v. Boškoski and Tarulovski*, it-04-82-T, 10 July 2008, para. 17.

87 Zwanenburg, M.C. (2005) *Accountability of peace support operations*, Netherlands: Martinus Nijhoff Publishers, p. 165.

88 Zwanenburg, M.C. (2005) *Accountability of peace support operations*, Netherlands: Martinus Nijhoff Publishers, 195–196, C. Greenwood, *International Humanitarian Law and*

The situation becomes slightly more complicated with regard to non-international armed conflicts. A non-international armed conflict is an armed conflict which takes place in the territory of a State between its armed forces and organised armed groups, or between such groups.[89] As such, an armed conflict between NATO and a non-State actor would be a non-international armed conflict, as both entities are not States. Other authors maintain that the intervention of an international organisation in an armed conflict would render the conflict automatically international, because of the fact that an international organisation is made up of States.[90] This view disregards, however, that international organisations may have international legal personality and should be seen separate from the member States.

It is held here that the intervention of an international organisation in support of an armed group fighting against the government would render the conflict international, while an intervention in support, or at least with the consent, of a State against such a group will *not* render the conflict international. Instead, it remains a non-international armed conflict. Some authors define such a conflict as an "internationalised" non-international armed conflict, but the term has no further legal relevance, other than to express the circumstance that other States or international organisation participate in the conflict in support of the State in whose territory the conflict takes place.[91]

In conclusion, an international armed conflict exists when there is an armed conflict between a State and NATO. A non-international armed conflict exists when there is a conflict between NATO – either in support or with the consent of the State in which the conflict takes place – and an organised armed group.[92] The next paragraph will examine the conditions to determine when NATO is a party in the armed conflict.

United Nations Military Operations, 1 Yearbook of International Humanitarian Law 3, 1998, p. 25, C. Emanuelli, *Les Actions Militaires de l'ONU et le Droit International Humanitaire*, 1995, p. 34.

89 Common article 2 of the 1949 Geneva Conventions.

90 Milanovic, M., *What Exactly Internationalizes an Internal Armed Conflict*, EJIL:Talk, 7 May 2010.

91 Gasser, H.P., *Internationalized Non-international armed conflicts: Case Studies of Afghanistan, Kampuchea and Lebanon*, American University Review, Vol. 33/1, 1983, pp. 145–161. ICRC https://www.icrc.org/casebook/doc/glossary/internationalized-internal-armed-conflict-glossary.htm.

92 ICTY, *Decision on the defence motion for interlocutory appeal on jurisdiction*, Prosecutor v. Dusko Tadic, 2 October 1995, paras. 66–70.

c The Conditions to Determine When NATO becomes a Party to an Armed Conflict

The next step is to establish the conditions which determine when NATO becomes a party to an armed conflict, since IHL is only applicable to the parties of the conflict. Before examining the conditions when the Alliance becomes a party an armed conflict, it is appropriate to discuss here whether NATO can become a party to an armed conflict at all. The question whether an international organisation is able to become a party to an armed conflict is examined extensively by various legal scholars.[93] As stated earlier, international humanitarian law is applicable to other entities than States, such as organised armed groups. In that sense, IHL may equally applicable to international organisations. There is no practice or explicit confirmation whether international organisations see themselves as potential parties to the conflict. However, the UN has considered itself as involved in an armed conflict because it considered IHL applicable.[94] Given the fact that NATO has international legal personality and is capable of bearing international rights and obligations, it does not seem entirely incorrect to assume that the organization is bound to norms of IHL when it is involved in hostilities in an armed conflict.

The deployment of NATO into a conflict zone does not automatically mean that NATO has become a party to an armed conflict. Certain conditions have to be met in order to become a party to an armed conflict. IHL sets different conditions for international and non-international armed conflicts, both situations will be examined in the following paragraph.

The applicability of IHL (*jus in bello*) is not dependent on the norms pertaining to the right to engage in hostilities (*jus ad bellum*). The norms on the conduct during armed conflict are strictly separated from the norms regulating the legality of engaging into armed conflict. In theory, the legal basis upon which an operation is conducted is not determinative to whether NATO is a party to an armed conflict.

The strict separation between the legal basis to use force and the application of IHL is on occasion blurred, in particular when forces are deployed in so-called peacekeeping operations, authorised under Chapter VI or so-called

93 Grenfell, K., *Perspective on the applicability and application of international humanitarian law: the UN context,* International Review of the Red Cross (2013), 95, p. 648; Zwanenburg, M.C. (2005) *Accountability of peace support operations,* Netherlands: Martinus Nijhoff Publishers.

94 Zwanenburg, M.C. (2005) *Accountability of peace support operations,* Netherlands: Martinus Nijhoff Publishers, p. 187.

Chapter "VI and a half"[95] of the UN Charter.[96] The neutral position that peacekeepers take in the armed conflict gives the impression that these forces will not become a party to the conflict, but the participation in armed conflict is not dependent on the formal characterisation of the forces, rather on factual circumstances.[97] If the UN mandate limits the use of armed force to invididual or unit self-defence actions, the peacekeeping mission maintains its neutral position and will likely not become a party to the armed conflict. However, if the mission goes beyond the initial peacekeeping mandate and resorts to offensive force, the mission does become a party to the armed conflict. Military forces in operations based on (collective) self-defence and peace enforcement operations based on respectively articles 51 and 42 of the UN Charter are likely to use armed force, but this is neither pre-determined. If the mission does not perform any offensive actions, it will not become a party to an armed conflict. Therefore, it is not possible to determine on the basis of *jus ad bellum* whether NATO will, or is to become a party to an armed conflict.

NATO only becomes a party to an international armed conflict if it resorts to armed force against another State. As soon as the Alliance detains prisoners or has control over a part of the territory of another State, then the norms of IHL pertaining to international armed conflict apply.[98] A minimal transgression, which expresses belligerent intent of one party is sufficient.[99]

An international armed conflict exists insofar there is evidence of belligerent intent of one party against the other. Belligerent intent exists when there is interference with another's 'sphere of sovereignty'.[100] This intent is deduced from factual circumstances and is deemed to exist when a party is involved in military operations or any other hostile act aimed at neutralising the enemy's personnel or resources, hampering its military operations, subduing it or

---

95 UN, *Question considered by the Security Council at its 749th and 750th meetings held on 30 October 1956: 2nd and final report of the Secretary General on the plan for an emergency international United Nations force requested in the resolution adopted by the General Assembly* on 4 November 1956, A/3302, 1956.

96 United Nations, Secretary General's Bulletin, ST/SGB/1999/13, 6 August 1999. Convention on the Safety of United Nations and Associate Personnel, 9 December 1994.

97 Convention on the Safety of United Nations and Associate Personnel, 9 December 1994.

98 Gasser, H.P., International Humanitarian Law: An Introduction, in: Haug, H. (ed.), *Humanity for All: The International Red Cross and Red Crescent Movement,* 1993, pp. 510–511.

99 Melzer, N., *Targeted Killing in International Law,* 2008, p. 250. T. Ferraro, *The Applicability of International Humanitarian Law to Multinational Forces,* International Review of the Red Cross, 2013, no. 95, Multinational Operations and the Law, pp. 575–576.

100 Melzer N., *Targeted Killing in International Law,* 2008, p. 250.

inducing its change in actions.[101] The temporal and geographical scope of the armed conflict extends beyond the exact time and place of the hostilities.[102] If NATO is involved in any of the situations as described here, it can be considered involved in an international armed conflict.

The conditions when an entity becomes a party to a non-international armed conflict are found in the 1949 Geneva Conventions, 1977 Additional Protocol II and jurisprudence, in particular that of the International Criminal Tribunal for the former Yugoslavia. Basically, there are two conditions to determine when a non-international armed conflict exists: (1) the fighting occurs between parties demonstrating a certain level of organization and (2) the fighting has reached a certain threshold of intensity. The level of organization is assessed by the existence of a command and control structure, the ability to conduct coordinated military operations, evidence of a certain level of logistics and the ability to respect and ensure respect for IHL.[103]

The intensity is measured by taking into account the number, duration and intensity of individual confrontations, types of weapons and equipment used, number and calibre of the munitions employed, number of forces and individuals involved in the conflict, the extent of destruction, the number of civilians fleeing, the number of casualties, the spread of the conflict.[104]

Given the structure of NATO as depicted in Chapter 4, the Alliance easily meets the criteria of organisation.[105] The next question would then be whether the conflict has reached the threshold for non-international armed conflict. Certainly, if NATO deploys in an already existent non-international armed conflict in support of a State, NATO will automatically become a party to the conflict and the norms of IHL pertaining to non-international armed conflict will apply.[106] The following paragraphs will examine whether NATO is a party to

101 Ferraro, T., *The Applicability of International Humanitarian Law to Multinational Forces,* International Review of the Red Cross, 2013, no. 95, Multinational Operations and the Law, pp. 575–576.

102 ICTY, Appeals Chamber, Decision on the Defence motion for interlocutory appeal on jurisdiction, *Prosecutor v. D. Tadić,* IT-94-I, 2 October 1995, paras. 66–70.

103 ICTY, Trial Chamber, Judgment, *The Prosecutor v. Tadić,* IT-94-I-T, 7 May 1997, paras. 561–568.

104 ICTY, Trial Chamber, Judgment, *The Prosecutor v. Boškoski,* IT-04-82-T, 10 July 2008, paras. 177–193.

105 Ferraro, T., *The Applicability and Application of International Humanitarian Law to Multinational Forces,* International Review of the Red Cross, vol. 95, no. 891/892, 2013, p. 577.

106 Ferraro, T., *The Applicability and Application of International Humanitarian Law to Multinational Forces,* International Review of the Red Cross, vol. 95, no. 891/892, 2013, p. 578.

an international or non-international armed conflict during its mission in the Balkans, Afghanistan and Libya.

d Application of the Conditions to NATO Operations

The abovementioned conditions can be applied to determine whether NATO has been a party in armed conflicts during its operations in the Balkan, Afghanistan and Libya.

Operations in the Balkans

The Alliance has been active in the Balkans since June 1992, initially performing monitoring tasks,[107] which later expanded to embargo enforcement activities[108] and the enforcement of a no-fly zone.[109] These operations continued throughout the international armed conflict in Bosnia-Herzegovina between the Socialist Federal Republic of Yugoslavia and the Republic of Croatia, at least until 19 May 1992.[110] After the independence of Bosnia-Herzegovina in May 1992, the armed conflict remained international between the Federal Republic of Yugoslavia – effectively controlling – the Bosnian-Serb Army (VRS) and forces of the Republic of Bosnia-Herzegovina.

NATO's operations expanded throughout the development of the ongoing international armed conflict in Bosnia-Herzegovina. The Alliance conducted close-air support operations in support of UNPROFOR and targeted e.g. command and control facilities.[111] From 1995, after the signing of the Dayton Peace

107 *Monitoring tasks*: Operation Maritime Monitor, 16 July – 22 November 1992, NATO warships patrolled the Adriatic Sea to monitor the United Nations Security Council's embargo on weapons to the warring parties during the fighting in Former Yugoslavia.

Operation Sky Monitor, 15 October 1992–12 April 1993, NATO aircraft monitored the No-Fly Zone declared by the United Nations Security Council against flights by military aircraft of the warring factions over Bosnia during the fighting in Former Yugoslavia.

108 Operation Maritime Guard, 22 November 1992–15 June 1993. Following a decision taken at a joint session of the North Atlantic Council and the Western European Union (WEU) Council, the separate NATO and WEU operations in the Adriatic Sea to enforce the United Nations' maritime embargo of weapons imports by the warring factions in Former Yugoslavia were combined into a single operation, Operation SHARP GUARD, 15 June 1993–2 October 1996.

109 Operation Deny Flight, 13 April 1993 – 20 December 1995. In contrast to Operation Sky Monitor, NATO was authorized in Operation Deny Flight to use "all necessary means" to enforce the no-fly zone.

110 ICTY, Appeals Chamber, Decision on the Defence motion for interlocutory appeal on jurisdiction, *Prosecutor v. D. Tadić*, IT-94-I, 2 October 1995, para. 72.

111 Operation Deny Flight, 12 April 1993–21 December 1995, Subsequent additions to the operation included Close Air Support to UN peacekeepers and air strikes in support of UN

Accord and the cessation of hostilities, the Alliance deployed military personnel in Bosnia-Herzegovina to conduct peacekeeping operations named subsequently IFOR[112] and SFOR.[113]

The ICTY established that an international armed conflict existed in Bosnia-Herzegovina from 1991 until 1995. NATO's operations from 1992 until 1995 were aimed at contributing to a peace settlement by enforcing the UN mandated embargo, no-fly zone and close air support. In doing so, NATO has used armed force, demonstrating belligerent intent against the Federal Republic of Yugoslavia as well as the Republic of Croatia. It is concluded that the Alliance has been a party to an international armed conflict from 1992 until 1995. After the conclusion of the Dayton Peace Agreement on 14 December 1995, the hostilities ceased and – in spite of the belief of the international community that violence would flare up again – no armed conflict re-emerged in Bosnia-Herzegovina. In the absence of hostilities, NATO did not continue as a party to any armed conflict during its operations IFOR and SFOR.[114]

NATO also deployed military personnel in Kosovo. From 1998, the Federal Republic of Yugoslavia (Serbia and Montenegro) violently opposed an ethnic Albanian minority. This minority formed the Kosovo Liberation Army (KLA)

---

resolutions. On 28 February 1994 NATO engaged in the first combat operations in its history when NATO aircraft shot down four Bosnian Serb fighter-bombers conducting a bombing mission in violation of the No-Fly Zone. Operations Deadeye and Deliberate Force, 30–31 August 1995 & 5–14 September 1995, after a mortar attack caused heavy loss of life at a marketplace in Sarajevo, UN peacekeepers requested NATO airstrikes, which began on 30 August against Bosnian Serb air defences (Operation Deadeye). When a bombing pause failed to result in Bosnian Serb compliance with the UN's demands to withdraw, Operation Deliberate Force targeted Bosnian Serb command & control installations and ammunition facilities. These airstrikes were a key factor in bringing the Serbs to the negotiating table and ending the war in Bosnia.

112 Operation Joint Endeavour (Implementation Force, IFOR), 20 December 1995–20 December 1996, NATO's first peacekeeping operation – IFOR – which had the mission of implementing the military aspects of the peace agreement for Bosnia (separation of warring factions and creating safe and secure conditions for the other tasks associated with the peace agreement). Approximately 60,000 troops from the 16 NATO members and 17 non-nato countries including Russia participated in IFOR initially.

113 Operation Joint Guard (Stabilisation Force, SFOR), 20 December 1996–20 June 1998. Following the end of Operation Joint Endeavour and the completion of the initial military tasks for implementing the peace agreement, NATO continued leading the international peacekeeping operation in Bosnia with a new focus and a smaller force now bearing the name SFOR instead IFOR.

114 Zwanenburg, M.C. (2005) *Accountability of peace support operations*, Netherlands: Martinus Nijhoff Publishers, p. 193.

with the aim to separate from the Federal Republic of Yugoslavia. After attempts to reach a peace accord failed, NATO conducted an air campaign under the name "Operation Allied Force" against positions of the armed forces of the Federal Republic of Yugoslavia (Serbia and Montenegro).[115] NATO's intervention was conducted without authorization by the UN Security Council. Operation Allied Force was not part of a peacekeeping mission like IFOR and SFOR. Rather, NATO was directly engaged in an international armed conflict against the Federal Republic of Yugoslavia.

A peace settlement followed and NATO initiated Kosovo Force (KFOR) to implement the agreement.[116] The operation is still ongoing in 2016. It is clear that NATO was in an international armed conflict with the Federal Republic of Yugoslavia (Serbia and Montenegro) during the period of Operation Allied Force. It has expressed belligerent intent by its bombing campaign on military objectives of the Federal Republic of Yugoslavia. After the peace settlement, the international armed conflict ended. While an armed conflict in Kosovo did not re-emerge, one could state that KFOR acted as an occupying force and that the customary norms of IHL pertaining to international armed conflict were applicable.[117]

---

115 Operation Allied Force, 24 March – 20 June 1999, NATO's air campaign against the Former Republic of Yugoslavia (FRY: Serbia & Montenegro) and its forces deployed in Kosovo. During this operation NATO used a wide range of aircraft and naval weapons against the FRY including submarine-launched cruise missiles, fighters, fighter bombers, air defence aircraft and AWACS. NATO also assembled a ground force in the Former Yugoslav Republic of Macedonia (FYROM) led by the ACE Rapid Reaction Corps (ARRC) headquarters. This force served as a confidence- building measure for the FYROM authorities and eventually became the Kosovo Force (KFOR).

116 Operation Joint Guardian, 12 June 1999 – Present (KFOR) The NATO-led KFOR (Kosovo Force) deployed into Kosovo to implement the peace settlement, which included the Military Technical Agreement signed by Serbia and the undertaking by the Kosovo Liberation Army (UCK) to demilitarise and transform itself. KFOR's mission was to establish a military presence, deter renewed hostilities, verify and if necessary enforce the terms of the MTA and UCK undertaking, establish a secure environment for the return of internally displaced persons (IDPs) and refugees and international organisations, provide immediate basic life support to IDPs in Kosovo, provide initial basic civil administration and other non-military functions pending the arrival of international organisations and control the borders of the FRY in Kosovo with Albania and FYROM. On 28 April 2005, the KFOR operation became part of OPLAN 10501 Joint Enterprise for the Entire Balkan Operation Area.

117 Zwanenburg, M.C. (2005) *Accountability of peace support operations*, Netherlands: Martinus Nijhoff Publishers, p. 181.

NATO's Operation ISAF in Afghanistan

The nature of the conflict in Afghanistan has been extensively debated in literature.[118] The conflict is generally viewed as an international armed conflict between a US-led coalition of States and Afghanistan from 1 October 2001 until 5 December 2001, on which date the Bonn Agreement was signed and an interim-government was established in Afghanistan. The US-led Operation Enduring Freedom (OEF) continued, but since the operations were not directed against the newly established Afghan government, the conflict changed into a non-international armed conflict. In parallel, another mission started on 20 December 2001 called the International Security Assistance Force (ISAF) mandated by the UN Security Council to assist the Afghan government to maintain security in the country. In 2003, NATO assumed command of ISAF.

ISAF supported the Afghan government in maintaining the security in areas of Afghanistan.[119] By 2003, the intensity and duration of the conflict between the Afghan government and ISAF on the one hand and the insurgency composed of both Al Qaida and Taliban members on the other, had reached the threshold of a non-international armed conflict.

There are divergent opinions regarding the status of the conflict between NATO and the Taliban. Some States have argued that there is no armed conflict in the region where their forces are operating,[120] or maintained that their activities do not involve the use of force and hence would not become a party to a non-international armed conflict.[121] These views disregard NATO's command relationship constituting effective control over the forces deployed in ISAF. As long as the forces act under the effective control of NATO, the Alliance as an international organisation is a party to the non-international armed conflict with the Taliban insurgency.

In 2014, the ISAF operation was terminated, but NATO continued to remain active in Afghanistan with a small training and mentoring mission under the name "Operation Resolute Support". The non-international armed conflict is

---

118 ICRC, *Conflict in Afghanistan II,* International Review of the Red Cross, Vol. 93, No. 881, March 2011. Y. Arai-Takahashi, *Disentangling legal quagmires: the legal characterisation of the armed conflicts in Afghanistan since 6/7 October 2001 and the question of prisoner of war status,* in, H. Fischer, A. McDonald, Yearbook of International Humanitarian Law, 2002, p. 61.

119 UNSCR 1510(2003), 13 October 2003, para. 1.

120 Boddens Hosang, J.F.R., *Aandachtspunten in de ISAF ROE vanuit het strategisch-juridisch kader,* Militair Rechtelijk Tijdschrift, no. 5, 2009, pp. 219–226. P. Ducheine, E. Pouw, *ISAF Operaties in Afghanistan,* 2010, p. 40.

121 Wilmshurst, E. (ed.), *International Law and the Classification of Conflicts,* 2012, p. 254.

still ongoing, although NATO cannot be considered a party to this conflict any more as it does not participate with armed force.

NATO Operation Unified Protector in Libya

During the NATO-led operation Unified Protector in Libya, NATO was a party to an international armed conflict with the Libyan government. The implementation of the no-fly zone required the destruction of Libyan air defence systems, such as surface-to-air missile sites and radar installations. In the execution to protect civilians under a threat of attack, NATO destroyed command and control centres, mobile rocket launchers, bunkers and ammunition sites.[122] There are some affirmative views from States considering that NATO is a party to an international armed conflict with Libya. Sweden adopted the position that *"the state or the organisation that exercises the factual control over the operation may become a party to the armed conflict if the operation is involved in hostilities with governmental forces."*[123] Norway adopts a similar position.[124] Intergovernmental organizations, such as the UN Human Rights Commission and non-governmental organisations,[125] such as Amnesty International,[126] also view NATO in this case as a party to the international armed conflict.

NATO has used force against the armed forces of the Libyan government. The use of force against Libyan forces interferes with the Libyan 'sphere of sovereignty' and therefore expresses a belligerent intent. The conditions to determine whether NATO is a party to an international armed conflict are therefore met. This also means that NATO is bound to the international obligations contained in customary IHL.

6.5.2 *International Obligations under Customary IHRL*

International Human Rights Law (IHRL) is the body of law designed to promote and protect human rights of individuals. IHRL formulates obligations for States in their conduct towards individuals under their jurisdiction. IHRL does not only oblige States to refrain from certain conduct, but also to actively

122 Press Briefing by the NATO Spokesperson and Brigadier General Mark van Uhm, Chief of Allied Operations, Allied Command Operations (SHAPE), 19 April 2011, www.nato.int.

123 Engdahl, O., *Multinational Peace Operations Forces,* in K.M. Larsen, C.G. Guldahl Cooper, G. Nystuen (eds.), Searching for a 'Principle of Humanity' in International Law, 2013, p. 257.

124 Engdahl, O., *Multinational Peace Operations Forces,* in K.M. Larsen, C.G. Guldahl Cooper, G. Nystuen (eds.), Searching for a 'Principle of Humanity' in International Law, 2013, p. 258.

125 UN Human Rights Council, *Report of the International Commission of Inquiry on Libya,* A/HRC/19/68, 2 March 2012.

126 Amnesty International, *The Forgotten Victims of NATO Strikes,* March 2012, p. 18.

prevent and suppress violations of international human rights, in particular international crimes. The ICCPR, Universal Declaration of Human Rights (UDHR), ECHR and others, include basic human rights, such as the right of self-determination[127] and the right to life,[128] the prohibition of torture,[129] discrimination,[130] arbitrary arrest[131] and slavery.[132] Several international conventions in particular impose obligations to prevent and suppress international crimes, which are referred to as 'positive human rights obligations'.

While these norms can undoubtedly be seen as having customary status, a comprehensive list describing the exact content of customary norms of IHRL – similar to the study done by the ICRC in relation to the customary status of IHL – is not (yet) available for IHRL. NATO is bound by customary IHRL, including positive human rights obligations, i.e. the obligation to actively prevent and suppress human rights violations, in so far as these are part of international customary law and as far as NATO is able to execute these obligations.

This paragraph examines whether customary IHRL is applicable to NATO during its operations. The first question to be answered in this regard is – similar to the question in relation to the norms of IHL – whether NATO can be an addressee of IHRL norms. Human rights norms require an entity that is capable to exercise jurisdiction. States obviously have the power to exercise jurisdiction, as an inherent part of their sovereignty. Paragraph (a) will examine whether international organisations may also be able to exercise jurisdiction, even in absence of being sovereign.

The second question regards the applicability of customary international human rights law during military operations, in particular NATO operations. While IHRL applies during peacetime as well as armed conflict, some of these norms may collide with norms of IHL. In these cases, it is relevant to examine which set of norms apply during activities that NATO may undertake. NATO conducts both operations involving the use of military force as well as operations that resemble law enforcement activities. Paragraph (b) will address the question whether IHRL applies during NATO operations.

The third and last issue that has to be resolved, is the applicability of customary IHRL and IHL during occupation. Occupation is a special situation in which a wide range of obligations under IHL and IHRL become applicable. Occupation is traditionally not associated with international organisations,

127 Article 1, ICCPR.

128 Article 6 ICCPR, article 2 ECHR, article 3 UDHR.

129 Article 7 ICCPR, article 3 ECHR, article 5 UDHR.

130 Article 2 and 3 ICCPR, article 14 ECHR, article 7 UDHR.

131 Article 9 ICCPR, article 5 ECHR, article 9 UDHR.

132 Article 8 ICCPR, article 4 ECHR, article 4 UDHR.

rather with States occupying another State's territory. However, recent practice of military operations conducted by international organisations, including NATO, shows that international organisations are capable of becoming an occupying force and, hence, are bound by norms of IHL and IHRL. Paragraph (c) will therefore examine the applicability of IHRL to NATO during occupation.

a The Element of Jurisdiction as a Condition for Applicability of Customary IHRL

All major IHRL conventions contain a clause that make their applicability conditional to the exercise of jurisdiction. For instance, Article 1 of the European Convention on Human Rights and Fundamental Freedoms (ECHR) states that *"The High Contracting Parties shall secure to everyone within their jurisdiction the rights and freedoms defined in Section I of this Convention".* Article 1 of the American Convention on Human Rights (ACHR) similarly notes that the Parties *"undertake to respect the rights and freedoms recognised herein and to ensure to all persons subject to their jurisdiction the free and full exercise of those rights and freedoms".*[133]

The term 'jurisdiction' is not defined in conventional human rights law, but the ICJ,[134] ECtHR and the UN Human Rights Committee[135] have made attempts to come to a definition. The ECtHR has provided by far the most jurisprudence on the subject. There are two strands of interpretation of the word 'jurisdiction'. The first strand is the so-called "spatial model of jurisdiction".[136] The spatial model interprets jurisdiction as a situation when one State exercises effective control over an area of another State. An example in this regard is the occupation of Northern Cyprus by Turkey.[137] The second model is the "personal model of jurisdiction". This model construes the existence of jurisdiction when one State exercises authority and control over an individual residing in

---

133 American Convention on Human Rights, 22 November 1969.

134 ICJ, Advisory Opinion, *Legal Consequences of the Construction of a Wall in the Occupied Palestinian Territory,* 9 July 2004, p. 181. ICJ, Judgment, *Democratic Republic of the Congo v. Uganda, Case Concerning Armed Activities on the Territories of the Congo,* 19 December 2005, p. 80.

135 ICJ, Advisory Opinion, *Legal Consequences of the Construction of a Wall in the Occupied Palestinian Territory,* 9 July 2004.

136 Milanovic, M., *Al-Skeini and Al-Jedda in Strasbourg,* 23 European Journal of International Law, No. 1, 2012, p. 122.

137 ECtHR, Grand Chamber, Judgment, *Loizidou v. Turkey,* Application no. 15318/89, 18 December 1996. ECtHR, Grand Chamber, Judgment, *Cyprus v. Turkey,* Application no. 25781/94, 10 May 2001, ECtHR, Grand Chamber, Judgment, *Ilascu et al. v. Moldova and Russia,* Application no. 48787/99, 8 July 2004.

another State. An example is a case were German State agents lured a German national residing in France to Germany.[138]

The exercise of jurisdiction is not a prerogative of States alone. International organisations can equally exercise jurisdiction, even though they do not possess a territory or have their own 'nationals'. For instance, NATO has exercised effective control over the territory of Kosovo during KFOR – albeit as part of the interim-administration of the UN under UNMiK.[139] Similarly, NATO has exercised jurisdiction over individuals by detaining persons during ISAF in Afghanistan and by targeting individuals during Operation Unified Protector in Libya.

The ECtHR abandoned the strict adherence to the application of the ECHR to the *espace juridique* of the State Parties[140] and leaned towards the "State agent authority model", but limited that model to situations in which the State exercises public powers.[141] This model was presented in a case concerning six individuals killed by British armed forces in Basra, Iraq. One Iraqi citizen was shot during a British patrol, another three were killed during a house search. A further two Iraqi individuals died during detention by British armed forces.

The Court confirmed the spatial model by maintaining that a State can exercise jurisdiction outside its national territory, if it exercises effective control over that territory.[142] The Court confirmed the personal model by affirming the possibility for a State to exercise jurisdiction if it has physical authority and control over the person in question.[143] The Court added, however, an extra condition to the personal model: the physical authority and control need to be part of *public powers* normally exercised by a State, thereby introducing some

138 ECtHR, *Stocke v. Germany,* Application no. 28/1989/188/248, 12 October 1989, Ser. A, Vol 199, 24, para. 166.

139 In *Bankovic* the ECtHR concluded that NATO did not exercise jurisdiction over Kosovo during Operation Allied Force, ECtHR, Decision of the Grand Chamber on admissibility, *Vlastimir and Borka Bankovic and others v. Belgium, the Czech Republic, Denmark, France, Germany, Greece, Hungary, Iceland, Italy, Luxembourg, the Netherlands, Norway, Poland, Portugal, Spain, Turkey and the United Kingdom,* 52207/99, 12 December 2001, para. 82.

140 ECtHR, Judgment, Grand Chamber, *Al-Skeini et al v UK*, Application no. 55721/07, 7 July 2011, para. 142.

141 ECtHR, Judgment, Grand Chamber, *Al-Skeini et al v UK*, Application no. 55721/07, 7 July 2011, para. 149–150.

142 ECtHR, Judgment, Grand Chamber, *Al-Skeini et al. v UK*, Application no. 55721/07, 7 July 2011, para. 138.

143 ECtHR, Judgment, Grand Chamber, *Al-Skeini et al v UK*, Application no. 55721/07, 7 July 2011, para. 136–137.

sort of control over a territory.[144] The house searches and patrols executed by the British armed force considered by the ECtHR were not only part of the exercise of authority and control, but also the exercise of public authority. The activities was an exercise of British jurisdiction, but only because of the occupation of Iraq and relevant UN Security Council resolutions.[145]

International organizations may also exercise jurisdiction based on the personal model, with the limiting principle of the exercise of *public powers* mentioned by the ECtHR in Al-Skeini. There are some instances where NATO personnel have exercised physical power and control over an individual, as part of a public function. For example, during KFOR, NATO has detained individuals as part of its public functions under the UNMiK interim-administration in Kosovo. Arguably, NATO exercised public functions – with the consent of the Afghan government – in Afghanistan.[146] The High Court of England and Wales held that NATO exercised jurisdiction in Afghanistan, but the Court did not put much emphasis on the "public powers" condition as mentioned by the ECtHR in Al-Skeini.[147] It is held here that NATO did exercise public powers in Afghanistan – on behalf and upon the request of the Afghan government – and has exercised physical power and control over e.g. individuals detained during its operations. As illustrated in Chapter 2, ISAF has detained – for a short period – individuals that posed a threat to the mission and transferred those to the Afghan government. Customary IHRL is, on the basis of the abovementioned circumstances, applicable to the detention and transfer of these individuals.

It is hard to maintain that NATO exercised physical control over individuals in Libya as part of public powers normally to be exercised by a State.[148] Indeed, NATO has exercised physical control by targeting individuals during an extensive air campaign, but it did not do so as part of exercising public powers in Libya. Similarly, Operation Allied Force in the Federal Republic of Yugoslavia (Serbia and Montenegro), NATO did not exercise jurisdiction. As pointed out above, in *Bankovic*, the ECtHR held that the control over the airspace could not be considered territorial control and hence NATO did not

144 ECtHR, Judgment, Grand Chamber, *Al-Skeini et al v UK*, Application no. 55721/07, 7 July 2011, para. 137.

145 Milanovic, M., *Foreign Surveillance and Human Rights, Part 3: Models of Extraterritorial Application*, EJIL: Talk, 27 November 2013.

146 Annex I to the Agreement on Provisional Arrangements in Afghanistan Pending the Re-establishment of Permanent Government Institutions, 5 December 2001.

147 High Court of England and Wales, *Serdar Mohammed v. Ministry of Defence*, 2014, EWHC 1369, OB.

148 ECtHR, Judgment, *Al-Skeini and others v. United Kingdom*, Application no. 55721/07, 7 July 2011, paras. 149–150.

have jurisdiction. If the criteria in *Al-Skeini* are applied, the same conclusion is reached, but the argument is slightly different. The actions of NATO, although constituting physical control over individuals during its air campaign, was not an exercise of public powers and therefore the individuals did not fall within its jurisdiction.

b The Scope of Obligations of IHRL during NATO-led Operations

NATO operations frequently take place during situations of armed conflict. In these situations, the norms of IHL predominantly regulate the conduct of hostilities. The norms of IHRL do not cease to apply during armed conflict, although some of its provisions may be derogated from in time of emergency.[149] Being both applicable and regulating often the same topic, the relationship between both sets of norms is fairly complex. It is relevant to the topic of this book to examine this relationship, as it affects the extent of obligations to NATO applicable during armed conflict.

It has been argued that in case of contradictory norms of IHL and IHRL, the issue should be resolved by reference to the principles of *lex specialis derogat legi generalis.* Often IHL has been seen as the *lex specialis* as it regulates a specific situation: that of armed conflict.[150]

The prevailing view currently is that both norms can apply in a given situation at the same time and can complement and reinforce each other. They complement each other especially during non-international armed conflicts, in which IHL does not regulate the conduct during these conflicts in such a detailed manner as it does in international armed conflicts. IHRL norms will thus take a more prominent role to fill in the gaps left open by IHL. Illustrative in this regard is the treatment of internees during non-international armed conflict. IHL is fairly silent on the conditions of internment during non-international armed conflicts, so that IHRL can provide additional guidance where possible.

The norms can also reinforce each other, mainly where both instruments seek to protect persons from abusive behaviour by those in whose power they are.[151] For example, both IHL and IHRL prohibit torture, which, as mentioned above, is a *jus cogens* norm. There is no definition of torture other than provided

149 ICJ, Advisory Opinion, *Legality of the Threat or Use of Nuclear Weapons,* ICJ Report 1996, 8 July 1996, para. 25.

150 ICJ, Advisory Opinion, *Legality of the Threat or Use of Nuclear Weapons,* ICJ Report 1996, 8 July 1996, para. 25.

151 Droege, C., *Humanitarian Law and International Human Rights Law in Situations of Armed Conflict,* Israeli Law Review, Vol. 40, No.2, pp. 337, 2007.

for in the Convention Against Torture and Other Cruel, Inhuman or Degrading Treatment or Punishment.[152] This definition can be used in interpreting the norms of IHL.[153] IHL also expands the prohibition of torture, so that it does not only apply to "public officials or other person acting in an official capacity"[154] but also to any party to the conflict including armed opposition groups.

There are few instances where the norms of IHL and IHRL collide. Obviously, the right to life enshrined in Article 2 ECHR, Article 4(1) ACHR, Article 6 ICCPR and Article 4 ACHPR will conflict with the right to use lethal force under IHL. In the event that a IHRL norm is in conflict with an IHL norm, the norm that regulates the matter more specifically (*lex specialis*) supersedes the more general norm, (*lex generalis*). As IHL regulates a specific situation to use lethal force in a situation of armed conflict, it is seen as the *lex specialis* to IHRL, which applies generically and at all times. But, the rule that IHL functions as *lex specialis* to human rights law in times of armed conflict is not absolute.[155] The relationship varies from case to case. Kleffner, Sassoli and Melzer argue that human rights law may, in certain cases, contain more specific standards in times of armed conflict, *"notably the case in situations that, while occurring during an armed conflict, closely resemble those for which human rights standards have been developed. Examples include the use of force in relatively calm situations of occupation for the purpose of maintaining public order and safety or in areas under the firm control of State authorities in times of non-international armed conflict."*[156]

For instance, if military forces are confronted with looting of individuals that do not pose a direct threat to the mission, the paradigm of law enforcement – which is governed by primarily IHRL – is applicable. This means that lethal force is only permissible in very exceptional circumstances, aimed at preventing an unlawful attack, necessary for the achievement of this purpose and minimizing to the greatest extent possible the recourse to lethal force. These prerequisites are based on primarily human rights norms.

Instead, if the military units use force to adversely affect the military operations or military capacity of the enemy, the paradigm of conduct of

152 Convention Against Torture and Other Cruel, Inhuman or Degrading Treatment or Punishment, 26 June 1987.

153 Article 31, Vienna Convention on the Law of Treaties, 23 May 1969.

154 Article 10, Convention Against Torture and Other Cruel, Inhuman or Degrading Treatment or Punishment, 26 June 1987.

155 Kleffner, J.K., *Human Rights and International Humanitarian Law,* in Gill, T., Fleck, D. (eds.), The Handbook of the International Law of Military Operations, 2010, p. 74.

156 Kleffner, J.K., *Human Rights and International Humanitarian Law,* in Gill, T., Fleck, D. (eds.), The Handbook of the International Law of Military Operations, 2010, p. 74.

hostilities – which is governed primarily by IHL – is applicable.[157] Lethal force is permissible when it is directed against a lawful object of attack, planned to avoid or minimize incidental civilian harm and not expected to cause civilian harm that would be excessive in relation to the concrete and direct military advantage anticipated. These conditions are derived from IHL.

There are at least two examples of NATO conducting law enforcement tasks during its operations. The first example are the counter-narcotics efforts in Afghanistan. Upon request of the Afghan government, the NAC agreed in October 2008 to act – in concert with the Afghan authorities – against drug facilities and facilitators.[158] Drug traffickers that were linked to the insurgency would be considered legitimate military targets, while others would be regarded as criminals and treated in accordance with the law enforcement paradigm.[159] If there was a nexus between the narcotics producer and the insurgency, the individuals and the facilities could be attacked as a military objective on the basis of IHL. If no nexus existed, the paradigm of law enforcement applies.[160]

The second example is the law enforcement task by KFOR forces. KFOR has been engaged in the restoration and maintenance of public safety and order and the supervision of demining activities.[161] In this regard it was often not engaged directly in the conduct of hostilities, rather with law enforcement activities. Therefore, the norms of IHRL apply, rather than the rules of IHL.

c IHL and IHRL Rules Applicable during Occupation

The previous two paragraphs examined the applicability of IHL and IHRL during armed conflict. This paragraph examines the applicability of the rules of IHL and IHRL during occupation. An occupation exists when a territory is actually placed under the authority of a hostile army.[162] For the application of the law of occupation it is irrelevant whether an occupation has received

157 Kleffner, J.K., *Human Rights and International Humanitarian Law,* in Gill, T., Fleck, D. (eds.), The Handbook of the International Law of Military Operations, 2010, pp. 40–41.

158 NATO Secretary General, Press Conference, Budapest, Hungary, (10 October 2008), cited in NATO Press Release, NATO Steps up Counter-narcotics Efforts in Afghanistan (10 October 2008).

159 Koelbl, S., *"NATO High Commander Issues Illegitimate Order to KIll"*, Der Spiegel Online, 28 January 2009.

160 Schmitt, M.N., *Targeting Narcoinsurgents in Afghanistan: The Limits of International Humanitarian Law,* Yearbook of International Humanitarian Law, Vol. 12, 2009, p. 304.

161 UN Security Council resolution 1244(1999), 10 June 1999, para. 9.

162 Article 42 Convention (IV) Respecting the Laws and Customs of War on Land and its Annex; Regulations concerning the Laws and Customs of War on Land, The Hague, 18 October 1907 (Hague Regulations), *"Territory is considered occupied when it is actually placed*

Security Council approval, what its aim is or whether it is called an 'invasion', 'liberation', 'administration', or 'occupation'.[163] Article 42 of the 1907 Hague Regulations define an occupation as a territory that is *"actually placed under the authority of the hostile army"*.[164]

Occupation brings along a plethora of obligations to the occupying party. The occupant is obliged to take all measures in its power to restore and ensure, as far as possible, public order and civil life.[165] Occupation also triggers the application of the Geneva Conventions of 1949,[166] which impose further obligations on the occupant, primarily embodied in the Fourth Geneva Convention Relative to the Protection of Civilian Persons in Time of War and Protocols I and II additional to the 1949 Geneva Conventions. Furthermore, during occupation certain parts of IHRL are also applicable.

The question whether international organisations can occupy a territory is answered in the positive by several authors dealing with peace support missions.[167] It is hard to equate a UN mandated military presence as an "authority of the hostile army". The term occupation therefore may be inappropriate for these operations. Examples of UN missions exercising functions and powers over a territory that could be compared to those assigned to an occupant are the missions in Cyprus, Cambodia, Eastern Slavonia, East Timor, Kosovo and the Congo in the 1960s.[168] International organisations could occupy territory other than pursuant to a UN Security Council resolution, but examples are scarce; only the EU operation in Mostar, Bosnia and Herzegovina, was based on

---

under the authority of the hostile army. The occupation extends only to the territory where such authority has been established and can be exercised."

163 ICRC, *Occupation and International Humanitarian Law*, https://www.icrc.org/eng/resources/documents/misc/634kfc.htm.

164 Article 42 of the 1907 Hague Regulations.

165 Article 43 of the 1907 Hague Regulations: *"The authority of the legitimate power having in fact passed into the hands of the occupant, the latter shall take all the measures in his power to restore, and ensure, as far as possible, public order and safety, while respecting unless absolute prevented, the laws in force in the country"*.

166 Common article 2 to the 1949 Geneva Conventions: "[…] *The Convention shall also apply to all cases of partial or total occupation of the territory of a High Contracting Party, even if the said occupation meets with no armed resistance."*

167 Zwanenburg, M.C. (2005) *Accountability of peace support operations*, Netherlands: Martinus Nijhoff Publishers; F. Naert, *International Law Aspects of the EU's Security and Defence Policy, with a Particular Focus on the Law of Armed Conflict and Human Rights*, 2010.

168 ICRC Report, Expert Meeting; Occupation and Other Forms of Administration of Foreign Territory, March 2012, p. 33.

a decision or the EU Council and not on a UN mandate.[169] The difference between a traditional occupation and an international administration mandated by the UN Security Council is that the powers of the UN occupational force is limited by the mandate given by the UN Security Council.[170]

Another difference is that occupation by peace support operations might be conducted with the consent of the host State, whereas in traditional occupations the consent is likely to be lacking. One could argue that an occupation with consent of the host State cannot be regarded as a belligerent occupation and that therefore the 1907 Hague Regulations and 1949 Geneva Convention do not apply. This is not to say that every occupation by a UN peace support missions is consensual. For example, in the case of the Democratic Republic of Congo, the consent of Kinshasa did not include the consent by warlords in the Eastern Congo for MONUC. Kosovo was administrated by UNMiK, in which NATO fulfilled the security tasks (KFOR). Although the host nation (the Federal Republic of Yugoslavia) did consent with the occupation, this consent was procured by the use of force during Operation Allied Force and the consent given should be regarded void according to Article 52 of the Vienna Convention of the law of Treaties. Whether or not an occupation is belligerent or consensual is relevant for the question of *jus ad bellum* rather than *jus in bello*. In other words, applicability of IHL and IHRL rules does not depend on the legitimacy of the occupation, but on the fact that there *is* an occupation.

Practice reveals that NATO considers the rules of IHL and IHRL applicable during occupation, at least in principle. KFOR policy documents refer to Articles 42 and 78 of the 1949 Fourth Geneva Convention relating to the powers of an occupant.[171] Similarly, NATO avoided language that could result in the perception that it was an occupying force in Bosnia-Herzegovina. Nevertheless, the detention policies of IFOR and SFOR contains language equivalent to that of the Fourth 1949 Geneva Convention regulating the detainment of persons in occupied territory.[172]

---

169 EU Bulletin, 1994/6, at 84, cited by S.R. Ratner, *Foreign Occupation and International Territorial Administration; The Challenges of Convergence,* The European Journal of International Law, Vol. 16, no. 4, 2005, p. 698.

170 Wolfrum, R., *International Administration in Post-Conflict Situations by the United Nations and Other International Actors,* Max Planck Yearbook of United Nations Law, Vol. 9, 2005, pp. 649–696.

171 COMKFOR Directive 42, 9 October 2001. A.S. Deeks, *"Administrative Detention in Armed Conflict"* Case Western Reserve Journal of International Law, Vol. 40, p. 417 and following.

172 Zwanenburg, M.C. (2005) *Accountability of peace support operations,* Netherlands: Martinus Nijhoff Publishers, p. 191.

6.6 Internal and External Rules of NATO

The 1986 Vienna Convention on the Law of Treaties between States and International Organizations or between International Organizations defines 'internal rules of the organisation' as *"the constituent instruments, decisions and resolutions adopted in accordance with them, and established practice of the organization."*[173]

Decisions of an international organisation can create rights and obligations for the organisation, to the extent that the act can be regarded as an obligation under international law. In other words, the internal rules of the organisation may have external effect so to become binding international obligations for the organisation. Purely administrative measures do not have any external effect. The most important internal rules with external effect are rules adopted for their own operational activities.[174]

In order for decisions to have external effect, they have to be formulated in such a manner that the intention to bind the organisation is sufficiently clear.[175] For instance, NATO Standard Operating Procedures, which state that the detention of individuals during NATO operations will be conducted in accordance with the *principles* of international humanitarian law, do not create international obligations for the Alliance. From the text itself, it is not sufficiently clear whether the Alliance's intent is to be bound to IHL norms.

Another factor that precludes the binding nature of internal rules of NATO is the classification of decisions. Most NATO rules relating to operational matters are classified and as such they are not publicly available. This does not mean that classified rules cannot bind the Alliance, rather these breaches of rules will likely not become under much scrutiny, as the content of these rules is not publicly known. If classified rules become publicly available – e.g. the temporary restrictions on detention in ISAF as illustrated in Chapter 2 of this

---

173 Doc. A/CONF.129/15, Vienna Convention on the Law of Treaties between States and International Organizations or between International Organizations, 21 March 1986, art. 2(1)(j), not yet in force. With regard to the Draft Articles on Responsibility of International Organizations the International Law Commission adopted a similar definition: *"the constituent instruments, decisions, resolutions and other acts of the organization adopted in accordance with those instruments, and established practice of the organization"*, Report of the International Law Commission on the work of its sixty-third session, 26 April – 3 June and 4 July – 12 August 2011 (A/66/10), at 54, para. 87, article 2.

174 Schermers, H.G. and Blokker, N.M. (2001) *International institutional law: Unity within diversity*, The Netherlands: Brill, para. 1208.

175 Schermers, H.G. and Blokker, N.M. (2001) *International institutional law: Unity within diversity*, The Netherlands: Brill, para. 758.

research – breaches of these rules may be subject to inquiry. The incident of the attack on the fuel trucks in Kunduz mentioned in Chapter 2 is illustrative in this regard. While the attack may or may not have been a breach of (customary) IHL, it certainly constituted a breach of certain operational directives or ROE, precluding NATO forces to attack militant forces when not under direct threat. Because the ROE and operational directives are classified they are considered purely internal documents without external effect.

6.7 Conclusions

Chapter 5 examined the international legal personality of NATO. International legal personality is relevant to the question of international responsibility, because without it, an international organization cannot carry international obligations. Chapter 5 concluded that NATO possesses international legal personality. NATO therefore can bear international rights and obligations. The current chapter examined to which international obligations NATO is exactly bound. The chapter concentrated on four potential sources of international obligations: NATO's constitutional documents (paragraph 6.2), the UN Charter and UN Security Council resolutions (paragraph 6.3), conventional and customary international law relevant to NATO-led military operations (paragraphs 6.4 and 6.5) and the internal and external rules of NATO (paragraph 6.6).

The North Atlantic Treaty imposes the obligation upon the Organization to act in accordance with the UN Charter. It is important to note that, in this respect, a violation of the UN Charter is a breach of NATO's constitutional document rather than a direct breach of the UN Charter. Whether the UN Charter and the decisions of the UN Security Council create direct international obligations, has been examined separately in paragraph 6.3. In one occasion, NATO has violated the provisions of the North Atlantic Treaty by intervening with armed force in Kosovo during Operation Allied Force, without a UN Security Council's mandate. The member States acknowledged that the operation constituted a breach of Article 2(4) of the UN Charter and therefore it had breached Article 1 of the North Atlantic Treaty.[176] The violation gave rise to claims submitted by the Federal Republic of Yugoslavia against several member States of

176 The *Deutscher Bundestag, Plenarprotokoll* 13/248/, 16 October 1998, at 23129, "*The decision of NATO* [on air strikes against the FRY] *must not become a precedent. As far as the Security Council monopoly on force* [Gewaltmonopol] *is concerned, we must avoid getting on a slippery slope*", quoted by Simma, B. (1999) '*NATO, the UN and the use of force: Legal aspects*', European Journal of International Law, 10(1), pp. 1–22. doi: 10.1093/ejil/10.1.1, p. 13.

the Alliance, but not directly against NATO itself.[177] It is submitted here that NATO can be held responsible for the violation of the Treaty, as the operation was a breach of the North Atlantic Treaty.

Other important documents, such as the NATO SOFA, Paris Protocol and Ottawa Agreement, contain very few international obligations for NATO. There is one obligation that is of relevance to the Alliance, which is the obligation to waive immunity of NATO personnel, if immunity would impede the course of justice without prejudice to the interests of the Alliance. This obligation, contained in Article XXII of the Ottawa Agreement, relates solely to international civilian staff working at international civilian headquarters such as NATO Headquarters in Brussels.

Since NATO is not a party to the UN Charter, the Alliance cannot be bound to its provisions. Nevertheless, the UN Charter plays a central role in the activities that NATO pursues. Its very creation relied upon a provision of the Charter, i.e. the right to take collective defensive action against an armed attack. The Washington Treaty makes ample reference to the UN Charter, which shows the commitment of the founding members to ensure that the UN Charter is adhered to when undertaking activities through the Alliance. Since all member States of NATO are also party to the UN Charter and, therefore, bound to its provisions and to the UN Security Council resolutions, NATO is *indirectly* bound to the UN Charter and to the UN Security Council resolutions. The Alliance needs to take due account of the terms and objectives of the UN Charter and resolutions of the Security Council, but it is not directly bound to them.

In similar fashion, NATO is not bound to conventional international human rights law or international humanitarian law, because it is not a party to these bodies of law. In theory, it would be possible for the Alliance to become, for instance, a party to the European Convention on Human Rights and Fundamental Freedoms if the required amendments to the convention would be made. However, NATO has not expressed (yet) any intention to accede to treaties relating to international humanitarian law or international human rights law.

NATO has entered into international agreements with States. The majority of these agreements regard the status of military forces. Mission SOFAs create few international obligations for NATO. One particular recurring theme is the respect of host nation law by NATO forces. Similar to obligations contained in NATO's constituent document relating to the UN Charter, the host nation laws are not directly binding to NATO, rather indirectly through the provisions of the mission SOFA.

177 International Court of Justice, Legality of Use of Force (Serbia and Montenegro v. Belgium, Canada, France, Germany, Italy, Netherlands, Portugal, Spain, United Kingdom and Yugoslavia v. United States of America), (1999), ICJ Reports 1999, 916.

Another international instrument commonly used between NATO and other international entities are Memoranda of Understanding (MOU). MOU can cover a range of topics including the gathering of intelligence, diplomatic assurances relating to the transfer of detainees, as well as financial regulations and host nation support arrangements. It is concluded that MOUs are politically binding documents and do not impose legally binding obligations. Therefore, MOUs are not a relevant source of binding international obligations to the Alliance.

In conclusion, the sources of international conventional law – including the constituent documents of NATO – are of relative minor relevance as a source of binding international obligations to NATO. The Alliance only bears the indirect international obligations to adhere to the UN Charter and UN Security Council, because of the circumstance that all of its member States are bound to them. With regard to the constituent treaty, Paris Protocol, Ottawa Agreement, mission SOFA and other agreements, contain barely any significant international obligations for the Alliance.

The situation is different with respect to international customary law. International customary law is an important source of international obligations for NATO. Customary international humanitarian law (IHL) and human rights law (IHRL) are of particular relevance to the international responsibility of NATO during its operations.

This chapter concluded that even though customary IHL and IHRL norm are directed to States and not to international organisations as such, there is no reason why international organisations could not be bound to these norms. International organisations can become a party to an international or non-international armed conflict and hence are obliged to abide by the norms of customary international humanitarian law. NATO has become a party to an international armed conflict in the former Yugoslavia against Serbia and in Libya against the Libyan government. The Alliance has been part to a non-international armed conflict in Afghanistan against the Taliban-led insurgency. As such, NATO is bound to customary IHL in these conflicts. For instance, the Alliance is obliged to protect the civilian population and civilian objects and to refrain from an attack which may cause incidental loss of civilian life, injury to civilians or damage to civilian objects or a combination thereof, which would be excessive in relation to the concrete and direct military advantage anticipated.[178] If NATO could have expected that the attack, as described in

178 Article 51(4), 52 and 57, *Protocol Additional to the Geneva Conventions of 12 August 1949, and relating to the Protection of Victims of International Armed Conflicts*, 1977, 1125 UNTS 3, 8 June 1977. Protocol I is applicable to international armed conflicts, but the customary norms are equally applicable to non-international armed conflicts. Henckaerts, J.-M.

Chapter 2 regarding the Kunduz airstrike, would result in excessive loss of civilian life, the Alliance would have violated the provisions of international customary IHL. Similarly, NATO allegedly breached the international obligations for failing to take precautionary measures to spare the civilian population, civilians and civilian objects in the course of the air strikes in Libya.[179]

Customary IHRL is another source of binding international obligation(s) on NATO. IHRL is only applicable when an international organisation exercises jurisdiction. From the outset it may look impossible for an international organisation to be able to exercise jurisdiction, as this is a feature particularly pertinent to States. Notwithstanding the lack of sovereignty, NATO is able to exercise jurisdiction over individuals or over a territory. One example are the activities conducted during KFOR operations as part of the public function under the UNMiK interim administration of Kosovo. Similarly, NATO exercised jurisdiction in Afghanistan in support of the Afghan government, when it detained insurgents for a limited period of time. During these activities, the norms of customary IHRL are applicable to the Alliance.

The last source of international obligations for NATO that has been examined in this chapter are the internal rules of NATO. The Alliance takes decisions and drafts rules for its own operational activities. The binding nature of these decisions and rules depend whether NATO has the intent to bind itself. Most decisions, policy and rules, by their formulation, are not binding. Others are purely internal without any external effect. The most problematic feature that inhibits enforcement of rules of the organisation is the fact that most of them are classified. Therefore, the internal rules of the organisation do not present any significant source of international obligations binding the Alliance.

---

and Doswald-Beck, L. (2005) *Customary international humanitarian law: v. 1: Rules*. United Kingdom: Cambridge University Press.

179 Article 57, *Protocol Additional to the Geneva Conventions of 12 August 1949, and relating to the Protection of Victims of International Armed Conflicts*, 1977, 1125 UNTS 3, 8 June 1977.

CHAPTER 7

Attribution of Wrongful Acts to NATO

7.1 Introduction

Responsibility arises when a breach of an international obligation is attributed to the organisation. The previous two chapters examined the international legal personality of NATO and the international obligations binding on the Alliance. This chapter examines the conditions under which an act constituting a breach of an international obligation committed by an individual participating in a NATO operation will be attributable to the organisation.

International organisations are legal entities that act in the physical world through individuals. Individuals carry out the actions of the organisation. Attribution is the link between the act of the individual to the organisation.

Two institutions have been particularly involved in describing the rules of attribution in international law. In 2004, the International Law Association (ILA)[1] prepared a study on the responsibility of international organisations and in 2011, the International Law Commission (ILC)[2] codified the practice of States and international organisations and existent jurisprudence[3] and formulated rules on the responsibility of international organisation, in particular on the attribution of wrongful conduct of agents and organs to the organisation.

This chapter will rely primarily on the codification efforts of the ILC for the reasons mentioned in the introductory chapter of this book. The ILC has a

1 International Law Association, Berlin Conference (2004) *Accountability of International Organisations*, Final Report of the Committee established by the International Law Associations, 2004.

2 International Law Commission, *Draft Articles on the Responsibility of International Organizations*, 2011.

3 International Court of Justice, *Reparations for Injuries suffered in the Service of the United Nations*, (1949), ICJ Reports 1949, 174. European Court of Human Rights, *A. Behrami against France*, application no. 71412/01 and *R. Saramati against France, Germany and Norway*, application no. 78166/01, Decision of 2 May 2007. UK, Opinions of the Lords of Appeal, *R (on the application of Al-Jedda) v Secretary of State for Defence*, 12 December 2007, UKHL 58. European Court of Human Rights, *Vlastimir and Borka Bankovic and others v. Belgium, the Czech Republic, Denmark, France, Germany, Greece, Hungary, Iceland, Italy, Luxembourg, the Netherlands, Norway, Poland, Portugal, Spain, Turkey and the United Kingdom*, Applicatino no. 52207/99, 12 December 2001.

 | DOI 10.1163/9789004354647_008

special status as it is directly tasked by the international community to codify and develop international law. When there is little available State practice and jurisprudence, it is important to receive agreement or at least acquiescence from States and international organisations that the rules represent a degree of *opinio juris*. Additionally, domestic and international courts and tribunals frequently refer to the ILC's Articles on the Responsibility of International Organizations, affirming that the ILC's work is an authoritative source.

The ILC differentiates between three categories of individuals through whom an international organisation acts and for which different conditions of attribution apply. The first category are individuals that pertain to an organ of the organisation and has such a status in accordance with the rules of that organisation. The second category consists of officials and other persons or entities, other than organs, who are charged by the organisation with carrying out, or helping to carry out, one of its functions, and thus through whom the organisation acts. These are defined by the ILC as agents of the organisations. The third, and last, category are organs of a State or an organ or agents of an international organisation that are placed at the disposal of another international organisation.

Below, the discussion on the attribution of conduct of NATO personnel will take place following the rules as established by the ILC's Articles on the Responsibility of International Organizations. The analysis will follow the same outline like the ILC's Articles. Paragraph 7.2 will examine the attribution of wrongful acts of agents and organs of NATO, followed by the analysis of attribution of wrongful acts of agents and organs placed at the disposal of NATO in paragraph 7.3. These two paragraphs reflect on the rules established in Articles 6 and 7 respectively in the ILC's Articles. Paragraph 7.4 discusses multiple attribution of wrongful conduct to both the States that participate in NATO-led operations and to NATO itself. Paragraph 7.5 will end this chapter with conclusions.

7.2 Attribution of Wrongful Acts of Agents and Organs of NATO

Wrongful acts of individuals are attributable to an international organisation if there is a link between the individual and the international organisation. The existence of such a link can easily be proven if there is an institutional relationship with the organisation, i.e. the status or position of the individual is formalized by the rules of the organisation. Such an institutional or 'organic' link with the international organisation exists with 'organs of the international organizations'. The ILC defines organs as *"any person or entity which has that status in accordance with the rules of the organization*"[4] and states in Article 6(1) of the ILC Articles that:

> the conduct of an organ or agent of an international organization in the performance of functions of that organ or agent shall be considered an act of that organization under international law, whatever the position the organ or agent holds in respect of the organization.

The link between the international organisation and its organ does not depend solely on what the organisation defines as its organs by its rules. International organisations may not exhaustively define all the entities that have the status of organs. In such instances, the powers of an entity and its relation to other bodies under internal law will be relevant to classify its status.[5] The ICJ noted that the official status of individuals is not relevant. It argued that

> *"any person who, whether a paid official or not, and whether permanently employed or not, has been charged by an organ of the organization with carrying out, or helping to carry out, one of its functions"* are organs of the organisation.[6]

The ILC adopted the same meaning for the term "agents" in its Articles.[7]There are thus two categories of entities with a defined link with the international organisation. One category is defined by its institutional or 'organic' link with the organisation which is established by the rules of the organisation. The other category is defined by its functional link, which means that the functions of the individual determine whether the individual is connected to the organisations. Any wrongful conduct, even *ultra vires* conduct,[8] of either category is

4 Article 2(c), ILC, Articles on the Responsibility of International Organizations (2011).

5 ILC, *Second report on responsibility of international organizations*, A/CN.4/541, 2 April 2004, p. 8.

6 International Court of Justice, *Reparations for Injuries suffered in the Service of the United Nations*, (1949), ICJ Reports 1949, 174, p. 177.

7 Article 2(d), Articles on the Responsibility of International Organizations, "[…] *an official or other person or entity, other than an organ, who is charged by the organization with carrying out, or helping to carry out, one of its functions, and thus through whom the organization acts."*

8 Article 8, ILC Articles on the Responsibility of International Organizations, 2011, *"The conduct of an organ or agent of an international organization shall be considered an act of that organization under international law if the organ or agent acts in an official capacity and within the overall functions of that organization, even if the conduct exceeds the authority of that organ or agent or contravenes instructions".*

automatically attributed to the international organisation in accordance with Article 6 of the ILC's Articles.[9]

NATO has both agents and organs with an institutional link defined in the rules of the organisation, as well as agents and organs with a functionally-defined link.

With respect to "organs", NATO's constituent document creates only one organ, the North Atlantic Council, but allows it to create subsidiary organs as required.[10] As examined in the previous Chapter 4, the NAC created a significant amount of subsidiary organs, including Supreme Headquarters Allied Powers Europe (SHAPE), Allied Joint Force Command Brunssum and -Naples and various other headquarters that are able to command and control, or otherwise support, NATO operations.

A large category of "agents" performing functions of the Alliance is civilian personnel. International civilian personnel are employees of the Alliance and, according to Article 6 of the Articles on the Responsibility of International Organizations, their conduct is automatically attributed to NATO.

There has been some debate on the attribution of conduct of other individuals working for NATO, in particular contractors.[11] NATO employs contractors during military operations for a variety of reasons. Contractors ease the burden on the military forces and can stimulate the local economy. NATO contracts personnel for, e.g. engineering, logistic (air and land) support and management of operational bases. Contractors do not have a direct employment agreement with NATO,[12] but are employees of private enterprises, who have a contractual agreement with NATO.[13]

Contractors are charged by NATO to carry out, or help it to carry out, one or more of its functions, and therefore they are considered agents of NATO. Wrongful conduct is ostensibly automatically attributed to the organisation.[14]

---

9 Tzanakopoulos, A. (2009) *'Attribution of conduct to international organizations in peacekeeping operations'*, EJIL Analysis, 10 March. Available at: http://www.ejiltalk.org/attribution-of-conduct-to-international-organizations-in-peacekeeping-operations/.

10 Art. 9, North Atlantic Treaty 1949, 34 UNTS 243, 24 August 1949.

11 Tzanakopoulos, A. (2009) *'Attribution of conduct to international organizations in peacekeeping operations'*, EJIL Analysis, 10 March. Available at: http://www.ejiltalk.org/attribution-of-conduct-to-international-organizations-in-peacekeeping-operations.

12 E.g. employed as NATO international civilian personnel, Article III(1)(b) Paris Protocol or as locally recruited civilians, article IX(4) NATO SOFA, or as civilian personnel in the employ of an armed force that is placed at the disposal of NATO, Article I(1)(b) NATO SOFA.

13 NATO Legal Deskbook, Second edition, 2010, p. 166.

14 Article 6 ILC Articles on the Responsibility of International Organizations. Tzanakopoulos, A. (2009) *'Attribution of conduct to international organizations in peacekeeping*

Practice shows that NATO acknowledges responsibility for contractors, evident from policy documents, e.g. in relation to the carrying of weapons by contractors.[15]

Besides international civilian employees and contractors, NATO relies heavily on personnel *seconded* to the various headquarters of the Alliance. Approximately 88%[16] of the total amount of personnel in NATO's military structure[17] are seconded to the Alliance. A prime example of a seconded official to NATO is the Supreme Allied Commander Europe (SACEUR), who is traditionally a US four-star general officer. Military personnel remain in the employment of their sending nation but are 'fully seconded' to NATO, i.e. they act in the exclusive interest of the Alliance; they sign a declaration of loyalty to the organisation and are subject to staff instructions. The ILC, in its commentary to the Draft Articles on the Responsibility of International Organizations, states that the rules of attribution under Article 6 apply to 'fully seconded' personnel like they do for other agents and organs of the organization. The ILC makes a sharp distinction between State organs and agents which are 'fully seconded' to the international organization, on the one hand, and State organs which to a certain extent still act in a national capacity during their secondment, such as national military contingents, on the other hand.[18]

It is unclear on which basis the ILC makes this distinction. NATO Member States always retain a significant degree of control, including that of criminal and disciplinary jurisdiction over both seconded military personnel placed within NATO (military) headquarters and military contingents provided for missions placed at NATO's disposal. In the absence of a precise distinction between fully seconded personnel and personnel placed at the disposal of NATO during its operations, the attribution of their conduct must be assessed by the degree of control that the sending State still retains, i.e. by the test of Article 7

operations', EJIL Analysis, 10 March. Available at: http://www.ejiltalk.org/attribution-of-conduct-to-international-organizations-in-peacekeeping-operations/.

15 NATO Policy on Contractor Support, C-M(2007)0004, 26 January 2007, NAC, Senior Nations Logisticians Conference, *NATO Policy on Contractor Support to Operations,* 12 January 2007, para. 50.

16 NATO Annual Manpower Plan 2016–2021, corrigendum 1, 2 March 2016.

17 This excludes personnel employed at NATO's International Staff and other international civilian headquarters.

18 Sari, A., Wessel, R.A., *International Responsibility for EU Military Operations: Finding the EU's Place in the Global Accountability Regime,* in Van Vooren, B., Blockmans, S. and Wouters, J. (eds.) (2013) *The EU's role in global governance: The legal dimension. United Kingdom*: Oxford University Press, pp. 126–141.

of the ILC Articles on the Responsibility of International Organizations. This test is discussed in the following paragraph.

7.3 Attribution of Conduct of Organs or Agents Placed at the Disposal of NATO

Like any other international organisation involved in military operations, the Alliance relies heavily on the contribution of military personnel by States. As described in chapters 4 and 5, NATO requests the required military forces and materiel from troop contributing nations (TCNs), who on their turn place their personnel under the command and control of NATO. The TCNs retain full command over their forces, i.e. the power to re-assign these forces to national command. TCNs also maintain criminal and disciplinary jurisdiction over their military forces. The military contingents therefore remain to a certain degree under the control of the TCN. Their acts can not automatically be attributed to the Alliance as would be the case for agents and organs that have a functional or institutional link with the organisation. Instead, conduct is attributed in accordance with a different rule. Article 7 of the ILC's Articles on the Responsibility of International Organizations states that

> [t]he conduct of an organ of a State or an organ or agent of an international organization that is placed at the disposal of another international organization shall be considered under international law an act of the latter organization if the organization exercises effective control over that conduct.[19]

The crucial part of this rule is the exercise of 'effective control'. This criterion for attributability has been considered by the ICJ, ICTY and ECtHR, as well as domestic courts. Unfortunately, the term has been interpreted by each court and tribunal in a different manner, making it difficult to define with certainty what is meant with 'effective control'.

In 1986, the ICJ determined in the *Nicaragua*[20] case that, in order to attribute the acts of the Nicaraguan Contras to the United States, the US had to

---

19 Art. 6, ILC Report on the work of its sixty-first session, 4 May to 5 June and 6 July to 7 August 2009, Supplement No. 10 (A/64/10).

20 International Court of Justice, *Case concerning the Military and Paramilitary Activities in and against Nicaragua* (Nicaragua v. United States of America), (1986), ICJ Reports 1986, 14, para. 115.

have "*directed or enforced the perpetration of the acts*". This could be either done by giving directions to the Contras or to force the Contras to carry out certain actions.[21] In 1999, the ICTY reflected on the attribution of conduct of the Army of the Serbian Republic of Bosnia and Herzegovina / Republike Srpska (VRS) to the government of the Federal Republic of Yugoslavia. The ICTY adopted a lower threshold: that of '*overall control*', by which the conduct is attributable in situations of mere assistance or coordinating in the planning of (para) military activities.[22] In 2007, however, the ICJ 'rejected'[23] the lower threshold of the ICTY and re-instated the *effective control* test in its *Bosnian Genocide* judgment.[24]

The ECtHR added extra confusion on the topic in its – widely criticized[25] – *Behrami and Saramati* judgment.[26] The circumstances of the joined cases regard the NATO operation "Kosovo Force" (KFOR). The case concerned two applicants, Mr. Behrami and Mr. Saramati. In *Behrami*, two boys, Gadaf and Bekir Behrami, played with undetonated munitions dropped by NATO in 1999 in the municipality of Mitrovica. The munitions detonated and respectively killed Gadaf and injured Bekir. The circumstances of Saramati were that Mr. Saramati was on various occasions arrested by UNMiK Police officers, by orders of COMKFOR, thereby allegedly violating his rights under the ECHR.

In order to assess whether the conduct of personnel of KFOR and UNMiK could be attributed to either the UN or NATO, the Court assessed whether the UN or NATO had "*ultimate authority and control*" over the wrongful conduct committed against Behrami and Saramati. The Court turned to the text of Security Council's resolution 1244(1999) and noted that the UN Security Council delegated some of its powers to KFOR and UNMiK to conduct their respective

21 Cassese, A. (2007) '*The Nicaragua and Tadić Tests Revisited in Light of the ICJ Judgment on Genocide in Bosnia*', European Journal of International Law, 18(4).

22 International Criminal Tribunal for the Former Yugoslavia, *Prosecutor v. Dusko Tadic*, IT-94-I-A, Judgment of 15 July 1999, para. 131.

23 Obviously, the ICJ is not bound to any *stare decisis* of the ICTY or any other international tribunal or court.

24 International Court of Justice, *Case Concerning the Application of the Convention on the Prevention and Punishment of the Crime of Genocide*, (2007), ICJ Reports 2007, 43, para. 401.

25 Milanoviç, M. and Papiç, T. (2009) '*As Bad As It Gets: The European Court of Human Rights' Behrami and Saramati Decision and General International Law*', International and Comparative Law Quarterly, 58.

26 European Court of Human Rights, *A. Behrami against France*, application no. 71412/01 and *R. Saramati against France, Germany and Norway*, application no. 78166/01, Decision of 2 May 2007.

missions.[27] In the opinion of the Court, the Security Council retained *ultimate* authority and control over the mission and therefore any conduct of UNMiK and KFOR is attributable to the UN.[28] The Court's decision is widely criticised for its conclusion that effective control exists when the UN "delegates" certain powers to entities. The issue of delegation is more a matter relating to institutional law than it is to the rules of international responsibility in general. The Court's judgment might be explained by the fact that the Court uses the test of *"overall authority and control"*[29] rather than the ILC's test of *"effective control"*, the former seemingly describing a more formal approach.

In a domestic ruling, the British House of Lords in the case of *Al-Jeddah* made no reference to *"overall authority and control"* formulated by the ECtHR. Instead it returned to the *"effective control"* test as established by the ICJ. This test was also confirmed as being the correct one by the ILC's Articles on the Responsibility of International Organizations.[30] Mr. Al-Jeddah was detained by British forces in Iraq and alleged that his human rights were violated. He maintained that the UK was responsible for the actions of the British forces as it had effective control over their actions. The House of Lords noted, by analogy, that the UN did not claim responsibility for the Abu Ghraib incident[31] – although UN had 'authorised' the mission – nor did the US or the UK deny responsibility

27 European Court of Human Rights, *Grand Chamber Decision as to the admissibility of Application no. 71412/01 by A. Behrami and B. Behrami against France and Application no. 78166/01 by R. Saramati against France, Germany and Norway*, 2 May 2007, para 43.

28 Milanoviç, M. and Papiç, T. (2009) *'As Bad As It Gets: The European Court of Human Rights' Behrami and Saramati Decision and General International Law'*, International and Comparative Law Quarterly, 58. It is debatable whether the differentiation between *"authorising"* and *"delegating"* truly exists. The Security Council usually authorises, rather than delegates in its UNSC resolutions. The Council has been granted such vast powers by the UN Charter under the premise of the restoration of peace and security, that one could barely imagine which powers would not befall the Security Council. To illustrate, the Security Council created the International Criminal Tribunals of Yugoslavia and Rwanda in the context of the maintenance of peace and security.

29 European Court of Human Rights, *Grand Chamber Decision as to the admissibility of Application no. 71412/01 by A. Behrami and B. Behrami against France and Application no. 78166/01 by R. Saramati against France, Germany and Norway*, 2 May 2007, para. 87, 134. The Court sometimes refers to *"ultimate authority and control"*, para. 133, 134, 135 and 140.

30 Opinions of the Lords of Appeal, R (on the application of Al-Jedda) v Secretary of State for Defence, 12 December 2007, UKHL 58, para. 22.

31 An incident relating to the abuse of Iraqi detainees by the US in the Abu Ghraib detention facility in Iraq in 2003.

for the conduct of their forces.[32] Although the UN had requested the UK and US to observe humanitarian law and to report periodically on the situation, his Lordship concluded that *"it is one thing to receive reports, another to exercise effective command and control"*.[33]

The last case that deserves mentioning in this regard here, is the *Nuhanović*-case before the Dutch Supreme Court. The case relates to the fall in 1995 of a Muslim enclave in Srebrenica that was under the protection of Dutch UN peacekeepers (DutchBat) serving in the UN-led mission UNPROFOR. Relatives of Mr. Nuhanović and mr. Mustafić, two local UN employees providing services at the Dutch compound, claimed that the Dutch forces did not provide adequate protection from attacks by Serbian forces against the Muslim population resulting ultimately in their deaths. The Supreme Court established that the Dutch government retained the power to reassign the forces placed at the disposal of the international organisation (i.e. Full Command) and had criminal jurisdiction as well as disciplinary and administrative powers over the military forces placed at the disposal of the UN. The UN was granted Operational Command and Control. However, the Court considered that the command relationship shifted when the situation deteriorated in Srebrenica. The UN ceased to give instructions to the Dutch contingent and the Dutch government progressively took more control over the continuosly developing situation. The Netherlands ordered the evacuation of the refugees and the retreat of the Dutch forces. The Court concluded that under these circumstances, the Dutch government exercised effective control over the Dutch military contingent and therefore their conduct has to be attributed to the Netherlands.[34]

---

32 Opinions of the Lords of Appeal, R (on the application of Al-Jedda) v Secretary of State for Defence, 12 December 2007, UKHL 58, para. 23.

33 Opinions of the Lords of Appeal, R (on the application of Al-Jedda) v Secretary of State for Defence, 12 December 2007, UKHL 58, para. 24.

34 Hoge Raad, *H. Nuhanović v. the Netherlands*, ECLI:NL:HR:2013:BZ9225, 6 September 2013. The Dutch Court examined whether the UN or the Dutch Government had exercised effective control over the Dutch contingent. It referred to article 6 of the ILC's Articles on Responsibility of International Organizations and concluded that the conduct of the forces can be attributed to the UN if the UN had effective control over the specific conduct. It also concluded that the same test applied to the attribution of conduct to the Dutch government. This conclusion is, however, in contradiction with the ILC's Articles and the Articles on the Responsibility of States. As the Dutch contingent is an organ of the Dutch government, there was no need to examine whether the Dutch government had effective control; this is to be presumed. The conduct of State organs is automatically attributed to the State.

The overall approach taken in jurisprudence and by academics is that international organisations involved in military operations are presumed to have effective control over military contingents during the period that they are placed at the disposal of the international organisation. By transferring Operational Command and Control to the international organisation, the contributing States cede a significant degree of control over their forces to the organisation to allow it to conduct operations. This gives rise to the initial presumption that the international organisation exercises effective control over the military contingents with respect to the conduct of operations.

Military contingents still act to a certain extent as organs of the TCN, since the contributing State retains disciplinary powers and criminal jurisdiction over the members of the contingent.[35] The lack of such powers certainly influences the degree of control that NATO has to enforce its decisions. Therefore, the existence of effective control must be assessed on a case-by-case basis. In most situations, however, the lack of disciplinary powers and criminal jurisdiction will not undermine the effective control that the Alliance has over forces placed at its disposal. As illustrated in Chapter 2 of this book, the Commander of Kosovo Force may have lacked criminal and disciplinary powers, but still had adequate measures at its disposal to enforce the prohibition for military personnel to visit areas known for human trafficking and forced prostitution. These measures may include to suspend alleged perpetrators from their duties, to conduct an operational investigation and to report potential misconduct to TCNs. This leads to the conclusion that NATO had effective control over the misconduct of KFOR personnel relating to human trafficking and forced prostitution.

Jurisprudence and the ILC's commentary on the Articles on Responsibility of International Organizations show that an international organisation may not have effective control in a situation when a TCN specifically interferes in the command relationship. The interference may either be *ad hoc*, as was the case of The Netherlands which issued orders to the Dutch military contingent in Srebrenica, or repetitive, during operation Allied Force, where military contingents continuously sought approval from their respective nations.[36] NATO

35 ILC, *Commentary to the articles on the responsibility of international organizations*, A/66/10, 2011, p. 87.

36 E.g. with respect to UNOSOM II, the UN did not have effective control over the peacekeepers, despite formal command and control arrangements. The *"national contingents [...] persisted in seeking orders from their home authorities before executing orders of the Forces Command"* impeding the UN to exercise effective control over the forces, G. Gaja, Special

did not have effective control over the military forces placed at its disposal for the time that the TCN interfered in the command relationship.

In some cases, a TCN may put restrictions and limitations on the degree of control that NATO may exercise over military contingents placed at its disposal. These limitations are agreed upon between the TCN and the Alliance prior to the execution of the mission and are a characteristic of the flexibility by which TCN may contribute to NATO operations. TCNs may 'veto' certain individual missions in which their military forces partake, e.g. the targeting of an object or individual or the use of special forces in a detention operation. The so-called 'red card' procedure is a practice in NATO operations that leaves some control to States when participating in domstically politically sensitive missions. Prior to the execution of a specific mission, a TCN can determine whether the mission could contravene national policies or obligations, and if so, may issue a 'red card'. The military contingent will not be used to conduct that particular mission.[37] TCNs may also notify NATO prior to the execution of an operation that its military forces may not participate in certain aspects of the mission. These restrictions are defined as "national caveats". These limitations may be based on domestic political or legal circumstances and limit the degee in which military forces operate. For instance, military forces may be confined to a defined geographical area or may be limited to partake in only specific military activities.

Obviously, when substantial limitations are set on the use military contingents either through red-card issuance or national caveats, the effective control

---

Rapporteur, Second Report on Responsibility of International Organizations, A/CN.4/541, 2 April 2004, p. 20. The same happened in NATO's operation Allied Force, where the NATO commander *"had to wait for the individual nations to answer back* [on the approval of targets], *having gone to their capitals and asked whether they should accept that target".* A. Wall, ed, *Legal and ethical lessons of NATO's Kosovo campaign,* US Naval War College, International Law Studies, Vol. 78, 2002, p. 25.

37 AJP 3.9, Section 0117, *"For targets of a politico-strategic importance, authority to prosecute will often be held at the national level. In the majority of other cases a designated officer will normally be empowered by his nation to authorise attacks against targets. Assuming that the officer has access to relevant legal, political and CD estimation information, and a full understanding of the military advantage anticipated in attacking the target, he will be able to perform the proportionality test and authorise his nation's military forces to attack targets in support of the JFC's operation plan (OPLAN) if appropriate. This authorisation may require some caveats, usually expressed in terms of the mitigation measures described in paragraph 0116, to ensure that his nation's obligation to minimise CD is discharged. Any targets that fall outside his delegated authority would be referred back to his nation for clearance."*

of NATO over these forces is limited and may – in certain specific cases – not exist at all.

In the case of detention operations in Afghanistan, as illustrated in Chapter 2, Canada informed NATO that it would not participate under NATO command when conducting detention operations. It placed the restriction that NATO would not have operational command once Canadian forces detain individuals. In this situation, Canadian forces would return under national command for the time that detention and transfer – or continued detention – would take place. In this situation, NATO does not have effective control over Canadian forces during detention operations and wrongful conduct during that period can only be attributed to the Canadian government.

The fact that personnel may act in contravention of orders or direction of NATO commanders, does not affect the effective control that the organisation has over individuals. Even *ultra vires* conduct is attributable to the organisation as long as the agent or organ acts in the capacity in which it has been placed at the disposal of the organisation.[38] In the case of the incident in Kunduz, Afghanistan, NATO exercised effective control over the German military contingent in Kunduz, Afghanistan, even though the German PRT commander acted allegedly contrary to COMISAF's orders and guidance. The result was the alleged wrongful conduct can be attributed to NATO.

7.4 Multiple Attribution of Wrongful Conduct in NATO-led Operations

Multiple attribution is the attribution of a single wrongful act to more than one entity. Although a rare occurrence in practice, multiple attribution is not new to international law. The ICJ's cases in the *Corfu Channel, Certain Phosphate Lands in Nauru, East Timor* and *Legality of the Use of Force* all consider

---

38 Article 8, Articles on the Responsibility of International Organizations, 2011, "*The conduct of an organ or agent of an international organization shall be considered an act of that organization under international law if the organ or agent acts in an official capacity and within the overall functions of that organization, even if the conduct exceeds the authority of that organ or agent or contravenes instructions.*" The article refers to the conduct of organs and agents of the organization and not specifically to organs and agents placed at the disposal of an international organization. In the latter circumstance its seems that in order to determine to which the ultra vires conduct must be attributed, it is necessary to determine the capacity in which the person was acting.

aspects of multiple attribution of conduct.[39] Likewise, the ECtHR has touched upon the subject in some of its cases.[40]

The Articles on the Responsibility of International Organizations and the Articles on the Responsibility of States consider multiple attribution of wrongful conduct to be theoretically possible. An act or omission of an agent or organ could trigger more than one rule of attribution, resulting in a contemporaneous application of two rules of attribution. For instance, if a joint organ is established by a State and an international organisation (e.g. the Coalition Provisional Authority in Iraq established in 2003 by a coalition of States), the conduct of that joint organ is attributable to the State under Article 4 of the Articles on State Responsibility and to the international organisation under Article 6 of the Articles on Responsibility of International Organizations.[41] Multiple attribution may also occur when an act or omission is carried out jointly by two or more entities, each of which is acting on behalf of a State or international organisation. For instance, if two soldiers, belonging to different coalition partners in Iraq, unlawfully harm civilians, the conduct is attributed to both States. As Messineo states, the issue here is not one of interaction of two rules of attribution, but of the simple application of the rules with relation to each subject of international law concerned.[42]

Multiple attribution of conduct may equally occur during NATO operations. For instance, NATO has established with the UN Office on Drugs and Crime a

---

39 International Court of Justice, *Corfu Channel* (United Kingdom of Great Britain and Northern Ireland v Albania), (1949) ICJ Reports 1949, ICJ Reports 1949, 4. International Court of Justice, *Certain Phosphate Lands in Nauru* (Nauru v Australia), (1992) ICJ Reports 1992, 240. International Court of Justice, East Timor (Portugal v Australia), (1995) ICJ Reports 1995, 90. International Court of Justice, Legality of the Use of Force (Yugoslavia v United States of America), Provisional Measures, 2 June 1999, (1999) ICJ Reports 1999, p. 916.

40 European Court of Human Rights, *Ilascu et al. v. Moldova and Russia*, Application no. 48787/99, Judgment of 8 July 2004; European Court of Human Rights, *M.S.S. v Belgium and Greece*, Application no. 30696/09, Judgment of 21 January 2011.

41 There are 21 permutations of the situation where the conduct of one actor could be deemed the conduct of two or more States or international organizations, Messineo, F. (2012) *Multiple Attribution of Conduct*. Available at: http://www.sharesproject.nl/wp-content/uploads/2012/10/Messineo-Multiple-Attribution-of-Conduct-2012-111.pdf (Accessed: 2012), p. 11.

42 Messineo, F. (2012) *Multiple Attribution of Conduct*. Available at: http://www.sharesproject.nl/wp-content/uploads/2012/10/Messineo-Multiple-Attribution-of-Conduct-2012-111.pdf (Accessed: 2012), p. 21.

joint counter-narcotics programme in several Central Asian countries.[43] The conduct of that joint organ may be attributable to both the UN and to NATO.

Still, multiple attribution is the exception rather than the rule. Article 7 of the Articles on the Responsibility of International Organizations prefers an alternative outcome. The conduct of military contingents placed at the disposal of NATO is attributed to NATO if it exercises effective control over the specific conduct. If the Alliance does not exercise such control, the wrongful conduct is attributed to the State by virtue of Article 4 of the Articles on the Responsibility of States. Article 7 of the Responsibility of International Organizations is designed to avoid the situation of multiple attribution. Multiple attribution is the exception,[44] rather than the default position.[45]

But, jurisprudence seems to confirm the possibility of multiple attribution in the case of military contingents placed at the disposal of international organisation.[46]

In *Nuhanović*, the Dutch Supreme Court held that the wrongful conduct of the Dutch contingent may be attributable to the UN under Article 7 of the ILC Articles on the Responsibility of International Organizations, as well as to the Netherlands for not taking action to prevent the wrongful conduct from happening. The court nuanced this by adding that the TCN would need to know

43 http://www.nato.int/cps/en/natohq/news_119956.htm?selectedLocale=en.

44 ILC, Comments and observations received from the United Nations, A/CN.4/637/Add.1, 13, para. 1.

45 ILC, Comments and observations received from the United Nations, A/CN.4/637/Add.1, 15. In this regard, the judgment of the Dutch Court on Srebrenica is somewhat surprising where it stated that it could not rule out that the conduct of the Dutch military contingent placed at the disposal of the UN could be attributed to both the Netherlands government as well as the UN. The Court may have misinterpreted the notion of effective control over the conduct of lent organs by considering which entity – the Netherlands or the UN – had such control. It is not relevant to examine whether the Dutch government had effective control over the Dutch military contingent. If the UN did not exercise effective control, the wrongful conduct of the military contingents is automatically attributed to the Netherland on the basis of article 4 of the Articles on the Responsibility of State, because it is an organ of the State. D'Argent, P. (2014) *'State Organs Placed at the Disposal of the UN, Effective Control, Wrongful Abstention and Dual Attribution of Conduct'*, Questions of International Law, p. 30.

46 Hoge Raad der Nederlanden, Judgment, The Netherlands v. H. Nuhanović, 6 September 2013, ECLI:NL:HR:2013:BZ9225. European Court of Human Rights, *Grand Chamber Decision as to the admissibility of Application no. 71412/01 by A. Behrami and B. Behrami against France and Application no. 78166/01.*

about the wrongful conduct.[47] Even with this nuance, there is little practice that supports this argument.[48] Responsibility does not exist by virtue of having the power to prevent wrongful conduct. There must also be a basis for an intervention, i.e. if there was an obligation of the UN peacekeepers to protect specific individuals, there would be a basis for The Netherlands to intervene within the chain of command.[49] As Crawford notes, the inaction is only significant if there is a legal duty to act.[50] The wrongful conduct of military contingents is only attributable to a State when there is an obligation for a State to prevent the conduct from happening, e.g. to prevent genocide.[51]

In the situation of ISAF as illustrated in Chapter 2 of this book, TCNs were obliged to prevent the transfer of detainees to the Afghan government, as there were substantial grounds for believing that the detainee would be in danger of being subjected to torture and there was an international obligation to prevent the detainees from being subjected to torture.[52] The TCNs had the power to prevent the transfers by reclaiming command over their forces. Therefore, and in addition to, the attribution of wrongful conduct to NATO, the conduct can be attributed to the involved TCNs as well.

7.5 Conclusions

International organisations are abstract entities that act in the physical world through individuals. International organisations are responsible for the actions of individuals, if their conduct is attributable to the organisation. The rules governing the attribution of conduct of individuals have been codified by

47 Hoge Raad der Nederlanden, Judgment, The Netherlands v. H. Nuhanović, 6 September 2013, ECLI:NL:HR:2013:BZ9225, para. 5.18.

48 Nollkaemper, A. (2013) *'Dual Attribution: Liability of the Netherlands for Conduct of Dutchbat in Srebrenica'*, Journal of International Criminal Justice, 9(5).

49 Nollkaemper, A. (2013) *'Dual Attribution: Liability of the Netherlands for Conduct of Dutchbat in Srebrenica'*, Journal of International Criminal Justice, 9(5).

50 Crawford, J., *State Responsibility: The General Part*, 2013, p. 218 cited by K.E. Boon, *Are Control Tests Fit for the Future? The Slippage Problem in Attribution Doctrines*, Melbourne Journal of International Law, Vol. 15, 2014, p. 34.

51 Article 1, *Convention on the Prevention and Punishment of the Crime of Genocide*, 1948, 78 UNTS 277, 12 January 1951.

52 Article 3(1), *Convention against Torture and Other Cruel, Inhuman or Degrading Treatment or Punishment*, 1984, 1465 UNTS 85, 26 June 1987.

the International Law Commission in 2011 in its Articles on the Responsibility of International Organizations.

Conduct of agents and organs that have an institutional link with NATO is automatically attributable to the organisation. Chapter 4 described the various organs and agents of NATO. The North Atlantic Council, Supreme Headquarters Allied Powers Europe and NATO's various operational headquarters all have an institutional link with the organisation and their actions are therefore automatically attributable to NATO under Article 6 of the ILC's Articles. For instance, the decision of the North Atlantic Council to initiate Operational Allied Force in Kosovo, without the authorization of the UN Security Council is attributable to NATO as is the decision to transfer detainees to the Afghan government during the ISAF operation (as described in Chapter 2 of this book).

The actions of agents and organs that are placed at the disposal of NATO are not automatically attributable to the organisation. Article 7 of the Articles on the Responsibility of International Organizations states that only conduct over which the organisation exercises effective control is attributable to the organisation. The Alliance relies for a significant part on agents placed at its disposal by States.

The Alliance is responsible for the conduct of those individuals only when it exercises effective control over the specific wrongful conduct. The test of effective control – as contained in Article 7 of the ILC's Articles – is complicated, as it requires detailed analysis of the factual circumstances of the conduct. Contrary to the *Behrami* case, effective control is not established by mere "authorization", such as a UN Security Council resolution. The command and control arrangements as described in Chapter 5 may give a general indication as to which entity has control over certain actions. In general, NATO is presumed to have effective control over agents placed at its disposal by States. States transfer Operational Command and Control over troops that they contribute to NATO. Operational Command is the authority to assign missions or tasks, to deploy units and to reassign forces. While TCNs retain disciplinary and criminal jurisdiction over their forces and have the authority to withdraw their forces from NATO command, NATO has considerable control in respect to leading of operations. The amount of control may vary, dependent on the influence that a TCN may exercise through the use of commonly used methods, such as national caveats and the "Red Card Holdership", but in general it is presumed that NATO has effective control over individuals placed at its disposal. COMKFOR had effective control over KFOR forces placed at its disposal, even in absence of criminal jurisdiction or disciplinary powers. The commander had the authority to issue orders to its personnel. Similarly, COMISAF had the authority to direct subordinate Regional Commanders to minimise the risks of civilian casualties. Therefore, the conduct of ISAF and KFOR personnel is attributable to NATO.

In some cases, conduct can be attributed both to NATO and the TCN or TCNs. Multiple attribution has not occurred in practice widely, but it is theoretically possible. A few examples have been given in how single conduct can be attributed to multiple subjects. With regards to NATO-led operations, it seems possible to attribute a single act to both NATO and the TCN in cases where one of the two had effective control over the conduct and the other – while having the authority – failed to intervene and thereby violated an international obligation.

CHAPTER 8

Conclusions and Recommendations

8.1 Introduction

The drafters of the North Atlantic Treaty could not have predicted in 1949 the course that NATO would fare. NATO was designed to portray collective trans-Atlantic resolve to counter a military threat from the Soviet bloc. It relied on numerous conventional forces stationed in various parts of Europe and on a nuclear deterrent. NATO was a static collective defence alliance in which the member States were the main actors.

After the Cold War NATO shifted its focus from defending the territorial integrity of the member States to crisis-management operations in areas outside the territory of NATO, where conflict has emerged or is about to emerge. The UN – tasked with the primary responsibility of the preservation of international peace and security – has relied many times on NATO's capabilities. In time, NATO became the only security institution capable of commanding large military operations at any place in the world.

The transformation also changed NATO from a legal and organisational perspective. While in 1949 the main actors of the Alliance were its member States, with the end of the Cold War the organisation gained a more distinct role, quite separate from the member States. In this new role, NATO broadened the scope of its military activities which inevitably invoked questions on the responsibility of the organisation.

Questions arose whether NATO could bear rights and obligations as an international legal entity. And, if so, to which international obligations would the Alliance be bound? Which conduct of NATO personnel can be attributed to the Alliance, given the fact that most of NATO personnel consists of military personnel contributed by nations?

In answering these questions, three cases were used to illustrate the relevance and practicality of responsibility of NATO during its operations. Chapter 2 is followed by chapters on, respectively, international legal personality, international obligations of NATO and rules of attribution for conduct of NATO personnel. This chapter will summarise the main conclusions drawn throughout the book and takes the liberty to provide in recommendations for NATO. Before coming to these conclusions and recommendations, the following paragraph will analyse the cases provided in Chapter 2 of this book.

 | DOI 10.1163/9789004354647_009

8.2 Analysis of the Three Illustrative Cases

8.2.1 *Human Trafficking and Forced Prostitution in Kosovo*

The case of human trafficking and forced prostitution in Kosovo illustrates two main issues relating to the responsibility of NATO. First, it addresses of international obligations binding upon the organisation. The Alliance could be held responsible for any violation of the prohibition of human trafficking and forced prostitution, if this is considered a binding international obligation resting upon the organisation. Second, the case illustrates the effective control that the Alliance has over its personnel.

Human trafficking and forced prostitution are acts that are criminalised in most domestic jurisdictions. The UN considers the trafficking in persons a serious crime and a grave violation of human rights. The United Nations Convention against Transnational Organized Crime and the Protocols thereto, in particular the Protocol to Prevent, Suppress and Punish Trafficking in Persons, obliges States party to the Protocol to criminalise in their domestic jurisdiction the act of human trafficking.[1] Forced prostitution is also considered a war crime and a crime against humanity under articles 7 and 8 of the Statute of the International Criminal Court.[2]

NATO is not a party to the UN Convention against Transnational Organized Crime and therefore is not bound to its provisions. Neither is the UN Convention part of international customary law. Even if it would have been considered international customary law, the Alliance would not have the possibility to implement its norms, as it has no power to adopt legislation criminalising the acts of human trafficking and forced prostitution.

The Statute of the International Criminal Court does not contain international obligations binding upon NATO. Instead, it obliges its personnel from nations that are parties to the Rome Statute to refrain from committing such acts. Given that COMKFOR has always been a national of one of the States party to the Rome Statute,[3] the NATO commanders would have been under the obligation to take all necessary and reasonable measures to prevent or repress such crimes. However, in the period that these crimes were reported,

---

1 United Nations Convention against Transnational Organized Crime and the Protocols Thereto, UN General Assembly resolution 55/25, 15 November 2000.

2 Articles 7 and 8, Rome Statute of the International Criminal Court, 1998, 2187 UNTS 38544, 1 July 2002.

3 The position of the Commander of KFOR has been filled by the United Kingdom, Germany, Spain, Italy, Norway and France.

the ICC Statute was not in force. Moreover, the ICC Statute creates individual criminal responsibility rather than a responsibility of the international organization under international public law. Therefore, the ICC Statute does not contain any international legal obligation for NATO.

In conclusion, NATO has no international obligation to prevent, suppress or refrain from committing human trafficking or forced prostitution. The Alliance cannot be held responsible for the alleged acts committed by NATO personnel.

The case illustrates a second aspect of international responsibility, which is the attribution of conduct. The case illustrates the degree of effective control over military personnel placed at the disposal of NATO by Troop Contributing Nations.

The Alliance relied on national commanders to issue policies to ensure that its personnel would not be involved in human trafficking and forced prostitution. In cases of violations of these policies, national commanders would then take necessary disciplinary action, or repatriate and criminal prosecute personnel before national courts.[4] NATO itself admitted that the issue of soldiers frequenting prostitutes was *"Hard to end"* as it does not have discipilinary or criminal jurisdiction over military personnel.[5] Non-governmental organisations voiced their dissaproval regarding the – perceived – impunity of personnel allegedly involved in these crimes. The question arises whether NATO has effective control over its personnel during military operations. This issue has been examined in Chapter 7 and concluded that the Alliance – in certain cases – does indeed exercise effective control.

It is true that NATO does not have criminal or disciplinary jursidiction over personnel. As discussed in the previous chapter, the lack of such powers does not by itself exclude the possibility that NATO has effective control. NATO could conduct a fact-finding investigation in cases where NATO personnel allegedly have been involved in human trafficking or forced prostitution and has the ability to suspend and remove personnel from posts. Moreover, the organisation has the power to report any misconduct to the Troop Contributing Nation.

In conclusion, NATO is not responsible under international law for acts of human trafficking of forced prostitution as it is not bound to these norms under international conventional or international customary law. The Alliance

4 The Times, *Colonel caught in brothel*, 6 July 2000; AFP, *Royal Marines sent home from Kosovo after strip-club booze up*, 11 January 2001; Associated Press, *10 French NATO peacekeepers caught at off-limits bar*, 6 December 2002.

5 Amnesty International (2004) *'So does it mean that we have the rights?' Protecting the human rights of women and girls trafficked for forced prostitution in Kosovo*. Available at: http://reliefweb.int/report/serbia/so-does-it-mean-we-have-rights-protecting, p. 53.

does have effective control over personnel allegedly involved in these acts as it could investigate, report the misconduct, and – where necessary – could take administrative actions.

8.2.2 *Detention Operations in ISAF*

Detention is – since the incidents at Abu Graib, Iraq in 2003 – a politically sensitive issue for most States involved in military operations. Detention operations are, relatively, also a very costly undertaking. For these reasons, the Alliance chose not to be involved in the long-term detention of individuals in the ISAF mission. Instead, NATO ordered the forces under its command to either release or transfer any captured person to Afghan authorities as soon as possible. NATO's rules of engagement for ISAF instructed Troop Contributing Nations to transfer persons to Afghan authorities within 96 hours after capture.

Even though the Alliance tried to avoid being implicated in the potential maltreatment of prisoners by NATO forces, the organisation remains responsible for the prisoners' well-being while in Afghan-led detention centres. The transfer of any prisoner from NATO forces to the Afghan government where he or she would run the risk of torture, would constitute a violation of international law, in particular Article 3 of the Geneva Conventions of 1949,[6] 5(4) of Additional Protocol II to the Geneva Conventions,[7] Article 7 of the International Covenant on Civil and Political Rights (ICCPR)[8] and Article 3(1) of the Convention against Torture, and other Cruel, Inhuman or Degrading Treatment or Punishment (CAT).[9] *Non-refoulement* – which constitutes the prohibition to transfer a prisoner to a State where there is a risk of torture – is considered a principle of customary international law.[10]

NATO intended to conclude a bilateral agreement with the government of Afghanistan to ensure that the treatment of transferred detainees would be in accordance with international law. The conclusion of such an agreement was, however, unsuccesful. Instead, the Troop Contributing Nations reached

6 Common article 3 of the Geneva Conventions of 12 August 1949.

7 *Protocol Additional to the Geneva Conventions of 12 August 1949, and relating to the Protection of Victims of Non-International Armed Conflicts*, 1977, 1125 UNTS 609, 8 June 1977. The article does not refer directly to the principle of *non-refoulement* but states that the detaining power has the responsibility over the well-being of the detainee when they release him.

8 *International Covenant on Civil and Political Rights*, 1966, 999 UNTS 171, 23 March 1976.

9 *Convention against Torture and Other Cruel, Inhuman or Degrading Treatment or Punishment*, 1984, 1465 UNTS 85, 26 June 1987.

10 Droege, C., *Transfer of detainees: legal framework, non-refoulement and contemporary challenges*, International Review of the Red Cross, Vol 90, no. 871, September 2008, p. 686.

bilateral agreements providing diplomatic assurances on the standards of treatment of the transferred prisoners.

The independent initiative of these Troop Contributing Nations received criticism from NATO as well as from human rights organisations. The diplomatic assurances are not considered adequate to avoid the risk that transferred detainees could be subjected to torture. Moreover, the bilateral agreements created different, and possibly contradictory, standards and procedures regarding the treatment of detainees.

As mentioned in Chapter 2, the transfer of detainees eventually resulted in a breach of the international obligation of *non-refoulement*, as reports showed that the detainees were allegedly tortured in some of the Afghan National Directorate of Security-led detention facilities.

NATO allegedly breached international obligations by ordering – through the adoption of the ISAF Rules of Engagement – the transfer of detainees to Afghan authorities. NATO was aware of the risks of torture to which the detainees would be exposed, but still continued to direct military forces placed at its disposal to transfer detainees.

The Alliance had effective control over the conduct of ISAF forces in this particular instance. In general terms, NATO has effective control over forces placed at its disposal as the TCNs transfer Operational Command and Control over these forces to the Alliance. The detention operations and the transfer of detainees fell within the scope of authority of NATO's Operational Command and Control as it related to mission accomplishment. It had indeed exercised such effective control by directly ordering these forces to continue the transfer of the detainees through its directives and ISAF ROE.

NATO's effective control ended from the moment when a TCN reassumed command over mission personnel. This has occurred in the case of Canada, when it reassumed command over the Canadian contingent and directed its personnel to suspend the transfer of captured persons. From 5 November 2007 until 26 February 2008 Canada had reassumed command and, consequently, NATO lost effective control over these forces with respect to detention operations. During this period, NATO can not be held responsible for wrongful conduct relating to the transfer of detainees by the Canadian contingent.

The bilateral agreements that certain TCNs concluded with the government of Afghanistan is relevant to the responsbility that States have with respect to the prohibition of *non-refoulement*. At the moment that Canada reassumed command over the Canadian contingent, the bilateral agreements would ensure that Canada fulfilled its obligations under international law. It remains unclear, however, whether from the moment that Canada placed its forces back under NATO command, the bilateral agreement is of any relevance to the responsibility of NATO or Canada.

In conclusion, NATO is bound to the prohibition of *non-refoulement* as it is part of international customary law. In the circumstances described above, NATO had effective control over Canadian forces during the period that detainees were regularly transferred to Afghan authorities. For this reason, the Alliance is responsible for any transfers that allegedly breached the prohibiton of *non-refoulement* by Canadian ISAF personnel.

8.2.3 *Kunduz Incident*

According to the UN, NATO air strikes accounted for the largest percentage of civilian deaths in Afghanistan. This, by itself, does not purport to be a breach of international law. Only attacks,

> *"which may be expected to cause incidental loss of civilian life, injury to civilians, damage to civilian objects, or a combination thereof, which would be excessive in relation to the concrete and military advantage anticipated",*[11] would be unlawful.

In order to comply with international law, NATO issued detailed guidance on targeting in an annex to the ISAF Operational Plan and – additionally – issued a directive that restricted the use of air-delivered ammunition even further than international law dictates. This directive was aimed to support the counter-insurgency efforts during the operation, as any incidental loss of civilian life could fuel anti-NATO and anti-governmental sentiment.

The airstrike on two fuel trucks in Kunduz in October 2009 resulted in significant civilian casualties, which called for a criminal investigation led by Germany on the conduct of the German personnel involved in the airstrike. The German Federal Prosecutor concluded that there was no indication of criminal conduct under domestic or international law. The United States of America did not (criminally) investigate the incident, nor did any other nation involved in the targeting process or decisions making process.

The case illustrated the complexity of conducting national investigations in a multinational operation. A NATO-led fact finding investigation is preferred to ensure a more comprehensive examination and analysis of the facts and circumstances of the incident. Such an investigation does not necessarily

11 Article 57(2)(iii), Protocol Additional to the Geneva Conventions of 12 August 1949, and Relating to the Protection of Victims of International Armed Conflicts, 8 June 1977.

jeopardise any national (criminal) investigation, as long as the NATO is given clear limits on the scope and intent of the investigation. The conclusion is that there was no breach of any norm of international law.

With regard to the attribution of conduct of wrongful conduct in this case, the following aspect can be observed. The Commander of ISAF issued strict guidance on the application of air-delivered munition during the mission. The PRT commander and the Joint Tactical Air Controller seemingly did not adhere to this guidance. It would be incorrect to conclude that NATO did not have effective control, solely based on the fact that NATO forces did not follow the directive given by the Commander of ISAF. Conduct of forces placed at the disposal of NATO shall be considered under international law an act of the organisation if the forces act in an official capacity and within the overall functions of NATO, even if the conduct exceeds the authority of the forces or contravene instructions.[12] Therefore, if there would been a wrongful act, the act could have been attributed to the Alliance, even though the Commander and Joint Tactical Air Controller contravened NATO instructions.

8.3 Final Conclusions

Conclusion 1: NATO is an International Organisation with International Legal Personality

The existence of international legal personality of NATO has both been disputed and acknowledged. Academic writers have been ambiguous regarding the status of NATO. There are a variety of reasons underlying the ambiguity. First, there is no evidence of an explicit intent of the founders of the Alliance to create an international organisation with international legal personality. Secondly, some academic writers look at NATO from a perspective of its earlier days when it operated mainly as an alliance of States and come to the conclusion that the Alliance does not possess international legal status. But, NATO undeniably possesses several of the indicia of international legal personality. The organisation has concluded international agreements with both States and other international organisations and enjoys immunity in the member States' territory. Therefore, there are indications that point toward the existence of international legal personality.

None of the international courts or tribunals have directly dealt with the question of international legal personality of NATO as of 2016, but with the increasing amount of operations that NATO conducts, the question may very

12 Article 8, ILC Articles on the Responsibility of International Organizations, 2011.

well arise in the near future. Already, there is a tendency of international actors in international law to treat the Alliance as having international legal personality, such as the ICTY. And, in the proceedings before the ICJ, States have confirmed that NATO exists as a separate entity from its members. In its inquiry in the events in Libya in 2011 the UN has also treated NATO as a legal entity. Finally, NATO itself, also, confirms that the Alliance has separate legal status from the member States.[13]

Conclusion 2: NATO Has Binding International Obligations under International Law

This book examined the international obligations that are relevant to NATO's operations. The main source of international obligations for NATO is found in the customary rules. Since NATO is not a party to any of the conventional norms, the obligations relating to *jus in bello* and *jus ad bellum* are limited to the customary norms. Most conventional international humanitarian law and convention international human rights law are customary in nature and therefore the substantive difference between conventional and customary rules is relatively marginal. International obligations prohibit NATO of committing certain acts or to engage in a certain activity. For instance, NATO is prohibited to target civilians and is obliged to prevent or suppress such actions. The latter category of obligations is defined as positive obligations, which are mainly

13 NATO Secretary General, *Strategic Airlift Capability (SAC) – Initiative Adoption of the NAMO charter*, 20 June 2007, *"It is accordingly agreed that only the member States of NAMO shall jointly and directly assume responsibility vis-à-vis NATO, and shall bear any resulting cost and liability for the implementation of the Airlift Management Programme, notwithstanding the fact that NAMO will be established, by the Council, pursuant to Article 9 of the North Atlantic Treaty and within the meaning of the Ottawa Agreement and will share in the international legal personality of NATO as well as the juridical personality possessed by NATO by virtue of Article IV of the Ottawa Agreement."* UN General Assembly, International Law Commission, *Responsibility of International Organizations, Comments and observation received from international organizations*, UN Doc A/CN.4/637, *"The following comments relate to the structure of the organization, its decision-making procedures and its practice with respect to claims. NATO is an international organization within the meaning of draft article 2(a) of the draft articles, and as such a subject of international law. It possesses international legal personality as well as treaty-making power."* Para. 2, p. 11. B. DeVidts, *Speaking notes on "aspects related to the Legal Status of the North Atlantic Treaty Organisation"*, 22 November 2004 (CJ(2004)0910), copy on file with the author. Only on one occasion, NATO's legal office of the International Staff has commented that NATO does not have international legal personality. Amnesty International, NATO/Federal Republic of Yugoslavia "Collateral damage" or unlawful killings? Violations of the Laws of War by NATO during Operation Allied Force, p. 13, 5 June 2000.

found in customary international human rights law. NATO was bound to take precautionary measures during air strikes in Libya in Operation Unified Protector. Likewise, in the case of Kunduz, it was obliged not to conduct attacks on military targets if the incidental loss of civilian life would be excessive to the military advantage anticipated. In relation to detention operations in ISAF, NATO was obliged to stop the transfer of detainees to Afghan authorities if there were substantial grounds to believe that they would be in danger of being subjected to torture.

Indirect obligations come into existence when all the member States of an international organisation are bound by a certain international obligation, but the organisation itself is not. In this situation, the organisation has to take "*due care*" that its actions do not violate the international obligations of its member States. The UN Charter and the resolutions of the UN Security Council are examples of indirect international obligations binding upon NATO. The Alliance itself is not formally bound by the UN Charter or by decisions of the UN organs as it is not a party to the UN Charter.[14] However, all of its member States are and therefore NATO is required to take note of these provisions.

Conclusion 3: NATO is Responsible for Conduct of Its Agents and Organs. With Respect to Personnel Placed at Its Disposal, the Alliance is Responsible for Their Conduct If It Exercised Effective Control

This book has examined the conditions under which wrongful conduct of personnel on NATO operations can be attributed to NATO. Based on the observations made in the chapter dealing with the institutional framework of NATO and having examined the conditions under which wrongful conduct is attributed to international organisations under international law, the following conclusions are made.

Wrongful conduct of agents or organs that have an institutional link with the Alliance can be directly attributed to NATO, if the conduct falls within the performance of functions of that agent or organ. NATO international civilians and contractors fall in the category of agents and organs that have a direct institutional link with the Alliance.

14 States that are not party tot he UN Charter are similarly not bound to UN Security Council resolutions. ICJ, Advisory Opinion of 21 June 1971, *Legal Consequences for States of the Continued Presence of South Africa in Namibia (South West Africa) Notwithstanding Security Council Resolution 276*, ICJ Reports 1971, p. 16, para 126; M.D. Öberg, *The Legal Effects of Resolutions of the UN Security Council and General Assembly in the Jurisprudence of the ICJ*, 16 European Journal of International Law, 2006.

The majority of NATO personnel, however, do not have an organic or institutional link with NATO. That is a result of the fact that nations which contribute troops retain full command over their forces as well as criminal and disciplinary jurisdiction. As a result, military contingents remain organs of the Troop Contributing Nations. Their conduct is attributed to the Alliance only when NATO exercises effective control over that conduct. In principle, NATO exercises effective control over military contingents placed at its disposal, because the Troop Contributing Nations transfer Operational Command and Control to NATO. Effective control can be undermined when military contingents continuously seek instructions from their national governments, as was the case in the NATO Operation Allied Force. As a consequence, the US government felt responsible for the incident regarding the bombing of the Chinese Embassy, even though NATO initially took responsibility for the action.

In general, NATO has effective control over military contingents placed at its disposal. NATO commanders have operational command and control and can direct forces to execute the operation. There are few cases known where TCNs completely reassume command over their forces so that NATO does not exercise effective control anymore over their conduct. This was illustrated by the case where the Canadian government assumed command over its forces with respect of detentions operations. Wrongful conduct during Canadian-led detention operations is in that case only attributable to Canada.

Conclusion 4: NATO Can be Responsible under International Law for International Crimes Committed by Its Personnel during Operations

International crimes may occur during NATO operations. It is inconceivable that NATO personnel would commit international crimes as part of Alliance' policy or instruction. However, the Organisation can be held responsible for a criminal act that per definition falls outside official functions of NATO personnel. Such acts lead to the individual criminal responsibility under international criminal law, but can also entail a breach of an international obligation of international customary law binding upon NATO, giving rise to the responsibility of NATO under international public law. For other international crimes, there may not be a prohibition for States or international organisations to commit the act under international public law. This is the case for e.g. human trafficking and forced prostitution where the act itself is not a breach of an international obligation, but the failure to prevent or suppress the crime is.

Positive obligations exist to prevent or suppress international crimes and are part of international customary law. NATO is, therefore, bound to these provisions in so far that it can implement these obligations. The Alliance is not able to criminalise conduct or to prosecute alleged offenders of international crimes as it lacks criminal jurisdiction. However, NATO has taken measures to prevent international crimes by providing training to NATO personnel prior and during operations. NATO does have the authority to investigate criminal conduct to a limited extent. The investigations are not intended to replace a criminal investigation by troop contributing nations. The Alliance can report allegations of criminal conduct to nations to pursue with criminal prosecution. NATO has also initiated ways to cooperate with States in order to prevent and punish perpetrators of international crimes. Finally, NATO is obliged to cooperate with – so far, only – the ICTY in accordance with its Statute.

8.4 Recommendations

Based on the conclusions made in the previous paragraphs, the following recommendations are made. Since the subject of this book is NATO and its responsibility for personnel during operations, the recommendations are primarily aimed at this organisation and relate to its responsibility under international law.

Recommendation 1: NATO Should Develop Guidelines to Respond to International Claims

This book demonstrated that NATO meets several indicia of international legal personality. It has entered into various international agreements and enjoys immunity from the member States' jurisdiction. On the other hand, the Alliance did not bring or receive international claims, which is another indicator of international legal personality. Seemingly, there is a reluctance to receive international claims. When such claims are presented, the member States assert the responsibility to process the claim on a national basis. This was evident with regard to the bombing of the Chinese Embassy in Serbia, where initially the Alliance did respond to the claim and issued formal apologies and where the US instantly took over. Instead, given the international legal personality of NATO, the organisation should take a more proactive role in the handling of international claims.

In that respect, NATO – as a legal entity under international law separate from its member States – should respond to inquiries from international organisations, such as the UN. The Alliance has done so in relation to the air strikes in Libya in response to the questions posed by the UN Human Rights Council's Commission of Inquiry.

Recommendation 2: NATO Should Incorporate Its International Obligations into Policy

This study concluded that the Alliance has binding obligations under international law. NATO does not consider itself bound to international law. It limits itself to state that it abides by the principles of international humanitarian law and international human rights law. Even though it does not run a large risk of violating international law, it nevertheless should express its international obligations in stronger terms. There is a risk that the Alliance is held responsible for violations of international law if it does not clearly state its obligations to Troop Contributing Nations participating in NATO operations.

Recommendation 3: NATO Should Advocate Non-interference in the Mission by TCNs

Troop Contributing Nations place their forces under the command of NATO for the duration of the operation, which leads to the assumption that NATO exercises effective control over the forces. However, practice shows that the nations quite often interfere in the command relationship by either directly issuing national orders, placing caveats on rules of engagement or positioning a 'red card holder' in targeting processes.

NATO is only responsible for wrongful conduct if it exercises effective control over the conduct in question. The interference of nations in the operation may result that the wrongful conduct is not attributable to the Alliance but to the troop contributing State.

The current tendency is that States interfere in order to avoid that their forces could violate national or international obligations and hence would be attributed to the State. This perception is somewhat unfounded, since the conduct of troops placed at the disposal of NATO is attributable solely to the organisation as long as it exercises effective control. Hence – as depicted in the illustrative cases – there would be no need for nations to enter into individual bilateral agreements with Afghanistan to regulate the transfer of detainees in order to ensure that their national obligations will be respected. Neither is there a need for a red-card holder or national caveats.

Recommendation 4: NATO Should Investigate and Report Breaches of International Law (Including International Crimes) Committed by Its Personnel

The book demonstrated that the Alliance is under direct and ancillary obligations to prevent and suppress breaches of international obligations, which include international crimes. Currently, NATO receives report on possible misconduct of NATO personnel during operations through an established reporting mechanism and the organisation has conducted more investigations into misconduct than it has done so in previous operations. It is recommended that NATO continues to investigate misconduct, in particular into allegations of international crimes. If no investigations are conducted by either NATO or the concerned TCN into allegation of international crimes, NATO breaches its obligations under international law and can be held responsible.

APPENDIX

NATO-led Military Operations

Operation	Mandate	Date	Aim	SOFA
Anchor Guard	–	10 August 1990–9 March 1991	Monitor S-E Turkey in case of an Iraqi attack during the first Gulf Crisis	–
Ace Guard	–	3 January 1991–8 March 1991	Air Defence in case of an Iraqi attack during the first Gulf Crisis	NATO SOFA
Allied Goodwill I / II	–	4-9 February 1992 and 27 February to 24 March 1992	Humanitarian assistance to post USSR.	–
Agile Genie	–	1–19 May 1992	AWACS coverage to monitor air approach routes from the North African littoral in relation to imposed sanction against Libya	–
Maritime Monitor	UNSCR 713(1991), 757(1992)	16 July–22 November 1992	Naval monitoring operation on weapons embargo in the Adriatic sea	–

 | DOI 10.1163/9789004354647_010

Operation	Mandate	Date	Aim	SOFA
Sky Monitor	UNSCR 781(1992)	15 October 1992–12 April 1993	Air monitoring operation on No-Fly Zone during the fighting in Bosnia-Herzegovina	–
Maritime Guard	UNSCR 787(1992)	22 November 1992–15 June 1993	Naval enforcement of the weapons embargo in the Adriatic	–
Deny Flight	UNSCR 816(1993)	12 April 1993–21 December 1995	Enforcement of the no-fly zone over Bosnia-Herzegovina	–
Sharp Guard	UNSCR 713(1991), 787(1992), 820(1993), 943(1994)	15 June 1993–2 October 1996	Combination of NATO and WEU operations on the maritime embargo of weapons in the Adriatic	–
Deadeye / Deliberate Force	UNSCR 836(1993)	30–31 August 1995 and 5–14 September 1995	Airstrikes against Bosnian Serb air defenses, command control installations and ammunition facilities	–
Joint Endeavour (IFOR)	1031(1995)	20 December 1995–20 December 1996	Implementation of the military aspects of the peace agreement for Bosnia-Herzegovina	Agreement between the Republic of Bosnia and Herzegovina and NATO, appendix IB to Annex A to the General Framework Agreement for Peace in Bosnia-Herzegovina of 14 December 1995 (Dayton Peace Accords)

(Joint Guard / Joint Forge (SFOR)	1088(1996)	20 December 1996–2 December 2004	Continuance of SFOR with smaller force and new focus	Agreement between the Republic of Bosnia and Herzegovina and NATO, appendix IB to Annex A to the General Framework Agreement for Peace in Bosnia-Herzegovina of 14 December 1995 (Dayton Peace Accords)
Eagle Eye	1199(1998)	30 October 1998–24 March 1999	Monitoring of Serb compliance in Kosovo	–
Joint Guarantor	1199(1998)	4 December 1998–20 March 1999	Assistance to OSCE monitors in Kosovo	–
Allied Force	–	24 March–20 June 1999	Air campaign in Kosovo against the Former Republic of Yugoslavia	–
Allied Harbour	–	16 April–30 August 1999	Assistance to Albania in relation to the influx of refugees from Kosovo	–
Joint Guardian (KFOR)	1244(1999)	12 June 1999–present	Peacekeeping force in Kosovo	UNMiK Regulation 2000/47, 18 August 2000
Essential Harvest	1371(2001)	27 August–27 September 2001	NATO support to ensure disarmament of Albanian National Liberation Army	Framework Agreement between the Republic of Macedonia and DPA / PDP,

Operation	Mandate	Date	Aim	SOFA
				13 August 2001 (Ohrid Agreement); Basic Agreement between the Republic of Macedonia and NATO for the Operation of NATO Missions in Macedonia, 24 December 1998.
Amber Fox	1371(2001)	27 September 2001–16 December 2002	Support to EU and OSCE monitors	Framework Agreement between the Republic of Macedonia and DPA / PDP, 13 August 2001 (Ohrid Agreement); Basic Agreement between the Republic of Macedonia and NATO for the Operation of NATO Missions in Macedonia, 24 December 1998.
Active Endeavour	Article 5	26 October 2001–present	Patrolling of the Mediterranean and monitoring shipping, boarding of suspected ships	
Eagle Assist	1368(2001)	9 October 2001–15 May 2002	NAEW&C support to defend airspace in relation to the attacks of Al Qaida on US territory on 11 September 2001	–

International Security Assistance Force (ISAF)	1386(2001)	11 August 2003–present	Security Assistance to the Islamic Republic of Afghanistan	Military Technical Agreement Between the International Security Assistance Force (ISAF) and the Interim Administration of Afghanistan ('Interim Administration'), 4 January 2002. Exchange of letters between NATO's Secretary General and the Afghan minister of Foreign Affairs, 5 September–22 November 2004.
NTM-I	1546(2004)	7 August 2004–31 December 2011	Training mission in Iraq to security forces	Exchange of letters between the National Security Advisor of the government of Iraq and NATO's Secretary General, 21/23 December 2008.
NATO Support to AMIS	1564(2004)	23 June 2005–31 December 2007	Airlift and mentoring support to AU	–
NATO Relief mission to US	–	9 September–2 October 2005	Humanitarian relief in relation to hurricane Katrina.	NATO SOFA

Operation	Mandate	Date	Aim	SOFA
NATO Relief mission to Pakistan	–	11 October 2005–1 February 2006	Humanitarian relief to northern Pakistan in relation to earthquake	Exchange of Letters between the government of Pakistan and NATO, 4 November 2006.
NATO support to AU AMISOM	1744(2007)	7 June 2007–present	Airlift support to AU	–
Allied Provider	1814(2008), 1816(2008), 1838(2008)	24 October–13 December 2008	Escort of vessels to counter piracy	–
Allied Protector	1816(2008), 1838(2008), 1846(2008), 1851(2008)	24 March–29 June 2009	Counter piracy operations in Horn of Africa	–
Ocean Shield	1851(2008)	17 August 2009–present	Assistance to States and counter piracy operations in Horn of Africa	–
Unified Protector	UNSR 1970(2011), 1973(2011	23 March–31 October 2011	No-Fly Zone and protection of Libyan civilian population	NATO SOFA

Bibliography

I Books

Amerasinghe, C.F., *Principles of Institutional Law of Internatioanl Organizations,* 2005.

d'Aspremont, J. (ed.), *Participants in the International Legal System*, 2011.

Bonafé, B.I., *The Relationship Between State and Individual Responsibility for International Crimes,* 2009.

Brownlie, I., *Principles of Public International Law,* Fifth Edition, 2001.

Collins, R., White, N.D. (eds.), *International Organizations and the Idea of Autonomy: Institutional Independence in the International Legal Order,* 2011.

Crawford, J., *State Responsibility: The General Part,* 2013.

Crawford, J., Pellet, A., Olleson, S. (eds.), *The Law of International Responsibility,* 2010.

Damgaard, C., *Individual Criminal Responsibility for Core International Crimes,* 2008.

Dinstein, Y., *War, Aggression and Self-Defence,* 2011.

Ducheine, P., Pouw, E., *ISAF Operaties in Afghanistan,* 2010.

Edström, H., Gyllensporre, D. (eds.), *New Security Challenges*, 2012.

Emanuelli, C., *Les Actions Militaires de l'ONU et le Droit International Humanitaire,* 1995.

Engberg, K., *The EU and Military Operations, A Comparative Analysis,* 2013.

Engström, V., *Understanding Powers of International Organizations,* 2009.

Fastenrath, U., Simma, B., *From Bilateralism to Community Interest: Essays in Honour of Judge Bruno Simma,* 2011, p. 41.

Fleck, D., et al (eds.), *The Handbook of the Law of Visiting Forces*, 2001.

Gazzini, T., *The Changing Rules on the Use of Force in International Law,* 2006.

Gill, T.D., Fleck, D. (eds.), *The Handbook of the International Law of Military Operations,* 2010.

Haug, H. (ed.), *Humanity for All: The International Red Cross and Red Crescent Movement,* 1993.

Henckaerts, J-M., Doswald-Beck, L. (eds.), *Customary International Humanitarian Law,* 2005.

Hendrickson, R.C., *Diplomacy and War at NATO: The Secretary General and Military Action After the Cold War,* 2006.

Kaniel, M., *The Exclusive treaty-making power of the European Community up to the Period of the Single European Act,* 1996.

Klabbers, J., *An Introduction to International Institutional Law,* 2009.

Klabbers, J., Wallendahl, Å. (eds.), *Research Handbook on the Law of International Organizations,* 2011.

Larsen, K.M., *The Human Rights Treaty Obligations of Peacekeepers*, 2012.

Larsen, K.M., Guldahl, C.G., Cooper, Nystuen, G. (eds.), *Searching for a 'Principle of Humanity' in International Law*, 2013.

Lazareff, S., *Status of Military Forces under Current International Law*, 1971.

Leurdijk, D.A., *The UN and NATO: The logic of primacy*, in Charles M. (ed.), *The United Nations and Regional Security: Europe and Beyond*, 2003.

Malanczuk, P., *Akehurst's Modern Introduction to International Law*, 1997.

Matthee, M., Toebes, B., Brus, M. (eds.), *Armed Conflict and International Law: In Search of the Human Face*, 2013.

Mayer, S. (ed.), *NATO's Post-Cold War Politics: The Changing Provision of Security*, 2014.

Mays, A.T., *Historical Dictionary of Multinational Peacekeeping*, p. xlvii, 2004.

Meijknecht, A., *Towards International Legal Personality: The Position of Minorities and Indigenious Peoples in International Law*, 2001.

Melzer, N., *Targeted Killing in International Law*, 2008.

Muller, A.S., *International Organizations and their Host State – Aspects of their Legal Relationship*, 1995.

Naert, F., *International Law Aspects of the EU's Security and Defence Policy*, 2010.

Portman, R., *Legal Personality in International law*, 2010.

Schlemmer-Schulte, S., Tung, K-Y (eds.), *Liber Amicorum Ibrahim F.I. Shihata: International Finance and Development Law*, 2001.

Schmalenbach, K., *Die Haftung Internationaler Organisationen*, 2004.

Shaw, M.N., *International Law*, 1997.

Sliedregt, E. van, *The Criminal Responsibility of Individuals for Violations of International Law*, 2003.

Sliedregt, E. van, *Individual Criminal Responsibility in International Law*, 2012.

Thies, W.J., *Why NATO Endures*, 2009.

Tomuschat, C, (ed.), *Kosovo and the International Community. A Legal Assessment*, 2002.

Verhoeven, J., *Droit Internationale Public*, 2000.

Voetelink, J., *Status of Forces, Strafrechtsmacht over militairen vanuit internationaalrechtelijk en militair-operationeelrechtelijk persepctief*, 2012.

Voetelink, J., *Status of Forces: Criminal Jurisdicition over Military Personnel Abroad*, 2015.

Van Vooren, B., Blockmans, S., Wouters, J. (eds.), *The EU's Role in Global Governance: The Legal Dimension*, 2012.

Wilmshurst, E. (ed.), *International Law and the Classification of Conlficts*, 2012.

Wilt, H. van der, Nollkamper, A., *System Criminality in International Law*, 2009.

Zwanenburg, M., *Accountability under International Humanitarian Law for United Nations and North Atlantic Treaty Organization Peace Support Operations*, 2004.

II Articles

Akande, D., Shah, S., *Immunities of State Officials, International Crimes, and Foreign Domestic Courts,* 21 European Journal of International Law, no. 4, 2011.

D'Argent, P., *State Organs Placed at the Disposal of the UN, Effective Control, Wrongful Abstention and Dual Attribution of Conduct,* Questions of International Law, 2014.

Bassiouini, C., *Crimes Against Humanity: The Case for a Specialized Convention,* Washington University Global Studies Law Review, Vol. 9, Issue 4, 2010.

Boddens Hosang, J.F.R., *Aandachtspunten in de ISAF ROE vanuit het strategisch-juridisch kader,* Militair Rechtelijk Tijdschrift, no. 5, 2009.

Boon, K.E., *Are Control Tests Fit for the Future? The Slippage Problem in Attribution Doctrines,* Melbourne Journal of International Law, Vol. 15, 2014.

Cassese, A., *When May Senior State Officials Be Tried for International Crimes? Some Comments on the Congo v. Belgium Case,* 13 European Journal of International Law, no. 853, 2002.

Cassese, A., *The Nicaragua and Tadić Tests Revisited in Light of the ICJ Judgment on Genocide in Bosnia,* 18 European Journal of International Law, 4, 2007.

Cerone, J., *Outlining KFOR Accountability in Post-Conflict Kosovo,* American Society of International Law, October 2000.

Cerone, J., *Minding the Gap: Outlining KFOR Accountability in Post-Conflict Kosovo,* 12, European Journal of International Law, no. 3, 2001.

Cock, C, de., *Operation Unified Protector: Targeting Densely Populated Areas in Libya,* Military and Strategic Affairs, Vol. 4, No. 2, September 2012.

Cohen-Jonathan, G., *Cour européenne des droits de l'homme et droit international général,* Annuaire Français de Droit International, 46, 2000.

Droege, D., *Transfer of detainees: legal framework, non-refoulement and contemporary challenges,* International Review of the Red Cross, Vol 90, no. 871, September 2008.

Ferraro, T., *The Applicability of International Humanitarian Law to Multinational Forces,* International Review of the Red Cross, 2013, no. 95, Multinational Operations and the Law.

Figà-Talamanca, N., *The Role of NATO in the Peace Agreement for Bosnia and Herzegovina,* 7 European Journal of International Law, 1996.

Gaeta, P., *Is NATO Authorized or Obliged to Arrest Persons Indicted by the International Criminal Tribunal for the Former Yugoslavia?* 9, European Journal of International Law, 1998.

Gaeta, P. (2007) *On What Conditions Can a State Be Held Responsible for Genocide,* European Journal of International Law, 18(4).

Gallis, P., *NATO's Decision-Making Procedure,* CSR Report for Congress, 5 May 2003.

Gasser, H.P., *Internationalized Non-international armed conflicts: Case Studies of Afghanistan, Kampuchea and Lebanon,* American University Review, Vol. 33/1, 1983.

Gazzini, T., *NATO Coercive Military Activities in the Yugoslav Crisis,* 12 European Journal of International Law 2001.

Greenwood, C., *International Humanitarian Law and United Nations Military Operations,* 1 Yearbook of International Humanitarian Law 3, 1998.

Hardtke, K.A., *The Actions of One, the Responsibility of a Nation: Charles Taylor's Conviction by the Special Court for Sierra Leone and Its Impact on State Responsibility Claims Against Liberia,* Wiscounsin International Law Journal, 2014.

Hartwig, M., *International Organizations or Institutions, Responsibility and Liability,* Max Planck Encyclopaedia of Public International Law.

Human Rights Watch, *"Troops in Contact", airstrikes and civilian deaths in Afghanistan,* September 2008.

Joines, J.R.W.D., *The Implications of the Peace Agreement for the International Criminal Tribunal for the Former Yugoslavia,* 7 European Journal of International Law, 1996.

Kempen, P.H.P.H.M.C. Van, *Four Concepts of Security – A Human Rights Perspective,* Human Rights Law Review 2013, Vol. 13, nr. 1.

Kennedy, D., *The sources of international law,* American University International Law Review, Vol. 2:1, 1987.

Klabbers, J., *The Life and Times of International Organizations,* Nordic Journal of International Law, 70, 2001.

Klabbers, J., *The Paradox of International Institutional Law,* International Organizations Law Review, 5, 2008.

Laursen, A., *NATO, the War over Kosovo, and the ICTY Investigation,* American University International Law Review, Vol. 17, Issue 4, 2002.

Limanowska, B., *"Trafficking in Human Beings in South-eastern Europe",* 2002.

Messineo, F., *Multiple Attribution of Conduct,* SHARES Research Paper 11, 2012.

Milanoviç, M., *State Responsibility for Genocide,* 17 European Journal of International Law, no. 3, 2006.

Milanoviç, M., *Al-Skeini and Al-Jedda in Strasbourg,* 23 European Journal of International Law, No. 1, 2012.

Milanoviç, M., Papiç, T., *As Bad As It Gets: The European Court of Human Rights' Behrami and Saramati Decision and General International Law,* International and Comparative Law Quarterly, Vol. 58, 2009.

Nollkaemper, A., *Concurrence Between Individual Responsibility and State Responsibility in International Law,* The International and Comparative Law Quarterly, vol. 52, No. 3, July 2003.

Nollkaemper, A., *Systemic Effects of International Responsibility for International Crimes,* 8 Santa Clara Journal of International Law 1, 2010.

Nollkaemper, A., *Dual Attribution: Liability of the Netherlands for Conduct of Dutchbat in Srebrenica,* Journal of International Criminal Justice, Vol. 9, Issue 5, 2011.

Nollkaemper, A., Nedeski, N., *Responsibility of International Organizations 'In Connection with Acts of State',* Amsterdam Center of International Law, No. 2012–05, 31 May 2012.

Pacquée, D., Dewulf, S., *International Territorial Administrations and the Rule of Law: The Case of Kosovo,* Essex Human Rights Review Vol. 4, No. 1, February 2007.

Ratner, S.R., *Foreign Occupation and International Territorial Administration; The Challenges of Convergence,* The European Journal of International Law, Vol. 16, no. 4, 2005.

Reichard, M., *Some Legal Issues Concerning the EU-NATO Berlin Plus Arrangement,* Nordic Journal of International Law, 73, 2004.

Ringmose, J., Rynning, S., *"Come home NATO? The Atlantic Alliance's new Strategic Concept",* Danish Institute for International Studies, DIIR Report, 2009:4.

Rosen, N., *How Are Multinational NATO Operations Responsible for International Humanitarian Law Operations,* The Fletcher Forum of World Affairs, Vol. 37:3 Special Edition 2013.

Ryngaert, C., *Member State Responsibility fort he Acts of International Organizations,* Utrecht Law Review, Vol. 7, Issues 1, 2011.

Sari, A., *Status of Forces and Status of Mission Agreements under the ESDP: The EU's Evolving Practice,* 19 European Journal of International Law 1, 2008.

Schmitt, M.N., *Targeting Narcoinsurgents in Afghanistan: The Limits of International Humanitarian Law,* Yearbook of International Humanitarian Law, Vol. 12, 2009.

Schmitt, M.N. (2011) *Investigating Violations of International Law in Armed Conflict,* Harvard National Security Journal, 2.

Seyersted, F., *International Personality of Intergovernmental Organizations. Do Their Capacities Really Depend upon Their Constitutions,* Indian Journal of International Law, Vol. IV, 1964.

Shraga, D., *The United Nations as an Actor Bound by International Humanitarian Law,* 5 International Peacekeeping 64, 1998.

Simma, B., *NATO, the UN and the Use of Force: Legal Aspects,* 10 European Journal of International Law 1, 1999.

Spinedi, M., *State Responsibility v. Individual Responsibility for International Crimes: Tertium Non Datur?,* 13 European Journal of International Law no. 4, 2002.

Vinopal, K., *Researching Public International Law,* American Society of International Law, Electronic Research Guide, 2013.

Wall, A., ed, *Legal and ethical lessons of NATO's Kosovo campaign,* US Naval War College, International Law Studies, Vol. 78, 2002.

Wendt, J.C., Brown, N., *Improving the NATO Force Planning Process,* Rand, 2008.

Wolfrum, R., *International Administration in Post-Conflict Situations by the United Nations and Other International Actors,* Max Planck Yearbook of United Nations Law, Vol. 9, 2005.

Yost, D.S., *"NATO's 1999 Strategic Concept",* Security Strategies: NATO, the United States and the European Union, NATO Defense College, 2005.

Zegveld, L., *Accountability of armed opposition groups in international law,* Cambridge studies in international and comparative law, 2002.

Zegveld, L., *Remedies for Victims of Violations of International Humanitarian Law,* IRRC, Vol. 85, No. 851, September, 2003.

Index